AF729956

ONE SIGNAL
PUBLISHERS

ATRIA

ALSO BY MIKE McINTIRE

Champions Way

RICOCHET

GUNS, GREED, AND THE AMERICAN WAY OF VIOLENCE

MIKE McINTIRE

ONE SIGNAL PUBLISHERS

ATRIA

NEW YORK AMSTERDAM/ANTWERP LONDON
TORONTO SYDNEY/MELBOURNE NEW DELHI

ONE SIGNAL PUBLISHERS

ATRIA

An Imprint of Simon & Schuster, LLC
1230 Avenue of the Americas
New York, NY 10020

For more than 100 years, Simon & Schuster has championed authors and the stories they create. By respecting the copyright of an author's intellectual property, you enable Simon & Schuster and the author to continue publishing exceptional books for years to come. We thank you for supporting the author's copyright by purchasing an authorized edition of this book.

No amount of this book may be reproduced or stored in any format, nor may it be uploaded to any website, database, large language model, or other repository, retrieval, or artificial intelligence system without express permission. All rights reserved. Inquiries may be directed to Simon & Schuster, 1230 Avenue of the Americas, New York, NY 10020 or permissions@simonandschuster.com.

Copyright © 2026 by Michael McIntire

All rights reserved, including the right to reproduce this book or portions thereof in any form whatsoever. For information, address Atria Books Subsidiary Rights Department, 1230 Avenue of the Americas, New York, NY 10020.

First One Signal Publishers/Atria Books hardcover edition September 2026

ONE SIGNAL PUBLISHERS/ATRIA BOOKS
and colophon are registered trademarks of Simon & Schuster, LLC

Simon & Schuster strongly believes in freedom of expression and stands against censorship in all its forms. For more information, visit BooksBelong.com.

For information about special discounts for bulk purchases, please contact Simon & Schuster Special Sales at 1-866-506-1949 or business@simonandschuster.com.

The Simon & Schuster Speakers Bureau can bring authors to your live event. For more information or to book an event, contact the Simon & Schuster Speakers Bureau at 1-866-248-3049 or visit our website at www.simonspeakers.com.

Interior design by Davina Mock-Maniscalco

Manufactured in the United States of America

1 3 5 7 9 10 8 6 4 2

Library of Congress Control Number: 2026933577

ISBN 978-1-6680-6306-4
ISBN 978-1-6680-6308-8 (ebook)

Scan here to get book recommendations, exclusive offers, and more delivered to your inbox.

This book is dedicated to my parents,
Joan and Lee McIntire,
the beloved yin and yang in my life

CONTENTS

RICOCHET

INTRODUCTION

GROWING UP IN southeastern Connecticut in the 1970s, I used to take school trips to see what was left of Native American tribes that once flourished there. A few remaining descendants lived in a sad collection of trailers on a reservation.

There was also a small museum. Someone would come out to greet the kids and our teacher and take us on a tour. We would learn how the Indigenous people were in sync with nature, always careful to not waste anything, turning leftover turtle shells into rattles after making soup.

Most of these little insights went in one ear and out the other. I was more interested in seeing the USS *Nautilus*, America's first nuclear submarine, docked at the navy base in New London. I'm quite sure, however, that if our school visits had included a description of the blood-drenched massacre of the Pequot tribe that had occurred nearby in 1637, my fourth-grade self would have perked up.

Like most American boys, I had a naive fascination with violence. It was a mythical and abstract fascination—had I actually witnessed something really bad, I would have run crying to my mother—but the attraction was there nonetheless. Culture played a role, starting at an early age. Comic books, cartoons, and toys were full of pugilistic energy. I discovered what it felt like to hold a gun when I was only five or six and my parents bought me a clear plastic bubble umbrella. Its handle was shaped like a derringer.

I must have had a dozen toy guns as a kid. One was a realistic-looking pump-action shotgun that fired plastic pellets. There were cap pistols that took rolls of paper with gunpowder embedded in it, causing a satisfying tiny detonation when you pulled the trigger. Dart guns shot suction-cup projectiles.

When I was old enough, I got a BB gun. I learned how to use it at a YMCA summer camp, where we fired air rifles at paper targets. At some point, my father took me to an abandoned gravel pit to shoot the real thing: a .22-caliber rifle. It was thrilling and scary and a little emotional. I was about twelve, and there was something about lifting the heavy firearm, all burnished wood and black metal, pointing it, and squeezing the trigger, hearing the loud crack, feeling the recoil—a bit of childhood innocence flew away with the bullet as it shattered an old amber beer bottle perched on a rock.

My dad had grown up in Maine, where his father was a licensed guide who would lead hunting and fishing parties into the wilderness. My grandfather had a log cabin on a lake in the northwestern part of the state that had deer heads and rifles hanging on the walls. Visiting it as a teenager, I wondered why the bed I was sleeping in felt lumpy, lifted the mattress, and found an antique lever-action Winchester tucked under it.

Though he was used to guns, my father viewed them the way his father did, as tools. They didn't fetishize them, make them central to their identities, or even think about them much at all. For my dad, who didn't hunt, that meant keeping them mostly for self-defense.

I'm sure my father thought he had convinced me never to fool around with a gun, and that he kept them secreted away where they couldn't easily be found. Wrong on both counts. I knew where his pistol and rifles were hidden, and more than once, when my parents were off somewhere, I took out the guns and played with them.

When I was a teenager, we lived in a semirural area. One day I got my father's .30-06 bolt-action rifle—the same type of powerful weapon used to murder Charlie Kirk—and fired a shot out an open window into the woods behind our house. I disposed of the shell casing and quickly stashed the gun back in the closet before my parents came home. I was lucky not to have killed someone.

Later, as an adult, I repeated the same ritual that my father had done with me, showing my nephew and then my son how to shoot a

.22 rifle when they had reached their teens (I keep my ammunition locked in a safe). The boys were thrilled.

But why? What did it matter whether they learned to shoot, and how come they enjoyed it so much? Was it because it felt manly, cool, and exciting? Or do the reasons go deeper than that?

Guns have been part of the wallpaper of growing up in America since before its founding. Originally, guns were utilized for hunting, varmint shooting, and, if necessary, self-defense or militia service.

But there also developed a romanticized idyll of firearms as the great equalizer, to be wielded by heroes who would save the day. They became ubiquitous in popular culture, to the point where they are now routinely marketed as manhood-affirming lifestyle accessories. These potent cultural reference points—one utilitarian, the other allegorical—merged into a sort of bland acceptance of firearms as something to be sold and kept around the house like almost any other product.

I've spent a big part of my career as a journalist writing about gun violence. I've also tried to investigate the larger forces at work. It's clear, for instance, that reckless commercial practices—making firearms nearly as easy to acquire as an iPhone—have contributed to the problem. In the modern era, a veritable witches' brew of money, politics, and ideology has warped gun rights, opening the door to irresponsible marketing and accessibility of powerful weapons.

But to lay blame solely with the selfish, craven, or deluded would be to miss the larger point. They are all responding to something embedded deep in the American psyche.

Like a volcanic eruption in the ocean that eventually cools and solidifies to form a verdant island, the American nation was born of violence. Our first two centuries were defined by armed revolution, subjugation of native peoples, civil war, expansionist conquest, and military dominance in two global conflicts. Guns were essential to that, and not just in the obvious sense. Helping blaze this foundational trail were entrepreneurs such as Sam Colt (mass production of revolvers), Richard Gatling (early machine gun), and household names such as Remington, Winchester, and Smith & Wesson.

American spirit, ingenuity, and capital put to work in the service of lethal force.

To acknowledge all this is not to paint the United States as a trigger-happy, unredeemable aggressor. Indeed, there is much laudatory tradition here. Viewed from another angle, American firepower helped end the institution of slavery, save Europe (twice), build a heritage of hunting and sport shooting, and create jobs for millions.

Accepting our uniquely complicated relationship with violence, and the history behind it, provides important context for the broader exploration of gun culture today. When you see firearms-industry marketing bathed in images of heroism, machismo, and the flag—well, it's not by accident.

This is where I should mention that I'm now a gun owner myself. I have four firearms and I have always believed Americans should be able to keep them, within agreed-upon limits, for self-defense, hunting, or sport.

What I have never understood, however, is our peculiar cognitive dissonance toward these things. We idolize guns and the power they confer, while at the same time blithely tuning out the carnage wrought: about forty thousand dead each year, an average of one mass shooting a day, and gunshots a leading cause of death among children. It wasn't always this way. Historically, Americans were more clear-eyed about guns as deadly tools and had little trouble balancing the right to own them against sensible restrictions.

Many states had gun-rights provisions in their constitutions, but also freely regulated when and where they could be put to use. A great irony of the Wild West mythos is that those dusty Tombstone towns were sometimes safer than big cities, since local sheriffs and marshals often banned the carrying of firearms. Other motivations were less civic-minded, such as early curbs on gun ownership by Black people.

Only in the last sixty years have we seen the ascendancy of a gun ethos that has corroded civil society in ways earlier generations would have found unimaginable. It is supported by a legal framework, suffused with ideological dogma, which recast the origins and purpose of the Second Amendment to fit a radical view of gun rights.

At its core is a stubborn minority of Americans who refuse to accept commonsense limits, even as advancements in lethal firearms technology make a grotesquerie of their insistence on ever-greater freedoms. In doing so, they have truncated the liberties of everyone who must live with the consequences: traumatic mass-shooter drills forced upon schoolchildren and office workers; a constant low-grade fear that spikes at the sound of a firecracker or car backfiring; police officers who must treat every traffic stop or domestic call as a potential gun battle.

Pondering all this, I sometimes think of that depiction of evolution in science textbooks showing the "ascent of man," where humans start out small and apelike and gradually grow larger and smarter. Except in the case of gun rights, it goes in reverse: We have become smaller and dumber.

The story of gun culture is essentially the American way but without guardrails. It is a cautionary tale of unfettered liberty, swagger, and free markets applied, in this case, to a product designed to result in our violent undoing.

Through my reporting over the years, my views on gun violence and the way we think about it have evolved. It's not enough to chronicle the killers and their victims, the politics of the Second Amendment, the role of industry, and the influence of social media—all important to understanding the problem. But they are embedded in a firmament of violence that stretches back across centuries to the nation's earliest beginnings.

That is why I start this book with the story of the 1637 massacre of the Pequots by English colonists and their Indian allies. Not to pass judgment—my family tree includes an English veteran of the Pequot War and a member of the Mohegan tribe—but to put the firmament in relief. It will continue to acquire shape and substance in succeeding chapters, which explore how the imperatives of war, slavery, westward expansion, crime, and commercialism intertwined with the development of firearms and fueled an ongoing debate over their use.

The book is divided into three sections—Violence, Power, and Freedom—which roughly correlate with America's historical narrative, while placing the role of guns within it.

The invention of firearms immensely altered the use of force, and with the Revolutionary War guns helped birth a superpower whose creators saw fit to embed them in the genome of its body politic with the Second Amendment. As the succeeding centuries witnessed a continuum of violence accompanied by new forms of firepower, there also developed a uniquely American mindset, recognized and articulated by the courts, that embraced armed resistance to more commonplace offenses—standing your ground.

Over the last hundred years, as gun violence became endemic in US cities, climaxing with submachine guns on the streets of Prohibition-era Chicago, and later came to include the assassinations of political leaders, public revulsion drove the first major attempts at government control. Backlash to those controls spawned what would become the modern gun rights movement.

The middle portion of the book chronicles the accumulation of power and turn to radicalism by the National Rifle Association, drawing upon previously unreported material, including internal NRA records and correspondence. The NRA, however, is only part of a larger story of how reactionary forces worked lawmakers and the judiciary to transform America's relationship with firearms. Congress granted extraordinary liability protections to the gun industry, while the Supreme Court reframed the Second Amendment, ignoring the long-held view that its reference to "a well regulated militia" was not a fusty preamble but a commonly understood restraint.

The third section of the book explores how these legal victories freed politicians, businesses, and Wall Street players to seek power and profits by making gun ownership a cultural identifier. And with the rise of social media and marketing aimed at a generation of alienated young men, freedom in this sense has often resembled the exercise of rights without responsibilities.

The book concludes with a look at what actions could be taken to change the trajectory that the country is on. This includes some thoughts on the larger societal forces at work beyond just the availability of guns.

The story of violence and guns in America is not always easy to tell or to hear. But it's one that I believe can ultimately be hopeful because knowledge is the only weapon more powerful than black powder.

VIOLENCE

A COWARDLY CONTRIVANCE

As a kid, I never learned about the Massacre at Mystic, despite living a hatchet's throw from where it happened and having a family connection to participants. It wasn't something the grown-ups in my life were prone to talk about. In part, that was because the ignominious episode could serve as a trailhead for any exploration of the American way of violence.

As an adult, I pieced that story together from firsthand accounts of English who were involved. What emerged offered an unnerving view of how my forebears, in the name of God and king, conjured the moral certitude to slaughter more than six hundred men, women, and children.

The tale begins in a moonlit encampment not far from a river, where a large group of militiamen could hear the distant, tremulous intonations of Native Americans singing. It was normally a sound that might send a shiver through the English.

But on that night, the hundred or so New Englanders were fortified with righteous rage. They believed it was the devil himself they heard, and yet God was with them. They settled in for a few hours of sleep before the sanctioned bloodshed to come.

It was the 26th of May in the year of our Lord 1637.

Rising before dawn, the men took up muskets, pikes, and swords and resumed their trek in silence toward where the midnight singing had been heard. They emerged from woods to find a field of newly planted corn before them. Just beyond was a large hill topped by a wooden fort that was the home base of the Pequots.

Accompanying Capt. John Mason and his party were more than

two hundred Native Americans from rival tribes who had joined them for the early-morning attack. The fort was actually a palisade of tree trunks encircling a village of about seventy wigwams, home to between four hundred and seven hundred men, women, and children in an area then called Mistick. These included the Pequot warriors who were the primary target of the English colonists.

Tensions between the colonists and Indigenous peoples had been building for years. The 1630s had seen the opening of floodgates as Puritans poured in and spread south and west from Massachusetts. Indigenous tribes, notably the Pequot, Narragansett, and Mohegan, previously had internecine conflicts over territory and resources, but now they jockeyed for advantage in dealing with the Europeans.

Trade with the Dutch and the English had worked for a while. The tribes exchanged wampum and animal skins for other goods, including firearms, whose value they immediately recognized. But clashes grew more common, and when a Pequot raiding party surprised a small farming colony along the Connecticut River, brutally killing nine men and women and kidnapping two girls, the enraged English vowed vengeance.

As the Puritans saw it, they had given the Pequots every chance to behave in a civilized manner, only to be repaid with bloodshed. A militia officer in Captain Mason's party, John Underhill, would later write:

"This insolent Nation, seeing we had used much lenity towards them, and themselves not able to make good use of our patience, set upon a course of greater insolence than before."

What happened next would arguably be recognized today as the start of a pogrom.

The Puritans kicked it off with a day of fast and prayer. Night watches were set throughout the colony and an edict was issued that no one leave their home without bearing arms. Most households had muskets to comply with mandatory militia training.

Militias in colonial America were not created to throw off the yoke of the state or to rebel against the monarchy. Their purpose initially was to defend against Indigenous raids and, occasionally, other European colonists (it would not be long before they also became an enforcement mechanism for slavery). The Massachusetts Bay Colony, starting in the 1630s, mandated that each household keep a pound of gunpowder and twenty bullets and be prepared to muster in thirty minutes. Connecticut law required all males, ages sixteen to forty-five, to have guns at home so their respective towns could create "trained bands" that would meet "four days in the year for instructions in military discipline."

The compulsory militia service, which afforded the colonists both weapons and some basic level of training, allowed them to come together as a fighting force following the Pequot assault on the farmers.

Before the English set off, a group of about fifty Mohegans arrived to join them, bringing along as proof of allegiance the severed hands of four Pequots, as well as a Pequot prisoner who was still alive. As the English watched, the Mohegans tied one of his legs to a post, and about twenty men used a rope to pull his other leg until his limbs separated; a militia officer put the dismembered man out of his misery with a pistol shot.

The Dutch, perhaps unnerved by the bloodlust and fury sweeping through the English colony, managed to secure the release of the two girls taken by the Pequots. The girls appeared physically unharmed and provided useful details about the Pequot fortifications. They also mentioned that the Indians had questioned them about how to make gunpowder.

The Pequots were going to need it.

There were two entrances to the Pequot fort, on opposite sides of the palisade, each blocked with a heavy brush pile. Captain Mason divided his men into teams to approach the entrances, while their Indigenous allies formed a wide circle behind them, to block the escape of any Pequots.

As the English crept forward, muskets in one hand and swords in the other, suddenly a dog started barking. A warning cry went up inside the fort.

"Owanux! Owanux!"

Pequot men raced to the palisade walls with bows and hatchets. Their presence known, the English stopped and raised their guns, firing a volley at the palisade. The thundering cracks reverberated through the forest.

Firing a seventeenth-century gun in battle was not a simple task. A typical musket is loaded from the muzzle end, gunpowder poured in first, followed by a wad of cloth (if available and time allowed) and a lead ball, all packed into place with a ramrod. Next, primer powder is put in a pan atop the breech of the gun. It is locked into place, the gun is cocked, and finally the shooter aims and pulls the trigger, causing a flint to spark into the pan and ignite the powder.

Experienced shooters could reload three or four times a minute. But most of the English colonists were not experienced—they were farmers, tradesmen, and merchants. Perhaps that is why Underhill, describing the sight of his men managing to successfully shoot up the Pequot fort, saw "the providence of God in it.

"That soldiers so unexpert in the use of their arms, should give so complete a volley," he said, it was "as though the finger of God had touched both match and flint."

While the initial round of gunfire had frightened the Pequots, it was not going to get the English into the fort. For that, they had to pull away the brush piles and charge through the entrances, whereupon they were immediately peppered with arrows. Some managed to make it far enough inside to engage the Indians, firing muskets, slashing with swords, and lunging with pikes.

But arrows were finding their mark. Englishmen were struck in the face, legs, neck. Several arrows bounced off Captain Mason's helmet. Underhill took arrows to the hip and between his shoulders.

Realizing their plans were faltering, Captain Mason made a fateful call. He grabbed a firebrand from inside a wigwam and set it ablaze. Underhill, who was essentially Captain Mason's second-in-command, followed suit, throwing gunpowder around and lighting it. Bloodied and out of breath, the English fled the fort and waited.

Soon, flames and columns of black smoke were rising high into the darkness. The predawn gloom was aglow in flickering firelight. And then came the screams.

Pequot men, women, and children tried to escape. Some made a dash through flames and smoke for the entrances, others clambered over the palisade walls. They were met with gunfire from the English who surrounded the fort.

Those who evaded the volleys of musket balls encountered the circle of Mohegans and Narragansetts waiting in the trees. They were butchered by their fellow Native Americans.

The slaughter was over in about an hour. Estimates are that about 150 of those killed were warriors, and the rest were more than 400 noncombatants, many of them elderly people, women, and children. Only a handful survived. Two English militiamen were killed—one of them accidentally by friendly musket fire.

Standing amid the carnage, some of the English were traumatized by the scale of it. Underhill later described the scene, providing a glimmer of introspection in the process:

"Great and doleful was the bloody sight to the view of young soldiers that never had been in war, to see so many souls lie gasping on the ground so thick in some places, that you could hardly pass along. It may be demanded, 'Why should you be so furious (as some have said), should not Christians have more mercy and compassion?'"

The militiaman had an answer.

"Sometimes, the Scripture declareth women and children must perish with their parents," he wrote, adding, "But we will not dispute it now. We had sufficient light from the word of God for our proceedings."

Some two centuries after the massacre, as the United States was celebrating its centennial, Connecticut authorities saw fit to honor Captain Mason with statuary and proclamations. A new state capitol building in Hartford featured an eight-foot-tall likeness of him, standing in a raised niche. Not far away, a stone relief entitled *Attack on an Indian Fort* depicted the captain heroically leading his men against Pequot warriors.

As a journalist working at the state capitol in the 1990s, I would pass by those commemorations frequently. Glancing up at them while hurrying to a press conference, I had what you might call an epiphany. It came shortly after a mass shooting at the Connecticut State Lottery headquarters, a story that I had been covering as a reporter for the *Hartford Courant*.

Guns had been on my mind, and I noticed for the first time that none of the sculpted depictions showed Mason with a firearm. Instead, they showed him and his men bravely charging with swords, in the face of arrows being shot by Native Americans hiding behind trees. Of course, swords had made an appearance during the attack. But mainly, the Pequots had fallen under repeated volleys of gunfire while defending themselves with comparatively primitive weapons as their homes burned to the ground.

Certainly, some of this historical distortion could be chalked up to the hagiography that often inflects commemorations of war. But this felt different to me. The absence of guns seemed intentional. If you squint hard enough at the stone relief, you can see small, faceless men in the rear with what appeared to be muskets over their shoulders. A sort of reluctant nod to the facts that didn't interfere with the implied message: There was something less honorable about the "savages" lobbing death from a distance while the white man courageously advanced with nothing but a blade.

Was I reading too much into it? Curious, I started looking up images that memorialized historical figures associated with wars. There was a statue of the Marquis de Lafayette in Hartford, not far from the capitol. The French aristocrat famously gave George Washington a set of flintlock pistols that he used throughout the Revolution. Lafayette had trained with guns at an early age, helped deliver five thousand muskets to American forces, and was shot in the leg during battle. But you wouldn't know that looking at his statue—it shows him on a horse waving a sword in the air. No gun. Similarly, good luck finding a statue of Washington holding one.

The same is true of Civil War commemorations of generals such as Ulysses Grant, William Sherman, and Robert E. Lee. In fact, all the way into the twentieth century, commanding officers, especially, were almost always celebrated with depictions of them gripping swords, while monuments featuring average soldiers sometimes included guns.

Some of this is no doubt attributable to the tradition of swords as a ceremonial accoutrement for military officers even in the modern era. But why should a sword somehow convey bravery and honor in a way that the far more common and useful gun does not?

As knowledge of black powder migrated from China to the Middle East and into Europe in the late medieval period, it was first put to use in cannons for Western warfare. It wasn't long before the mechanics of these weapons gained efficiency and shrank, resulting in hand-size versions that shot a ball from a rough iron pipe.

These early "hand cannons" were dangerous, inaccurate, and capable of firing only short distances. If they didn't blow up in your face, your best chance for striking the enemy was to aim in the general direction of a cluster of soldiers and hope to hit one of them.

Hand cannons were eventually replaced by the harquebus, an early long gun that could fire hundreds of yards but was heavy and often required a stand on which to rest the barrel. These, too, gradually improved and by the sixteenth century were increasingly common on European battlefields alongside traditional swords, bows, and pikes.

The benefits were obvious. Bladed weapons, along with arrows and bolts, usually required repeated application to find their mark, while a single ball blasted from a firearm often punctured early types of armor, inflicting grievous injuries. Yet, some military leaders initially did not take to guns.

Sir John Smyth, a high-ranking English officer, complained to the Crown in 1591 that guns were "very complicated things which get out of order in many ways" and tired the soldiers who had to carry them. "Whereas, also a bowman can let off six aimed shots a minute, a musketeer can discharge but one in two minutes."

More than practical considerations, there was also resistance to the way firearms altered the nature of conflict itself. An early-sixteenth-century chronicler of Ottoman wars, Ibn Zunbul, observed that Mamluk knights of that period rejected the firearm as dishonorable and unmanly—deadly "even if a woman were to fire it"—and he blamed Christian crusaders for polluting the battlefield with them. "You have brought with you this contrivance artfully devised by the Christians of Europe when they were incapable of meeting the Muslim armies on the battlefield," he wrote, adding, "How darest thou shoot with firearms at Muslims!"

This sense of unfairness, that a gun imbued any ignorant serf (or woman!) with unearned power, was probably best expressed by the

Chevalier de Bayard, a sixteenth-century French knight. Bayard was known to hang enemy prisoners who were found to have wielded firearms. Combat, he believed, should be waged face-to-face by men of strength and skill, not cowardly tykes plinking at noble soldiers from a safe remove.

"It is a shame," Bayard declared, "that a man of spirit should be exposed to be killed by a miserable stone or iron ball against which he cannot defend himself."

Whatever the drivers, institutional hesitancy to embrace the new technology meant that early advancements in firearms occurred mostly in the civilian sector, only later finding their way into wider acceptance by armies. And acceptance did eventually arrive. The brutal logic of the thing was overwhelming.

A musket or harquebus ball carried about twenty times the kinetic energy of an arrow, did not depend on the bowman's strength to fire it, and could fell the enemy with one shot; it was not uncommon for soldiers to fight on with multiple arrows sticking out of them, whereas a single iron ball could lay waste to their anatomy. Importantly, a firearm could do the same against a horse, degrading cavalry units more quickly.

The inevitability of the gun eventually overtook its chivalrous detractors, ushering in a new age of ever more ruthless and remote efficiency in the ability to kill. For Bayard, probably the most famous of the firearms naysayers, fate delivered the verdict early.

Leading French troops in battle at the Sesia River in Italy in 1524, Bayard had his horse shot out from under him—twice—by an enemy heavily armed with the relatively new harquebuses. Bayard and his men fought bravely with swords and pikes, but were no match for the relentless hail of balls fired from a distance.

A harquebus ball struck Bayard in the loins, fracturing his spine. He refused to leave the battlefield and instead had his men prop him up against a tree to await the advancing enemy, saying, "There is no need to pity me. I die as a man of honor ought."

When the great knight was finally vanquished, sword still in hand, he was surrounded by lesser men whose deadly black-powder contrivances carried a message from the future.

It is a great irony, given how guns are marketed today as totems of masculinity, that many seasoned fighters in that earlier era rejected them as unworthy gadgets wielded by weaklings. The glib, smashmouth tone of modern gun influencers on Instagram and YouTube would seem to validate our ancestors' skepticism of how firearms fit into traditional conceptions of honor, grace, and courage.

There have been plenty of studies purporting to show an association between men's attraction to guns and feelings of insecurity related to economic status, relationships, or social standing. I tend to be skeptical of some of these, for the simple reason that correlation does not necessarily equal causation. That said, I've known guys in my life who would, regrettably, seem to fit this scenario.

And gun companies appear to believe it. So much of firearms advertising is based on an unabashed appeal to men who, well, want to feel like a man. I can easily imagine a twenty-first-century marketer's resurrection of Capt. John Mason as a steroidal hero, ammo belts strapped across his chest and wielding a smoking rifle.

The gunless depictions of Mason in the Connecticut state capitol, however, only drew my attention to the reality that firearms created a fundamental imbalance in the conflict that favored the English over the Pequots—similar to what Bayard and his men encountered a century before. To be sure, the Pequots had learned how to use guns and would try to barter for them or seize them whenever possible. But they could not hope to match the scale of armaments, ammunition, and training of the English, who enjoyed the support of the Crown.

After the Mystic Massacre, what was left of the Pequot tribe in the region fled west along the Connecticut coast until reaching a swamp where English militias caught up to them. A final confrontation ensued in which the English again relied heavily on musket fire to end it. This time, before finishing off most of the Pequot fighters, they allowed women and children to surrender—only to send most of them into slavery later.

The Connecticut Pequots were effectively destroyed as a cohesive political unit and culture. Rival tribes mopped up those who were left wherever they found them. When Sassacus, a Pequot sachem who had escaped the swamp battle, sought refuge with Iroquois Mohawks, they killed him and sent his head to the English as a show of solidarity.

The militiamen had vanquished their fiercest enemy, but it was far from the end of conflict with the Native Americans. Skirmishes would continue, culminating in the late 1670s in what became known as King Philip's War, the biggest and bloodiest of the New England clashes.

The war was a sprawling series of battles across several states, and this time the English faced Indigenous people who were frequently armed with guns, despite efforts in the intervening years to rein in the spread of firearms through treaties with various tribes. There were thousands of casualties before the war ended in 1678, and atrocities were committed on both sides. Hundreds of women, children, and other noncombatants were killed or burned out of their homes—an echo of the seminal Massacre at Mystic decades earlier.

King Philip's War, and the brutal way it was conducted, marked the end of any hope of peaceful coexistence between the Europeans and Indigenous peoples. It was also a turning point for the New England militias, which had been forced to improve their military prowess in repeated engagements over many years. Their weaponry and training had ultimately proved decisive.

By the dawn of the eighteenth century, the militias had solidified their place in the social and political fabric of the emerging nation. The concept of citizen soldiers had proven to be an effective model for conquest and settlement in the absence of significant troops, which Great Britain did not initially commit.

By the time the Crown finally did send more of its army to America, mainly to fight the French in an endless geopolitical great-powers contest, the colonies had developed a rudimentary military capability of their own. It would prove useful when they decided to turn their muskets on a new enemy—one wearing red coats.

DIN OF ARMS

SHOTS FIRED, PEOPLE on campus with guns, students and teachers running. A chaotic and frightening scene—but then, the hasty formation of a well-regulated militia always was.

It was the morning of July 5, 1779, and a lookout with a telescope atop the chapel at Yale College had spied British Gen. William Tryon arriving at New Haven with a fleet of ships and thousands of troops. Alarm guns sounded, word spread, and soon professors, students, farmers, and shopkeepers scrambled to take up positions, wielding the firearms they were expected to keep for just such an emergency.

"Men rushed madly about, some hatless, without their coats, but all armed with their long muskets," a witness later recalled. "All seemed to be making for the green, where already men were forming into line."

Drums pounded. Dogs barked and boys ran. Among those seen responding to the New Haven green was Prof. Naphtali Daggett, a former president of Yale, holding the reins of a skinny old horse while waving a musket aloft with his free hand.

Daggett's experience that day was typical of many citizen-soldiers whose courage outpaced their military skills. A man of letters in his early fifties, old for that time, Daggett presumably had only basic proficiency with a firearm. As he attested later in an affidavit, he joined other militiamen on the morning of July 5 to take up positions on a hilltop and await the British. But the enemy advanced faster than expected.

Daggett saw redcoats coming up the hill, and as he sought cover behind some bushes, he was immediately spotted. He ran without taking a shot.

"They instantly fired upon me," he wrote, "which they continued till I had run a dozen rods, discharging not less than fifteen or twenty balls at me alone."

The shots all missed. Daggett made it to the bushes, managed to level his musket at one of the soldiers, and fired. He, too, missed. Reloading his musket, he quickly "determined not to discharge it any more" because the enemy was upon him. Daggett offered himself in surrender, but found that the British regulars were not sticklers for the rules of combat.

The redcoats called him a "damned old rebel" and demanded to know why he fired at them. Daggett's scholarly response—"Because it is the exercise of war!"—seemed to infuriate them further, and they beat him with rifle barrels, gashed his head and torso with a bayonet, and stole his shoes, handkerchief, and tobacco box. They then forced him to walk, bleeding and bruised, into town, where he collapsed in "such acute and excruciating pain as I have never felt before."

Daggett died the following year.

From where we sit today, centuries removed from that fraught time, it's hard to imagine what it was like for average citizens to drop their pitchforks or quills, grab a musket, and rush out to confront professional soldiers who were far better trained and equipped. It took a special kind of mettle.

Over the years I've interviewed people who think of themselves as carrying on the tradition of citizen militias. These are mostly weekend warriors who like to run around the woods in camo with AR-15s. Some are nice people, with families, who believe in being "prepared" in case of disaster, whether natural or the political kind.

Others just seem lost. They might buy a DON'T TREAD ON ME flag, watch TikTok videos by paid influencers hyping the latest gear, and spout pseudohistory over beers or pot. Some of them showed up at the US Capitol on January 6, 2021, and occupied statehouses during the protests over COVID-19 restrictions.

Most of the aspiring citizen-soldiers I've talked to seemed to truly believe they were constitutionally empowered to take up arms against government acts they didn't like—for some, being told to wear a mask in a pandemic was their Boston Massacre.

You might say that these were the ignorant serfs so feared by the likes of Chevalier de Bayard. A lack of knowledge and perspective, combined with easy access to extremely lethal weaponry, had created a dangerous subculture untethered from any sense of civic responsibility.

A good example of how misinformation, politics, and commercial interests can come together to hijack history is the 2020 plot to kidnap Michigan's Gov. Gretchen Whitmer. Thirteen men, at least half of whom had ties to self-proclaimed militia groups, were charged with planning the abduction as retaliation for pandemic-related lockdowns. In their own recorded words, the suspects came across at best as trash-talkers, at worst, as dangerous insurrectionists. They complained about being "robbed and enslaved by the state" and vowed resistance "manifested through bullets."

Following the news coverage at the time, I thought that more attention should have been paid to two important elements: firearms and the misguided self-justification for using them.

One of the plot's ringleaders, Adam Fox, lived in the basement of a vacuum repair shop in Grand Rapids. Down there, amid the hoses, nozzles, and broken canister vacs, the unemployed Fox slept with his dogs and guns, occasionally taking to social media to vent about COVID-19 restrictions. He took a video of himself, alone in the cellar, practicing with an unloaded AR-15–style rifle, quickly slapping in a fresh magazine before dropping the gun and whipping out a semiautomatic pistol. His T-shirt depicted an American flag superimposed with the silhouette of an assault weapon.

The semiautomatic rifle that Fox was toying with can fire about forty-five rounds per minute, with each .223-caliber bullet traveling six hundred yards in one second. The gun is lightweight and has ten times the accuracy of a musket, can hold a hundred-round magazine, and is generally equal in firepower to about thirty colonial-era minutemen with the guns of their period. On impact, a single bullet will blow apart a skull or vital organs, leaving a gaping exit wound the size of a fist. If you're still alive when the slug leaves your body, you will bleed out quickly.

I don't own an AR-15, but I've fired them, and I'm always struck by the sense of sheer lethality. There are more powerful rifles—

my 30-06 bolt-action hunting rifle uses larger ammo that travels farther—but the lighter, fast-loading punch of an AR-15 gives it a menacing charisma.

There are tens of millions of these semiautomatic weapons circulating in the civilian population of the United States today. They are easy to purchase online, and, in many states, you can arrange to have them delivered to a licensed dealer for pickup near your home. Those bought through private sales, rather than through a dealer, generally do not require a background check.

In short, AR-15s are weapons of war, dumbed down slightly by not having the option of fully automatic firing. The gun industry is happy to help you get one to live out your patriotic fantasies.

One company sells a semiautomatic military-style rifle called the Militia Model. Another company says on its website it was "founded with one goal, to restore the idea of the Militia. As citizens of a free country, it is our duty to be well equipped and well trained." With a few mouse clicks and a credit card, self-imagined minutemen can arrange to have an AR-15 shipped to a dealer near them.

Some of those arrested in the Whitmer kidnapping plot trained with self-described militias while planning the kidnapping. These organizations have a long and checkered history in Michigan that includes occasional criminal investigations, yet have enjoyed tacit acceptance by some Republican leaders, who find it politically expedient to appear with them at rallies or even inside the state capitol in Lansing.

However, what militia members do not seem to recognize, or choose to ignore, is that the US Constitution granted primary control over militias to the states—and the laws of every state prohibit unauthorized, private military activities. In Michigan, the state constitution explicitly requires that military forces "in all cases and at all times be in strict subordination to the civil power."

In other words, subordinate to the governor.

The Whitmer kidnapping case lurched to a muddled conclusion. Nine suspects pleaded guilty or were convicted, while five others were acquitted, owing in part to allegations of FBI overreach in the use of informants. Fox was sentenced to sixteen years.

The whole affair was quintessentially modern American in its absurdity and danger. Regardless of whether the hapless schemers—more middling men than minutemen—ever really intended to pull it off, they easily obtained enough firepower to kill many people. They also armed themselves with a rationale and sense of mission based on a misreading of history that has proven convenient to business and political interests.

Real militias don't exist anymore. But appreciating their place in American history is vital to understanding gun culture today. The Constitution's references to the militia are an object of consternation or adoration, depending on point of view, and have generally made it more difficult for the country to find agreement on anything involving firearms.

Citizen militias in America have only mustered once to fight government tyranny. And it wasn't the American government they were fighting.

The lookout who spotted the British ships from atop the Yale chapel that July 5 morning in 1779 was none other than Naphtali Daggett's successor as college president, Ezra Stiles. The townsfolk had been warned that such an assault could occur, but as Stiles described it later in a diary, "a lethargy seemed to have seized the inhabitants" as they hoped, without reason, that the invasion force might pass them by.

They were soon disabused of that notion.

General Tryon and his second-in-command, Gen. George Garth, landed two raiding parties of roughly three thousand British regulars and Hessian mercenaries. The first redcoats to arrive read aloud, to anyone within earshot, an "Address to the Inhabitants of Connecticut," which was an exquisitely English blend of menace, leniency, and sneer at the threat posed by the rebel militias:

"Can the strength of your whole province cope with the force which might at any time be poured through every district in your country? You are conscious it cannot. Why, then, will you persist in a ruinous and ill-judged resistance?"

The challenges faced by the citizen militias were apparent in how they coped with the New Haven invasion. On the plus side, they were well armed.

The first English colonists had received regular shipments of firearms to equip their militias for fighting the Pequots and whatever else was required of them. But over the next hundred years, as the colonies grew, so, too, did their ability to make their own guns, increasingly flintlocks, superior to the unwieldy and less accurate matchlocks, which were inoperable in bad weather.

Gunsmithing, made possible by the abundance of natural resources in the New World combined with Old World skills, began as small apprenticeships. A lone gunsmith, wearing a blackened cowhide apron, might take weeks to fashion a custom-made musket, forging the iron and cutting maple or cherry wood for the stock.

During the eighteenth century, gun manufacturing expanded to full-blown factories in the cities, such that, by the start of the Revolution, it didn't matter when the British Crown finally halted arms shipments. The Americans were capable of producing tens of thousands of muskets per year (though they relied heavily on weapons imported from France and Spain as the war progressed).

But even as the availability of firearms increased, the training requirements of New England militias had gradually scaled back before the war, as the threat from native populations receded. General training days had slipped from monthly to eight times a year in Massachusetts, four in Connecticut, and two in Rhode Island.

They were, after all, not a standing army of professional fighters, but everyday people with jobs, families, and homes to worry about. Even Stiles acknowledged that the first things he did after sounding the alarm were to set about safeguarding Yale's important papers, saving his furniture, and sending his daughter out of harm's way.

The local men, he wrote, had a decidedly uneven response to the approaching British forces.

"Perhaps one-third of the adult male inhabitants flew to arms and went out to meet them. A quarter moved out of town doing nothing, the rest remained unmoved, partly Tories, partly timid Whigs."

One of those Tories was Joshua Chandler, a wealthy businessman whose family manse overlooked the town center. As a loyalist, he welcomed the arrival of His Majesty's troops to dampen the spirit of rebellion, which was, to his mind, sowing division and disorder.

Two of Chandler's four sons were cooperating with the British and helping guide them into New Haven. According to a journal kept by one of Chandler's daughters, on the morning of July 5, another of Chandler's sons relayed to the family the disconcerting news that the arriving British would likely be met with stiff resistance:

"Jim Hillhouse and his men have picketed the whole coast for miles, and by my faith, if General Tryon lands he'll get a reception that he little expects."

Capt. James Hillhouse was a militia commander who was among the first to engage the British when they landed shortly after dawn. Indeed, despite the fear or indifference described by Stiles, hundreds of men did heed the call to defend the city. Hillhouse—who in real life was a lawyer and builder—had his unit drag cannons into place and take up hiding positions along roads leading from the shore.

The British made a lot of mistakes. The temperatures that summer day were scorching, making long marches in their woolen uniforms barely tolerable, and their commanders had underestimated the militia resistance. At one point, General Garth, bogged down by American musket and cannon fire near a bridge, sent a dispatch to General Tryon saying, "We have had a little difficulty with the rebels in coming hither" and his men were "greatly fatigued through heat." Tryon himself wrote in a report of his raiding campaign that his troops had been "under a continuous fire" from militia units in and around New Haven.

Ultimately, however, the militias were no match for the British forces, who overran the city by early afternoon. At the Tory household of Joshua Chandler, the arrival of Tryon's troops was not the welcome event the family had expected. As British regulars moved house to house accompanied by Hessian mercenaries, whose dark uniforms and tall hats were distinct from the red coats of their counterparts, the day descended into horror for most residents.

Soldiers got drunk, stole valuables, and shot cattle. Hessians dragged young women, screaming, into the streets and molested them. Old people and children were beaten and humiliated.

One house that was spared was the Chandlers'. Before the day's atrocities, Joshua had arranged to host General Tryon for dinner. Now, as the setting sun cast shadows across a battered New Haven cityscape, the British officers arrived at his door to keep their appointment.

Writing later in her journal, Joshua Chandler's daughter gave an unnerving description of the evening:

"Gen. Tryon was very polite and courteous, his remarks were well chosen and his conversation witty, and during dinner caused much merriment. It was hard to believe so cultured a gentleman was at heart so wicked as to lead such cowardly murderers."

The citizen militias of early America indisputably made a difference during the war with Britain. As in the case of the battle of New Haven, their main benefit was to add an unpredictable and harassing element, degrading enemy strength and forcing the British to factor them in when making plans.

Small militia units, unable to avail themselves of regimented lines of trained musketeers who alternated firing and reloading, adapted the use of their guns for guerrilla warfare. Because each man was effectively on his own, he had to shoot from a hiding place where he could take the time needed to reload his musket without fear of being killed.

Not surprisingly, the militias' record of success was spotty. Militia units supplemented the newly raised Continental Army, sometimes to great effect, as when Vermont minutemen beat back German mercenaries at Bennington in 1777 and patriot militias defeated their loyalist opposites at Kings Mountain in South Carolina in 1780. Even the battle of New Haven saw General Tryon's troops pull out the very next day as militia reinforcements moved into the area, though the decision to leave was also attributable to the weakening of British forces from drinking and oppressive heat.

Other times, it was the militias' own lack of discipline that was disastrous. Hundreds of militiamen cut and ran at the battle of Camden, handing the British a significant victory in the Southern Campaign. Of course, the Continental Army itself, burdened by short-term enlistments, haphazard supply chains, and interstate rivalries, had its own problems with consistency.

When the war ended, hard decisions had to be made on how to maintain a peacetime military capability and what role the militia would play. Who would compose it? Would the new national government or individual states control it? Should there even be a citizen militia, as opposed to a professional army?

Driving the debate was the inexorable tension between Federalists, who favored a strong national government, and Anti-Federalists, concerned primarily with states' rights. The philosophical differences were most stark on the militia question, since an existential fear of the founding generation was that a standing army could be misused by a despotic ruler. Of all the big questions, they had to get this one right.

The Constitutional Convention came up with a compromise. The task of putting it down on paper fell largely to James Madison, who not long afterward would also craft the Second Amendment.

Bookish, five feet four, and slightly built, the diminutive future president of the United States suffered from health problems, including anxiety, which would consume him toward the end of his life. He served as an officer in the Virginia militia during the Revolution but never saw battle, largely due to his frail condition. Unlike his contemporaries Alexander Hamilton, John Adams, and Thomas Jefferson, Madison was not a lawyer, though he had studied the law.

His real talents sprang from a restless intellect, nurtured by a classical education at what would become Princeton University and almost immediately put to use in the political affairs of the fledgling nation. Within five years of graduating in 1771, Madison joined Virginia's House of Delegates, and at age twenty-nine became the youngest member of the Continental Congress. In these early legislative roles, he quickly garnered a reputation as an indefatigable, if unassuming, participant in the major issues of the day—qualities that served him well when he later emerged as a guiding force at the convention.

Madison, who came to be regarded as the "Father of the Constitution," sought to balance the periodic military requirements of a central government with the desire to decentralize power over that military among the states. The founding document that emerged from the convention declared that Congress would "provide for organizing, arming, and disciplining, the Militia, and for governing such Part of them as may be employed in the Service of the United States," but leave "the Appointment of the Officers, and the Authority of training the Militia" to the states.

And what was the purpose of the militia that Madison and his compatriots envisioned? Was it, as would be argued by self-described "militia" gunmen of today, to empower citizens to engage in armed resistance to laws they didn't like or even insurrection against their own government?

Article I, section 8, clause 15, of the Constitution spelled it out. Congress had the power "to provide for calling forth the Militia to execute the Laws of the Union, suppress Insurrections and repel Invasions."

In other words, the precise opposite of what constitutional extremists of the modern era choose to believe.

This should come as no surprise. While the framers rightly worried about the specter of a standing army—Madison called it "one of the greatest mischiefs that can possibly happen"—they also were acutely aware of the need for order and the rule of law. As Hamilton would remark, on the occasion of the federal government deploying the militia to quash an armed rebellion by farmers opposed to a new tax, there was "no such thing as a 'constitutional resistance' to laws constitutionally enacted."

When it came time to ratify the Constitution, Madison went to the ramparts to argue the Federalist position. Writing in Federalist 46 in January 1788, he sought to knock down arguments that it would effectively disarm states and leave them at the mercy of a central tyrannical force, deriding them as "the misjudged exaggerations of a counterfeit zeal" rather than "the sober apprehensions of genuine patriotism."

He went on to do the math, making the case that, at best, the new federal government might be able to raise an army of twenty-five thousand to thirty thousand men:

"To these would be opposed a militia amounting to near half a million of citizens with arms in their hands, officered by men chosen from among themselves, fighting for their common liberties, and united and conducted by governments possessing their affections and confidence."

Even in Madison's worst-case scenario of an uprising against federal oppression, it would be "conducted by governments"—meaning the states that controlled and regulated their militias—and not armed individuals acting on their own.

Six months later, on June 14, 1788, Madison joined Virginia delegates to debate ratification and again tangled with Anti-Federalists on the subject of the militia. He continued to thread the needle between the need for a federal military component and states' demands for control. Madison made the point that when left solely to state legislatures, militia units during the war had been "neglected and rendered unfit," and that the Constitution offered a safe remedy.

"I cannot conceive that this Constitution, by giving the general government the power of arming the militia, takes it away from the state governments," said Madison. "The power is concurrent, and not exclusive."

When the Constitution was eventually ratified, it did not end the squabbling over the militia—or many other things. It is important to recognize that while the militia question was certainly of major concern, it was hardly the *only* subject confronting the founders. Commerce, taxation, and the structure of government itself were front and center. The Constitution laid down the foundation for all that, but many Americans, particularly Anti-Federalists, who continued to worry about centralized power, believed it did not go far enough in protecting basic rights and freedoms.

To win votes during ratification, Federalist supporters had reluctantly agreed to address the concerns by adding a bill of rights later, through amendments. Madison initially opposed the idea, thinking it unnecessary.

Among the champions of the bill of rights was Jefferson, Madison's fellow Virginian and a mentor. Jefferson, who was in Paris at the time, had written to Madison in December 1787 to share his thoughts about the new Constitution, including a list of "what I do not like":

"First the omission of a bill of rights providing clearly and without the aid of sophisms for freedom of religion, freedom of the press, protection against standing armies, restriction against monopolies, the eternal and unremitting force of the habeas corpus laws, and trials by jury in all matters of fact triable by the laws of the land and not by the law of Nations."

What Jefferson was enumerating was, essentially, an embryonic list of amendments, and the reference to "standing armies" underscored, yet again, the crucial context from which the Second Amendment would soon emerge.

Madison gradually came around to accepting the need for a well-defined set of amendments, mostly as a way of staving off the dreaded specter of another constitutional convention. Ratification had been a bitter and hard-won battle, and its Federalist victors were increasingly concerned that rabble-rousers out in the states could succeed in reopening the entire process. A bill of rights could quiet the agitators.

For Madison, there were also personal reasons in the mix. He had narrowly defeated James Monroe to win a seat in the new House of Representatives, in part by promising to support a bill of rights. Not a fan of retail politicking, he had to be browbeaten into taking to the hustings, but now that he had done it—and won—he intended to keep his campaign pledge.

Ever the dutiful and learned grind, Madison took on the task of drafting the amendments. He collected proposals from the states and set about distilling them into a coherent and comprehensive list to be approved through a committee process in Congress.

It is generally understood that little meaning should be attached to how the Bill of Rights is ordered. In fact, Madison didn't initially even envision listing them at all—he wanted them woven into the text of the Constitution, an idea Congress rejected for fear that it would look like a stealth rewriting of the document. Instead, they were appended to the end.

For guidance, Madison leaned heavily on the Virginia Declaration of Rights, which preceded the Declaration of Independence. There are many echoes from the 1776 Virginia treatise that appear in the Bill of Rights, including that "freedom of the press is one of the great bulwarks of liberty" and that "all men are equally entitled to the free exercise of religion."

That earlier declaration had also dealt with the issue of the militia, plainly asserting the reason for securing a right to bear arms:

"That a well regulated militia, composed of the body of the people, trained to arms, is the proper, natural, and safe defense of a free state; that standing armies, in time of peace, should be avoided as dangerous to liberty; and that in all cases the military should be under strict subordination to, and governed by, the civil power."

On the question of bearing arms, other states also addressed it in their constitutions, and while each placed it in the context of a militia, some went further. Vermont and Pennsylvania declared that "the people have a right to bear arms for the defence of themselves and the state," making a point of safeguarding self-defense in addition to militia service. Others, such as Massachusetts and North Carolina, only made references to the "common defence" or "defence of the state."

Madison's first crack at what would become the Second Amendment was similar, but contained some curious differences. When submitted to the House in June 1789, the text read:

"The right of the people to keep and bear arms shall not be infringed; a well armed and well regulated militia being the best security of a free country: but no person religiously scrupulous of bearing arms shall be compelled to render military service in person."

The last part of the amendment made an allowance for conscientious objectors. By stipulating that they would not be forced to take part in the militia "in person," Madison was acknowledging a practice in that era of using a substitute or paying a fee to fulfill military service. The "religiously scrupulous" clause also demonstrated, lest there remain any doubt, how the right to bear arms was inherently bound up in the desire to maintain a well-regulated—meaning well trained and disciplined—military capability.

Madison had initially placed the right to bear arms *before* the reference to a militia. The best explanation for this is that it reflected his original intent to work it into the body of the Constitution, specifically the section outlining other curbs on federal power. But the House rejected that approach, and when a committee reworked

Madison's list, it flipped around the amendment's wording so that it was closer to a freestanding statement with an introductory preamble.

Second Amendment scholar Saul Cornell, who has written extensively on the importance of the militia in colonial-era gun rights deliberations, said, "The decision to recast the language had enormous constitutional significance."

"Framing the right to bear arms as a corollary of a preamble focusing on the need for a well-regulated militia clearly signaled that the purpose of the amendment was to protect the militia," Cornell wrote.

By the time the final wording had cleared the House and the Senate in September 1789, the reference to religious objectors had been dropped. The set of twelve proposed amendments then went out for ratification by the states, which failed to agree on the first two dealing with congressional apportionment and pay raises. That meant that everything else on the list got bumped up.

What had been the third of the amendments—freedom of religion, speech, and the press—became first, and bearing arms second.

George Washington had his doubts about putting too much stock in the militia.

The first president initially argued in favor of maintaining a few reduced standing regiments, augmented by militias that would serve as the initial line of defense until a full army could be raised, much as had been done during the Revolution. Washington knew firsthand the risk of overreliance on citizen units. In a letter to John Hancock in 1776, the general complained that militiamen had often caused more harm than good in battle:

"To place any dependence upon militia, is, assuredly, resting upon a broken staff. Men just dragged from the tender scenes of domestic life—unaccustomed to the din of arms—totally unacquainted with every kind of military skill, which being followed by a want of confidence in themselves when opposed to troops regularly trained—disciplined, and appointed—superior in knowledge & superior in arms, makes them timid, and ready to fly from their own shadows."

In the postwar period, however, militias enjoyed wide political support. Beyond existential concerns about standing armies, America's founding generation had conjured a romantic idyll of the citizen-soldier grabbing his musket and racing to the people's defense. Congress rejected several of Washington's military proposals before eventually agreeing to retain a rump force of one-year enlistments from various states, to be supplemented by militia units when necessary.

The United States did not have to wait long to test this new arrangement. Washington was barely into his first term as president when he was faced with deploying a force of nearly fifteen hundred men—the vast majority of them militia members—to drive out Indigenous warriors blocking American expansion in the Northwest Territory. It was an unmitigated disaster, the first of several in that conflict between 1790 and 1791, resulting in a total of more than a thousand US casualties and emboldening the British to increase support for their Native American allies.

The military failures in the West forced an early reckoning, leading to the creation of larger, more permanent regiments that ultimately formed the basis for the modern army (though it took the War of 1812 to put an exclamation point on the folly of a militia-based defense of the nation). It was becoming painfully apparent as early as 1790 that an emerging geopolitical power, with expansionist designs, could not rely on shopkeepers and farmers as its tip of the spear.

By the time the Second Amendment was ratified in December 1791, the rationale for it was already in doubt.

THE AMERICAN MIND

A FEW MONTHS BEFORE the Bill of Rights was ratified in December 1791, the governor of South Carolina, Charles Pinckney, wrote an urgent letter to George Washington.

Pinckney explained that he had received a request for assistance from the French colonial rulers of Saint-Domingue (modern-day Haiti), who were struggling to quell a violent uprising by enslaved Africans. It seemed that the enslaved people, who vastly outnumbered their white European and mixed-race overlords on the island, had staged a sweeping revolt that threatened to inspire similar insurrections in other slaveholding societies.

"I am afraid if not checked in time," Pinckney wrote, "it is a flame which will extend to all the neighbouring islands, & may eventually prove not a very pleasing or agreeable example to the Southern States."

Had the Second Amendment actually been created for the purpose of empowering any individual to take up arms in self-defense rather than for the maintenance of a well-regulated militia—the argument of the modern-day gun lobby—rebellious slaves might have benefited the most. But the amendment had not, and the slaves did not.

From the earliest days of colonization, white authorities made sure to qualify laws on gun ownership so that Black people, Native Americans, and certain other minority groups were excluded. Fear of armed uprisings was especially prevalent in slave-dependent states in the South, where in many places enslaved people outnumbered whites.

In September 1739, about twenty enslaved Africans in South Carolina escaped in what became known as the Stono Rebellion and decided to make their way to Spanish Florida, where Spain had issued a proclamation promising freedom to slaves from the British colonies. The first thing they did was target a cache of firearms, as recounted later by an unnamed colonial official, who wrote that the rebels "surprised a warehouse belonging to Mr. Hutchenson."

The band of rebels marched on toward Florida and gained followers, eventually numbering close to one hundred, as they burned houses and killed white families along the way. In response, the white settlers raised a militia and caught up to the Africans, killing most of them before they could make it to the border. In the colonial official's written account, the militiamen's decision to shoot even those rebels who tried to surrender was depicted as admirable forbearance:

"This is to be said to the honour of the Carolina Planters, that notwithstanding the Provocation they had received from so many Murders, they did not torture one Negroe, but only put them to an easy death."

South Carolinians responded to this massacre with a new law, the Act for the Better Ordering, of 1740, cracking down on the few liberties enslaved Black people had up to that point, including a provision that "it shall not be lawful for any slave, unless in the presence of some white person, to carry or make use of fire arms."

Keeping guns out of the hands of Black people was a recurring theme in eighteenth-century debates over the formation of government. Thomas Jefferson's early drafts of a Virginia state constitution contained the phrase, not included in the final version, "No freeman shall be debarred the use of arms" (keyword "freeman"). Arguing over ratification of the US Constitution, Virginia convention delegate Patrick Henry fretted that it limited the use of the militia only to defending against foreign invaders, and not "an insurrection of slaves" (Federalists assured him it did not).

The Second Amendment ended up making no distinction between white and Black bearing of arms. But it didn't have to. The Constitution, while not explicitly addressing the issue of slavery, contained enough references to make clear that Black people were not afforded the same rights as others. Among other things, it required that escaped slaves be returned to their owners and not granted freedom.

More to the point, by largely remaining silent for political expediency, the founders allowed states, mostly in the South, to write their own laws denying Black people the right to possess firearms. For the most part, the prohibitions worked.

Slave rebellions in the early nineteenth century rarely involved widespread use of guns because they were hard to acquire. The most famous of them, led by Nat Turner in Virginia in 1831, was carried out by more than seventy people armed almost entirely with bladed or blunt weapons, who managed to kill about sixty white people before being suppressed by militia units with guns (the rebels also chose not to use the few firearms they found to avoid drawing attention).

Virginia had laws dating to the mid-seventeenth century preventing even free Black people from having guns. After the Turner uprising—in which some freemen were accused of being conspirators—other states that didn't already have such restrictions followed suit, including Georgia, which banned gun possession for freemen entirely, and Delaware, which instituted a licensing requirement.

To be sure, many free Black Americans, including active abolitionists, obtained firearms when they were able to, particularly after passage of the Fugitive Slave Act in 1850. The law allowed agents from slaveholding states to pursue and reclaim enslaved people who had escaped to the North. There was fear that even free Black Americans could be handed over into slavery because of poor documentation around the keeping of enslaved people.

By the time of John Brown's raid on Harpers Ferry, Virginia, in 1859, many abolitionists had accepted that only armed revolt could overturn the institution of slavery. Supporters in the North sent almost two hundred rifles for Brown's raiding party, but because Brown believed most of the enslaved blacks that he envisioned joining him were not familiar with guns, he also had nearly a thousand metal pikes delivered for them to use. Almost none of them saw action because the hoped-for uprising never happened.

A desire to disarm "the other" is a persistent vein that has coursed through gun control efforts ever since firearms were invented.

English laws dating back to the sixteenth century limited access to firearms by the poor and, later, Catholics, a religious minority deemed to be a potential threat after the Protestant Reformation. Edicts issued in feudal Japan were aimed at keeping guns and swords out of the hands of peasants. The Nazis banned possession of guns and other weapons by Jews in the prelude to the Holocaust.

Given the prevalence of guns in my family when I was growing up, I was surprised to discover that my own ancestors faced varying experiences with state control over firearms depending on their ethnic or racial origins. My mother's American lineage traces to an English settler who arrived in the Massachusetts Bay Colony in the early seventeenth century, belonged to a militia, and fought the Pequots.

But her ancestors also include members of the Mohegan tribe, who were among those denied the right to obtain firearms in Connecticut under restrictions dating to at least 1642. A law passed that year declared that no colonist "shall sell or give to any Indean, directly or indirectly, any such gun or gunpowder, or shott, or lead."

By the late nineteenth century, my father's Scottish ancestors had settled in rural Maine and had little trouble arming themselves for hunting, trapping, and, eventually, guiding others on paid excursions into the wilderness. Meanwhile, Irish immigrants on my mother's side found a less welcome reception in the urban areas where they arrived.

Crime associated with Irish and Italian immigrant communities that were swelling in big cities led to new gun laws in Northern states in the late 1800s and early 1900s. Lawlessness was a very real problem, made worse by a proliferation of cheap revolvers, some costing as little as fifty cents, the equivalent of about twelve dollars today. But in practice, some of the restrictions, such as New York's Sullivan Act of 1911, allowed police to discriminate based on nationality or ethnicity when issuing gun permits.

With time the Irish assimilated—by the 1930s, my maternal grandfather was a city police officer carrying a gun, a big step up from his father, a jail custodian. But the African American experience was different.

Well into the twentieth century and beyond, Black people have faced discriminatory treatment when attempting to exercise basic rights, including gun ownership. After his house was bombed in Alabama in 1956, Martin Luther King Jr. tried to obtain a permit to carry a pistol but was deemed "unsuitable" by the local sheriff, who had wide discretion to deny applicants.

In California in the 1960s the Black Panthers began utilizing their right, under state law, to openly carry guns in the form of "cop watching" patrols in minority neighborhoods where tensions with the police were high. The state legislature responded by passing the Mulford Act, a bipartisan law that barred open carry of loaded weapons without a permit.

Even when following the guidelines and tradition of legal gun ownership hallowed by the NRA, African Americans do not always enjoy the same benefit of the doubt afforded others. When Philando Castile was pulled over for a faulty brake light in Minnesota in 2016, he announced he had a licensed pistol on him but was shot and killed anyway while apparently reaching for his ID. In Alabama in 2018, Emantic "EJ" Bradford Jr., a soldier on leave, pulled out his licensed handgun after someone started shooting inside a shopping mall and was shot to death, from behind, by officers who mistook him for a suspect.

These and similar cases were never recognized in the same way that gun rights proponents made a cause célèbre of, say, Kyle Rittenhouse, the white teenager who said he came to Kenosha, Wisconsin, with an AR-15–style rifle to protect local businesses during unruly civil rights protests and ended up shooting three people. Unlike Castile and Bradford, Rittenhouse, seventeen, had willingly inserted himself into a dangerous situation, and it wasn't even clear if he should have had a gun in the first place—a judge threw out a charge of illegal possession by a minor amid debate over the confusingly worded law. Rittenhouse, who claimed self-defense, was acquitted of the remaining charges.

To understand the antecedents of this dichotomy, one has to return to the institution of slavery, which arguably contributed to the metastasizing of violence in the American body politic more than anything else. Its secondary effects spread into the culture and psyche of the nation, particularly in the South, long before the Civil War and have in some ways lingered ever since.

"The relation of master and slave begins in violence," wrote Theodore Parker, an early-nineteenth-century abolitionist and minister. "It must be sustained by violence—the systematic violence of general laws, or the irregular violence of individual caprice."

The antebellum period saw a slow-boiling change in public attitudes as the national cancer that was slavery became increasingly untenable. Cultural and political hostility became entrenched. Americans hated each other.

Murder rates rose, especially in Southern states, where the perverse enforcement requirements of slaveholding had instilled an almost casual acceptance of violence. Historian Randolph Roth documented the uniquely vicious tendencies found in the South, which he connected to a slavery-induced coarsening of the culture as a whole, fueled by a "tradition of ruthless vigilantism."

"Murderers elsewhere in the United States were certainly capable of sadistic violence," Roth said, adding, "But northern whites rarely tortured other whites."

At the same time, westward expansion was fostering a frontier ethic that emphasized individual action in the absence of state-imposed law and order. Settlers were essentially on their own, expected to defend themselves against all manner of threats, whether they be resistant natives, thieves, or violent drunks.

The Civil War flooded the country with firearms, and in its aftermath there was a need both to restrict their usage by extrajudicial militias such as the Ku Klux Klan and other white vigilantes in the South, and also to empower newly emancipated enslaved people to defend themselves. The rise of "black codes" during Reconstruction included many attempts at the state and local levels to continue the old practices of denying guns to nonwhites, sometimes through local ordinance, other times violently through nighttime raids by the Klan.

Washington responded with laws and military orders that sought to counter them. The federal government banned public and concealed carrying of guns in parts of the former Confederacy, but also sought to balance that with a recognition of a right to self-defense. The dichotomy can be found in a General Order of 1866, which declared that the "constitutional rights of all loyal and well-disposed inhabitants to bear arms will not be infringed; nevertheless this shall not be construed to sanction the unlawful practice of carrying concealed weapons," adding for good measure, "And no disorderly person, vagrant, or disturber of the peace, shall be allowed to bear arms."

In 1866, Congress also passed the Fourteenth Amendment, which sought to ensure equal protection of rights, including to bear arms, for African Americans. The intention of the amendment was to push the federal recognition of various rights down to the states and require that any constitutionally permissible limits be race neutral.

Indeed, the nineteenth century saw a profound evolution in the way guns were regulated across the country, not only because of the postwar legal and military restrictions imposed in the South but also because of larger societal shifts. In what Patrick Charles, a scholar and historian for the US Air Force, calls the "armed citizenry model," the right to bear arms gradually moved away from its original militia context to one where individuals kept firearms for self-defense. Colonial-era militias became obsolete, replaced by corps of paid volunteers that eventually formed the basis for the National Guard.

As the growing nation attempted to deal with interracial violence in the South and lawlessness on the western frontier, firearms usage was being legislated and adjudicated based on common law and state constitutions.

Post–Civil War constitutions in many states included a right to bear arms that contained qualifiers allowing for government regulation where necessary. The 1869 Texas constitution declared, "Every person shall have the right to keep and bear arms, in the lawful defense of himself or the State, *under such regulations as the Legislature may prescribe*" (emphasis added).

Florida in 1885 enshrined a right to bear arms, adding "but the Legislature may prescribe the manner in which they may be borne." The Idaho constitution of 1889 contained a similar clause, saying, "The legislature shall regulate the exercise of this right by law."

What all of this meant, legally, was that the Second Amendment protection of gun ownership for militia purposes was increasingly irrelevant in the courts. This trend reached an apotheosis of sorts with the US Supreme Court's decision in *United States v. Cruikshank* in

1876, which almost glancingly shoved aside efforts to find an individual right to bear arms in the Second Amendment outside of the militia context.

Cruikshank dealt with larger issues than just gun rights. The high court overturned the convictions of whites prosecuted under federal law for taking part in a horrific massacre of Black people in Louisiana that arose from a political dispute in which both sides were armed. Federal prosecutors had argued that the white mob denied the victims their First and Second Amendment rights of free assembly and bearing of arms.

The court, however, declared that those constitutional rights offered protection only from federal government interference and did not apply to states or individuals. The plaintiffs, in other words, should have sought justice at the state level and not have invoked federal authorities.

In explaining itself, the *Cruikshank* court made some significant observations about gun rights. It said, in essence, that the Second Amendment was intended only to ensure that states would not have their militia powers usurped by the federal government; it was not written to protect an individual right to keep and bear arms because there was no need for that:

"This is not a right granted by the Constitution. Neither is it in any manner dependent upon that instrument for its existence. The Second Amendment declares that it shall not be infringed, but this, as has been seen, means no more than that it shall not be infringed by Congress. This is one of the amendments that has no other effect than to restrict the powers of the national government."

There was much to regret about the *Cruikshank* decision, which effectively derailed attempts to use federal power to safeguard the rights of African Americans in the South and delayed, for a hundred years, incorporation of federal rights into state law. Unable to rely on the national government for security, Southern Black people were subjected to the rise of Jim Crow laws that enshrined racial discrimination far into the twentieth century.

Purely from a gun rights perspective, however, the high court's interpretation of the Second Amendment, coming much closer in time to the founding era, arguably captured its intent more faithfully than the court's twenty-first-century successors. Its premise was reaffirmed ten years later in *Presser v. Illinois*, in which the high court ruled that only states have the power to authorize militias and regulate the bearing of arms.

The *Presser* court did make clear that states could only go so far in restricting firearms before impinging on the federal government's own security needs. States could not "prohibit the people from keeping and bearing arms, so as to deprive the United States of their rightful resource for maintaining the public security, and disable the people from performing their duty to the general government."

But the federal government's need for armed citizen-soldiers in reserve would further erode in the years ahead. Passage of the Militia Act of 1903 began formalizing the National Guard, which soon replaced local militias altogether.

The post–Civil War period proved to be a crucible for annealing the American way of violence into something that resembles what we recognize today. It took shape out in the land, but would be saluted and codified in the halls of legislatures and the courts.

There were a handful of authorities from that era who best articulated the changes taking place. One was William Ellis Niblack. A nineteenth-century Democratic congressman from Indiana and a champion of westward expansion, Niblack had briefly been talked about as a possible presidential candidate in 1876. It was the country's centennial and patriotic passions were running high.

That year had seen the crushing defeat of George Armstrong Custer at the Battle of the Little Bighorn, and there was a general impatience with native tribes standing in the way of America's Manifest Destiny to claim the entire western continent. In fact, hundreds of years had passed since the battles with the Pequots, and Americans were *still* waging bloody wars against the Indigenous population. During that time, the country had also emerged from a bloody revolution and an even bloodier civil war.

Viewed from the outside, violence seemed to be the country's creed. Yet the national mood was one of pride, if not jingoistic fervor, and there was little appetite for introspection.

After seven terms in Congress, Niblack chose not to run again and instead launched a successful campaign for a seat on the Indiana Supreme Court—where he almost immediately was confronted with a case that would become critical to understanding, and shaping, America's relationship to violence.

Niblack had overcome a hardscrabble upbringing on the frontier. He attended classes in a log schoolhouse and had to drop out of college when his father died, yet managed to become a surveyor and eventually a lawyer. In Congress, he enthusiastically voted for the integration of Minnesota and Oregon into the Union and, in 1860, favored Kansas's admission despite a raging debate over whether it would be a proslavery state.

Taking to the House floor in April 1860, Niblack had made the case that the issue of slavery did not matter because the Kansas territory met every qualification necessary to join the United States. He referred to the "irrepressible conflict," a term recently coined by William Henry Seward to describe the country's need to once and for all reckon with the slavery question. It was an issue, Niblack said, "reaching down to the very foundations of our government and involving fundamental principles of society itself.

"An issue which, when interpreted as John Brown and his followers seem to have understood and interpreted it, would deluge this land in blood."

Conservative in his politics, he also expressed serious reservations about giving too much power to the federal government and insisted on the need to protect individual liberty from state-sanctioned oppression. In another speech before Congress, this one in the years after the Civil War, Niblack warned against continued military occupation of the South, saying the army could not be trusted to administer civil duties safely.

On election day in 1876, as Niblack was waiting in his hometown of Vincennes to learn if Indianans would elevate him to their Supreme

Court, one of those voters, John Runyan, was headed to the polls in New Castle on the other side of the state. Niblack and Runyan had never met, but fate would soon intertwine their paths.

Runyan, a Democrat in a largely Republican community, intended to vote for Samuel Tilden in the presidential election. But on his way there, Runyan was accosted by a big loudmouth named John Spell. Despite name-calling and threats from Spell, a supporter of Republican Rutherford B. Hayes, Runyan got to the polling place and cast his ballot.

Spell didn't let up, however. Returning home, Runyan was again harassed by the larger man. Unnerved by the experience, Runyan, who had a disability preventing the full use of his right arm, asked a friend if he could borrow a pistol for safety. Now armed, he went out later that evening to try to learn about the election results.

Outside the polling place, where a crowd was gathering, Runyan soon found himself again drawn into partisan bickering. This time, a man named Charles Pressnall began bullying him. What happened next was a matter of dispute—Runyan claimed Pressnall physically attacked him, other witnesses said it was only verbal—but it ended with Runyan pulling out his gun and shooting Pressnall, who later died.

Runyan was charged with manslaughter. At his trial, the judge issued a lengthy set of instructions to the jury, which included a disquisition on self-defense. After affirming the right of individuals to protect themselves from assault, sometimes even to the point of killing the aggressor, the judge laid down an important caveat: "If the person assailed can protect his life and his person by retreating, it is his duty to retreat, and thus avoid the necessity of taking human life."

The judge was articulating a very old concept. English common law, dating back centuries, favored retreating in the face of aggression when in public spaces, all the way "to the wall"—a legal term—before resorting to deadly force. That canon informed jurisprudence that had developed in the American colony and was generally recognized as an attempt to minimize homicides by requiring at least one party in a dispute to de-escalate.

In fact, by the late nineteenth century some state courts, particularly in the North, were increasingly seeing firearms as a threat to the established order. The Maine Supreme Court, dismissing a self-defense claim in an 1865 shooting case, declared that people "should not be permitted to carry deadly weapons in a civilized community. Their possession tends to induce their use."

Runyan was convicted and sentenced to eight years in prison. He appealed to the Indiana Supreme Court, where he challenged the part of the jury instructions pertaining to self-defense. He found a receptive audience in newly elected Justice Niblack.

Writing for the majority, Niblack found that the lower court had erred—not in explaining the legal concept of avoiding violence if at all possible, but, rather, in failing to make clear that it just wasn't the way we do it in America:

"A very brief examination of the American authorities makes it evident that the ancient doctrine, as to the duty of a person assailed to retreat as far as he can, before he is justified in repelling force by force, has been greatly modified in this country. Indeed, the tendency of the American mind seems to be very strongly against the enforcement of any rule which requires a person to flee when assailed, to avoid chastisement or even to save human life."

The message was clear: Don't tread on me.

Niblack's rumination on "the American mind," written as the nation was still abuzz with its centennial celebration of independence from the British throne, was getting at something foundational to how his countrymen viewed the world. Americans were different. Not just in the form of government they chose to create, but in the violence that gave birth to that great experiment and, crucially, the continuing embrace of violence as necessary not just to survive but to do so with honor.

Not violence for the random sake of it. But violence that was directed, relied upon, and justified as a means to an end.

Wiping out the native populations was excused as being in the service of God, king, and country. Brutally enforcing slavery was deemed necessary for the economic growth of the colonies. Violently rebelling against Britain was seen as an inalienable right. And responding with force when confronted by belligerence was expected.

As Richard Maxwell Brown, one of the foremost historians of

American violence, wrote, "Apart from its role in the formation and preservation of the nation, violence has been a determinant of both the form and the substance of American life."

"One significant feature of the Revolution is that the example of violent resistance to the mother country, and all the acts of violence associated with that great event, served as a grand model for later violent actions by Americans in behalf of any cause."

Of course, Niblack's ruling—one of the first to assert a uniquely American right to *not* retreat in the face of aggression—did not sanction the proactive use of violence to achieve a goal. As a legal matter, it was simply moving the goalposts for what was allowable when defending oneself.

But his tantalizing reference to a basic, almost feral ingredient of the American condition was memorable and in some ways more important. He didn't simply reject the notion that Americans had to back down when assailed—he suggested they needn't do so "even to save human life."

Niblack's ruling would be cited in a landmark 1895 US Supreme Court case, *Beard v. U.S.*, which established a common law right to stand one's ground against an aggressor. The justices in *Beard* also cited a second state court ruling, this one from Ohio, that was similar to Niblack's and also coincided with the centennial. In that case, the Ohio Supreme Court had found that forcing someone to retreat in the face of aggression was essentially legalized cowardice, and that "a true man who is without fault is not obliged to fly from an assailant."

The cases represented a seismic expansion of the sanctioned use of deadly force, which had previously enjoyed legal protection only in the context of defending oneself at home—the "castle doctrine," which had existed in English common law for centuries. The cases also laid the groundwork for contemporary stand-your-ground laws and case precedents that today exist in all but a handful of states.

The concept was successfully invoked in 2013 by George Zimmerman, the neighborhood watch volunteer who shot and killed Trayvon Martin in a Florida suburb. Zimmerman had confronted and questioned Martin, an unarmed Black teenager walking through the area, and ended up shooting him during a fight in which Zimmerman said he feared for his life. A jury acquitted him of second-degree murder.

In 2025, a Philadelphia jury acquitted Maurice Byrd, a Black man charged with first-degree murder for shooting Stephen Strassburg, who had repeatedly harassed Byrd with racist taunts until the two men wound up scuffling in a parking lot. Byrd argued his actions were justifiable under the state's stand-your-ground law.

The degree to which the proliferation of guns contributed to the judiciary's reinterpretation of self-defense was underscored in another state supreme court decision around the turn of the twentieth century. In Minnesota in 1905, the justices overturned the murder conviction of a frontiersman who had shot a neighbor during an argument, ruling that the duty to retreat had become effectively outdated because of firearms:

"The doctrine of 'retreat to the wall' had its origin before the general introduction of guns. Justice demands that its application have due regard to the present general use and to the type of firearms. It would be good sense for the law to require, in many cases, an attempt to escape from a hand to hand encounter with fists, clubs, and even knives, as a condition of justification for killing in self-defense; while it would be rank folly to so require when experienced men, armed with repeating rifles, face each other in an open space, removed from shelter, with intent to kill or to do great bodily harm."

Collectively, these court decisions were not only making a statement about what it meant to be an American, but allowed for a reinterpretation of other laws in a way that was compatible with a generalized acceptance of violence as a societal feature, not a bug. Central to that would be regulation of the use of firearms.

The Second Amendment, in the plain reading of its text, had seemed to preserve the right of the people to keep arms for the purpose of mustering together as a well-regulated militia to protect the state. It said nothing explicitly about an individual right to have a gun for everyday self-defense.

But if individuals had the right to quickly resort to lethal force to defend themselves, especially against someone with a gun, it followed that they should have the right to arms useful for that purpose. Locating that additional right in the Constitution became the grand project of the modern-day gun lobby, which seized upon the nineteenth-century explication of the American mind and ran with it.

One thing that rarely came up in those century-old courtroom debates over the limits of self-defense was the rapidly evolving technology of firearms during that period. It wouldn't be long before the increasing lethality of guns made their expanding presence in public life appear untenable.

From a young age, whenever I had the opportunity in a library, flea market, or used-book shop, I'd seek out the oldest-looking books and peruse them. That's what I was doing when I came across an appealingly antiquated book called *With Sherman to the Sea: The Civil War Letters, Diaries and Reminiscences of Theodore F. Upson*. It's a fascinating read, both for the poignancy of its guileless narrator—a child going off to war—and for the unexpected insights into how firearms technology was evolving just as the country's relationship to violence was also changing.

Upson was a sixteen-year-old farm kid, living with a foster family in LaGrange County, Indiana, when he volunteered to join the Union Army early in the Civil War. Like a lot of brave young men from the North who signed up, Upson was basically a decent sort, even if he didn't give much thought to the Black people who stood to benefit the most from his service. In a journal he kept, he said he once turned down the chance at a captaincy with a Black regiment.

"The truth is," he wrote, "none of our soldiers seem to like the idea of arming the Negroes. Our boys say this is a white man's war and the Negro has no business in it, but a good many say they have stood for emancipation which came, of course, as fast as our armies occupied slave territory."

Growing up on a farm, and being a teenager, Upson had no military skills, but he knew something about firearms, having learned to shoot a musket at a young age. He quickly discovered, though, the gun's limitations in combat.

The musket had evolved since the Revolution. By the time of the Civil War, there were rifled versions with grooves on the inside of the barrel, allowing for more accurate shots that traveled farther. But they still required loading each ball or bullet manually, greatly slowing the pace of shooting.

Traveling with Gen. William Tecumseh Sherman's army, Upson and his comrades kept hearing about a new type of weapon, a "repeating rifle," capable of firing multiple shots without reloading. The Spencer rifle could fire seven bullets before having to be reloaded, while the Henry rifle could shoot sixteen.

Because they were so new, and not yet in production on a scale necessary to outfit regiments, most of the Union men who managed to get one had to buy it themselves. The inventors of them were in the North, and the weapons were mostly unavailable to the Confederacy.

While in Snake Creek Gap in Georgia in May 1864, Upson finally acquired a Henry rifle from an injured soldier who wanted to sell his. He paid $35—all the money he had, the equivalent of about $700 today. It wasn't long before he saw the results.

Upson's journal is filled with references to how the Confederates—"Johnnys" he called them—lived in fear of the more powerful firearms:

"I think the Johnnys are getting rattled; they are afraid of our repeating rifles. They say we are not fair, that we have guns that we load up on Sunday and shoot all the rest of the week. This I know, I feel a good deal more confidence in myself with a 16 shooter in my hands than I used to with a single shot rifle."

When the war was over, Upson was among those sent to Washington, DC, to celebrate. They were treated as conquering heroes, having taken part in Sherman's famously brutal march through Georgia. While spending time with local police officers at a shooting range, he found that none of them were aware of the power of the new repeating rifles and that "some of them rather doubted that one could be sure of hitting a man at the distance named, some 500 yds."

Upson said "that would be easy" and offered to show them.

"I took off my coat and put 12 shots, one after another, into their target and did not half try," he wrote. "Those fellows opened their eyes; said they had no idea such shooting could be done."

The group of men gathered at the range that day could not have known they were witnessing a technological leap forward destined to change the course of wars—if not society itself.

A REAL MENACE

UNION STATION IN Kansas City, Missouri, is a massive beaux arts monument to early-twentieth-century railway dominance, when hundreds of trains a day would pass through. It opened to the public in 1914 and quickly became an object of local pride as a major Midwest transportation hub.

The station is a short drive from another landmark, in Kansas, with a more complicated relationship to Missouri and its citizenry: the US Penitentiary at Leavenworth.

At 7:15 a.m. on June 17, 1933, a Missouri Pacific train from Fort Smith, Arkansas, arrived at Union Station. On board, Frank Nash, in handcuffs, was accompanied by two FBI agents and an Oklahoma police chief. The lawmen were returning Nash to Leavenworth, from which he had escaped three years earlier.

Nash was a career criminal with a long record of robberies, safe-cracking, and assault. He was part of a loosely connected gang of outlaws, including the notorious "Pretty Boy" Floyd, that knocked over banks and committed other violent mayhem throughout the Prohibition-era Midwest.

The law enforcement officers escorting Nash that morning were on edge. It was not uncommon for gangsters in the lawless milieu of the late 1920s and early 1930s to attempt prison breaks, ambush cops, and carry out brazen crimes that were shockingly ruthless and bloody. They had an invaluable tool that made it all easier: the machine gun.

Firearms technology had come a long way since young Theodore Upson scrounged the cash to buy his Henry rifle during the Civil War.

That conflict had seen a burst of innovation in the development of more efficient, faster ways to kill on the battlefield. In addition to repeating rifles, one of the biggest advancements was the widespread adoption of metallic cartridges.

No longer did soldiers need to fumble through multiple steps of loading powder, paper, and balls. Thanks largely to French gunsmiths, the essential ingredients now came neatly compacted in a brass or copper casing with the bullet affixed to the tip. It was what made repeating rifles and pistols possible.

With that step solved, it was only a matter of time before increasingly rapid-fire weapons were developed. The next huge leap forward came with the invention of semiautomatic firing, which does not require manually ejecting the spent cartridge and chambering the next round. These guns are essentially self-loading, unlike bolt action or lever action, which slow the pace of shooting. With a semiautomatic firearm, you simply squeeze the trigger to fire each shot and do not need to do anything else.

But technology didn't stop there. The ultimate goal of firearms inventors was the ability to spray the maximum number of bullets in the shortest time. In other words, a *fully* automatic gun, which required only a single squeeze of the trigger to fire a continuous burst of rounds. With a fully automatic—otherwise known as a machine gun—there was no need to depress the trigger for each shot. Squeezing it once was enough.

Invention of the first machine gun is credited to Hiram Stevens Maxim, a quirky British tinkerer who also patented a fire sprinkler system, hair curling iron, and various flying machines. Early versions of the Maxim gun, mounted on stands, were heavy and complicated to operate, some of them featuring hand cranks and multiple rotating barrels. They were water-cooled, allowing for longer stretches of shooting, and could fire hundreds of rounds per minute. World War I saw the first widespread use of them, and afterward came smaller, lighter adaptations that could be wielded by hand.

One of the most popular was created by John Thompson, a US Army officer, and because his design relied on pistol-type cartridges, the gun was therefore classified as a submachine gun, a step below its more powerful cousin, which took larger rifle rounds. Thompson's version became known as the tommy gun.

Tommy guns were a favorite of bank robbers during the gangster era. Even if it wasn't fired, just the sight of one, with its recognizable black drum magazine that could hold a hundred rounds, was enough to scare victims into compliance. The gun quickly worked its way into popular culture as a strangely compelling motif of American violence.

Unfortunately for the G-men (slang for "government men," which is credited to gangster George "Machine Gun" Kelly) escorting Frank Nash to Kansas City that June morning in 1933, such lethal firepower was not yet part of their arsenal. In fact, FBI agents were not even officially authorized to carry guns at that time, although some did anyway.

The three lawmen with Nash were met at the station by two more FBI agents and two police officers, who scanned the area and kept a lookout for suspicious activity. They carried shotguns or pistols.

The armed group walked briskly through the station, footsteps echoing off the polished rose-brown marble floors and the ornate ceiling nearly one hundred feet above, strung with thirty-five-hundred-pound crystal chandeliers. It was a Saturday morning and the swell of early summer travelers was growing as trains arrived and departed.

Exiting the station, the men hurried toward two cars parked out front. They put Nash in the front passenger seat of a Chevrolet sedan, and three of the agents and officers got into the back. As FBI Special Agent Raymond Caffrey, thirty-one, was getting into the driver's seat, someone nearby shouted, "Up! Up!"

Two men, one with a submachine gun, suddenly appeared from behind a green Plymouth parked nearby. A third man popped up from the back of another car.

"Let 'em have it!"

A fusillade of bullets sprayed the agents' cars, mowing down everything in its path. It was over in thirty seconds and the gunmen fled, leaving behind four dead law officers, including Caffrey, as well as their prisoner, Nash.

When word of what became known as the Kansas City Massacre got back to Washington, DC, FBI Director J. Edgar Hoover decided to level the playing field. Going forward, his agents would no longer go unarmed. If the criminals were going to have tommy guns, then, by God, law enforcement would have them, too.

The Prohibition era saw a perfect storm of violence. The rise of criminal elements competing to fill an insatiable public demand for alcohol dovetailed with the availability of increasingly lethal firearms.

By 1933, the murder rate would nearly double compared to pre-Prohibition times, and violent crime overall shot up 13 percent. Prisons filled—the number of inmates at Leavenworth, outside Kansas City, was more than twice the maximum capacity of fifteen hundred. The consequences would be far-reaching.

Faced with growing calls for action, Congress took up the issue of gun control in a serious way for the first time. Up to that point, state and municipal governments had responded haphazardly to the growing problem of gun violence, exacerbated by the easy availability of the six-shot revolver. The American experience with gun crime, however, was not evenly distributed across the country and in some ways belied what has come to be the modern understanding of it.

An enduring myth of the Wild West was that nineteenth-century frontier towns were lawless free-for-alls where everyone was armed to the teeth and on a hair trigger to blow one another away. The reality was far different. Guns were prevalent, yes, but so were local regulations aimed at controlling their use.

Dodge City and Tombstone both banned the carrying of guns within municipal limits without obtaining a permit. With little sense of irony, the NRA today points to the gunfight at the O.K. Corral to argue that Tombstone's gun control ordinance "proved to be almost entirely ineffective." But one could just as easily argue that the lesson of O.K. Corral was that good guys with guns successfully stopped bad guys who refused to obey the law. The NRA's main argument has, after all, always been that we need stronger law enforcement against criminals.

Because so much of the sprawling western frontier was open land with little or no judicial infrastructure, gun regulation was often left to private organizations that effectively controlled vast territories. The Wyoming Stock Growers Association adopted a resolution in 1887 declaring that "the custom of carrying firearms by those engaged in the round-up and in working the cattle ranges is productive of great evil and frequently results in the damage of persons and property:

"Be it therefore resolved, that the custom of carrying firearms, except in the immediate vicinity of Indian reservations, should be discountenanced, and it is hereby made the duty of the members of this Association, foremen of round-ups, and foremen of ranges, to use every effort in their power to prevent the carrying of firearms by cattle men at all times and places except when absolutely necessary."

Much of this was driven by concerns about drunken cowboys going off half-cocked. A report in the *Texas Live Stock Journal* in 1884 lamented that "the six-shooter loaded with deadly cartridges is a dangerous companion for any man, especially if he should unfortunately be primed with whiskey.

"In almost every section of the West murders are on the increase, and cowmen are too often the principals in the encounters." The report added, "Cattlemen should unite in aiding the enforcement of the law against carrying of deadly weapons."

It is important to note that while homicide rates were indeed high in many Old West towns, they were almost entirely the result of fights between men (often intoxicated) and were not reflective of broader crime problems. In fact, to this day it is still the case that a majority of homicide victims in the United States are killed by someone they know, and usually with a gun.

Historian Roger McGrath, who taught the course "The American West" at UCLA, studied crime statistics for nineteenth-century frontier towns in California and Nevada and found that rates of offenses such as robbery, burglary, and larceny were quite low compared to those in urban areas in the North. He attributed this, in part, to an "armed citizenry"—composed largely of men with military experience in the Mexican War and the Civil War—that came together in the absence of dependable law enforcement. But he also identified other factors that may have served as deterrents to criminal behavior: "full or near-full employment, religion, and a collective sense of optimism."

"While men have hope, no matter what their present circumstances, they are probably less likely to resort to crime," McGrath said.

In many Northern cities, meanwhile, hope was in short supply.

The compounding pressures of immigration, poverty, and overcrowding were resulting in rampant crime. In New York, gangs roamed parts of lower Manhattan. Street brawls and full-blown riots broke out between Irish Catholics and Protestants. There were spasms of gun-related mayhem.

The New York Times in May 1873 reported on a dispute between two Brooklyn boys armed with pistols, "with the shocking result that the mother of one of them, in the endeavor to separate the combatants, was shot dead." The *Times* called for stronger regulation:

"The proper way is to begin at the beginning, and regulate the sale of such weapons so that they may fall as nearly as possible only into proper hands."

It took a while, but New York did eventually pass the Sullivan Act, which required obtaining a police-issued permit to own or carry a handgun. The city of Chicago had adopted a similar ordinance three years earlier.

But leaving it to states and localities to regulate where, when, and how people could use firearms resulted in a patchwork of laws that often canceled each other out with the crossing of a border. It made no difference that an Italian immigrant named Giuseppe Zangara probably could not buy a handgun in New York when he could—and did—easily buy one at a pawnshop in Florida and then use it to try to assassinate Pres. Franklin D. Roosevelt in February 1933. His shots missed and instead mortally wounded Chicago Mayor Anton Cermak, standing nearby.

By the time of the Kansas City Massacre four months later, the White House and Congress had seen enough.

"For some time," Congressman Robert Doughton intoned from the House floor, "this country has been at the mercy of the gangsters, racketeers, and professional criminals. The rapidity with which they can go across state lines has become a real menace to the law-abiding people of this country."

Doughton, a powerful Democrat from North Carolina, worked with the Roosevelt administration to introduce the National Firearms Act in 1934. The argument behind it was that criminals could take advantage of the uneven patchwork of state laws unless there were federal restrictions that applied to all. To avoid uncertainty over whether outright bans would pass muster in the courts, the bill instead imposed heavy taxes on certain firearms—$200, the equivalent of almost $5,000 in 2026—as well as strict registration requirements.

Hearings were held that spring to consider a draft of the proposed legislation. Among those who spoke was the president of the NRA, Karl T. Frederick, a Harvard-trained lawyer and Olympic gold medalist in competitive shooting. Frederick's testimony in April 1934 is crucial to understanding the evolution of gun rights in the twentieth century.

I was surprised when I read the full transcript of Frederick's appearance before the House Committee on Ways and Means. I had always assumed that, back then, NRA leadership was much more moderate than today. That is partly because critics of the NRA have long cited a quote from Frederick at the 1934 hearing:

"I do not believe in the general promiscuous toting of guns. I think it should be sharply restricted and only under licenses."

While it may be satisfying to highlight the hypocrisy of the modern NRA, the cherry-picked quote doesn't begin to reflect Frederick's actual views on firearms regulation, let alone the impact of his testimony on the law being considered. Because, contrary to the mythology of his being the "moderate" NRA man, Frederick arguably put a more diplomatic and erudite gloss over a fundamentalist view of gun rights that could easily find a home in his grandson's NRA.

For starters, Frederick's endorsement of licenses and restrictions applied only to public carrying of handguns, which wasn't the central point of the hearing. The draft law being considered focused on curbing the criminal use of guns of all kinds by imposing an onerous tax and registration on the purchase of them. As originally conceived, that would also have included handguns.

But the NRA objected to that idea. It sent another official of the organization, army Gen. Milton Reckord, to the Justice Department to lobby against including pistols and revolvers in the legislation. The group had also encouraged its members to send telegrams of protest to members of Congress, although Frederick later claimed he was unaware of any organized campaign.

Frederick's mission at the hearing was slightly different and, in some sense, more important. He began by drawing attention to the portion of the draft bill that would sharply restrict machine guns, which it defined as "any weapon designed to shoot automatically or semiautomatically twelve or more shots without reloading." The key word was *semiautomatically*.

It is worth dwelling on that for a minute. Congress was poised to adopt the most far-reaching firearms restrictions in history—and it may not have even realized it. The bill would have made it all but impossible for the average person to purchase not just a fully automatic machine gun, but virtually *any* kind of firearm capable of firing twelve or more rounds that didn't require manual chambering of each bullet. In the modern era, that could have meant large-capacity semiautomatics such as AR-15s and Glock pistols were as tightly regulated as machine guns, which are unobtainable by most people.

It's clear from the questions posed by committee members that many didn't understand the difference between fully and semiautomatic. Frederick was almost certainly aware of this. Rather than straightforwardly objecting to the inclusion of semiautomatics, he couched his criticism as an attempt to *strengthen* the legislation, not weaken it. Pointing to the part of the definition that required a machine gun to be capable of firing twelve or more shots, he said that was "wholly inadequate and unsatisfactory.

"A gun which fires automatically or semiautomatically less than twelve shots is not under this definition a machine gun," Frederick said. "And yet, in my opinion, it is in fact a machine gun and should be so classified."

Committee members were impressed that the NRA man seemed to be proposing to make the law tougher. This sparked a discussion about magazine sizes and whether restrictions should be imposed on the number of bullets they could hold. That wasn't what Frederick wanted, however, and he quickly sought to nip it in the bud, saying he would like to instead "suggest a definition of machine gun which I think obviates" the concern about magazines.

"The definition which I suggest is this: A machine gun or submachine gun as used in this act means any firearm by whatever name known, loaded or unloaded, which shoots automatically more than one shot without manual reloading, by a single function of the trigger."

It was a deft sleight of hand. Frederick framed his revised definition as a way to toughen the bill by addressing the number of shots fired. But at the same time he deleted the reference to semiautomatic and added the requirement of a single trigger pull to fire multiple rounds—drastically limiting the types of guns it would apply to. Initially, this appeared to go over the heads of many committee members.

But one congressman, Samuel Billingsley Hill, a Democratic lawyer from Washington State, smelled a rat. Noting that "in one sense you are limiting the scope of this definition and in another you are broadening it," he questioned Frederick's inclusion of "single function of the trigger." Frederick replied that he was simply trying to capture "everything that I think is a machine gun instead of including only those machine guns which fire twelve or more shots without reloading."

Hill wasn't having it: "The point I am making is why include in your definition the phrase 'with one function of the trigger'?"

"Because that is the essence of a machine gun," Frederick responded. "Otherwise you have the ordinary repeating rifle. You have the ordinary shotgun, which is in no sense and never has been thought of as a machine gun."

This was a mischaracterization that seemed designed to alarm members of the committee unfamiliar with firearms. The proposed bill would not have restricted repeating rifles or shotguns. It is commonly understood that "ordinary" repeating guns are not semiautomatic because while they are capable of firing successive shots, they require manual cycling of the chamber—sliding a bolt, cocking a lever, or pumping. This distinction was well-known even in 1934, since semiautomatic long guns were already in circulation, growing in popularity and on the verge of being adopted by the US Army as its standard-issue rifle.

Eventually the committee moved on, delving into an almost philosophical colloquy over what makes a criminal and whether gun laws are justified. Here, Frederick's rather fatalistic views sound strikingly similar to those of the modern NRA, challenging the need and effectiveness of virtually any restrictions. Criminals will always get their hands on guns, he opined, and trying to stop that will only inconvenience "law-abiding citizens."

Frederick said, "I do not believe that Congress or the people back home want us to attempt miracles. In my opinion, based upon a rather extensive experience with this subject and study of it, very little of practical value can be accomplished by federal legislation."

Congressman Hill, who had emerged as Frederick's chief antagonist at the hearing, tried to get the NRA man to "concede there is a necessity for *something*" in the law to address gun violence, but he wouldn't even do that. Finally, Hill got to the heart of the NRA's position: It was better to have none of the proposed restrictions if it would inconvenience even a single gun owner.

"I take it that your objection to this character of legislation is that the restrictions which it would impose upon the law-abiding citizen in the matter of firearms outweigh the advantages which might be gained in the hunting down and catching of the criminal," said Hill.

"In general," Frederick agreed, "I think it is best for the public interest."

In the end, the NRA got most of what it wanted—much to the dismay of Asst. Atty. Gen. Joseph B. Keenan, who pronounced the final bill "a joke." It lowered the tax his department had sought on firearm manufacturers from $5,000 to $1,000; the definition of a machine gun was changed to exclude semiautomatic weapons; and pistols and revolvers were not covered by the law. On its face, the latter exemption didn't make a lot of sense, since handguns were the most concealable of all firearms and that was a major focus of the new law; it was why sawed-off long guns were to be restricted.

Women's groups, which had lobbied for the strongest bill possible, were outraged at the decision to drop handguns from its language. Following a raucous convention in Hot Springs, Arkansas, in May 1934, at which women rose to their feet to condemn the NRA, the General Federation of Women's Clubs sent a telegram to Doughton's committee saying, "We hold you accountable for your responsibility to the people of your state and your country, and demand that the bill to regulate the sale and possession of firearms include pistols and revolvers."

During legislative debate, Doughton conceded that protests had been heard from "some ladies' organizations throughout the country." But, he said, it had been determined that the typical law-abiding American should not be penalized by restricting handguns that were "essential in his home for the protection of himself and his family."

The men making the decisions had chosen to ignore the concerns of women who believed they had reason to fear guns kept "in *his* home" being turned on them or their children. Domestic violence had, after all, been a driving force behind the temperance movement, and the nation was slow in recognizing and addressing its dangers—it wasn't until 1920 that wife beating was formally outlawed in all states and 1993 that marital rape was illegal nationwide.

Sponsors of the bill calculated that passage would be easier if it focused on weapons associated, in the public's mind, with the gangster-style mayhem that made headlines. That did not include the types of guns men might use to hunt deer, defend their households, or, possibly, shoot their wives.

On April 4, 1939, a farmhand in Oklahoma found the bullet-riddled body of a professional thief named Jack Miller lying near a dry creek bed. Miller, a notorious thug and gang member who the day before had brandished a shotgun while stealing $80 at a dive bar named the Route 66 Club, had been shot four times with a .38.

It was an unusual denouement for someone with a case pending before the US Supreme Court.

U.S. v. Miller challenged the constitutionality of the National

Firearms Act. It was one of the few cases since the founding of the republic to reach the high court that directly implicated the Second Amendment. The ruling that arose from it is also one of the most debated, since its wording and logic was maddeningly opaque and offered thin reeds to both sides of the gun control issue.

Miller was a big, bearish ne'er-do-well from small-town Oklahoma who had been given more than enough chances in life, only to blow them every time. While working as a bouncer at a bar in 1924, he killed an unruly customer but avoided a lengthy prison sentence. Later, after years of getting away with petty crimes, he joined the O'Malley Gang, a ruthless scrum of bank robbers, kidnappers, and murderers who terrorized the Depression-era Midwest.

Finally, after stealing about $22,000 from a bank in Fort Smith, Arkansas, in 1935, Miller and the gang were brought down by police with help from the FBI, which by then was fully committed to avenging the Kansas City Massacre of two years earlier. Miller was indicted and promptly flipped, in exchange for immunity.

To the joy of prosecutors, Miller ratted everybody out and was rewarded with a promised acquittal. But he returned to his old ways, and in April 1938 he and a partner, Frank Layton, were pulled over by state police in Arkansas and found to have in their car a short-barreled shotgun, without the required $200 tax stamp. The men were charged with violating the NFA.

The criminal case quickly became mired in intrigue. Miller and Layton pled guilty. However, the district court judge who heard their case, Hiram Ragon, dismissed the indictments and issued an opinion saying the NFA violated the Second Amendment. Miller and Layton were reindicted, and again Ragon batted it away, with no explanation or evidence presented to support his contention.

Speculation immediately surfaced that Ragon, a Roosevelt appointee who as a congressman had supported stiffer gun regulations, was positioning *Miller* as a test case to win Supreme Court approval of new federal firearms laws. At the same time that the *Miller* case was ping-ponging around Ragon's court, Congress was contemplating another major gun bill, the Federal Firearms Act, which would impose regulations on dealers and manufacturers.

Sure enough, the government appealed directly to the high court. It made for a strange tableau, since Miller and Layton had long disappeared after being set free and were not part of the legal proceedings that ensued in their names. In fact, no one represented them during oral arguments before the Supreme Court on March 30, 1939.

The government offered a medley of points, including that the Second Amendment, with its reference to a well-regulated militia, protected the bearing of arms in the context of "the collective body and not individual rights." But it also argued, narrowly, that the NFA regulated weapons that were uniquely suited to criminals and had no relation to uses covered by the Constitution.

Somewhat surprisingly, the Supreme Court took only a month and a half to issue a unanimous opinion. It was relatively short. Frustratingly for historians and future firearms scholars, it dealt with the Second Amendment in the most convoluted of ways. Rather than decide the question of collective-versus-individual rights, the court first set about determining if the amendment was in fact concerned with militias—and then confined itself to assessing if a sawed-off shotgun could plausibly be considered a militia weapon.

Regarding militias, the court concluded that, yes, the amendment was intended to assure that Americans could muster when needed to defend the state:

"With obvious purpose to assure the continuation and render possible the effectiveness of such forces, the declaration and guarantee of the Second Amendment were made. It must be interpreted and applied with that end in view."

That would seem to beg the "rights" question. But the court sidestepped it, moving instead to the strangely cramped matter of firearms functionality. It decided that the short-barreled guns restricted under the NFA were of no use for militia purposes and therefore did not enjoy constitutional protection:

"In the absence of any evidence tending to show that possession or use of a 'shotgun having a barrel of less than eighteen inches in length' at this time has some reasonable relationship to the preservation or efficiency of a well regulated militia, we cannot say that the Second Amendment guarantees the right to keep and bear such an instrument."

And that was that. For the next seventy years, the *Miller* ruling would be cited, occasionally, to support arguments on both sides of the gun rights debate. It probably proved most useful for those endorsing the militia-centric view that the Second Amendment did not confer an individual right to bear arms. But even there, it had its limits.

Brian Frye, a University of Kentucky law professor, prepared an in-depth analysis of the case decades later. In it, he posed the question "What does *Miller* tell us about the meaning of the Second Amendment?" His answer: "Maybe nothing."

Frye wrote, "At a minimum, it held the Second Amendment permits Congress to tax firearms used by criminals. At the maximum, dicta suggest the Second Amendment protects an individual right to possess and use a weapon suitable for militia service. And in general, it implies the Second Amendment permits reasonable regulation of firearms."

A little something for everybody, and not enough to satisfy anyone.

During the April 1934 congressional hearing, NRA President Frederick was asked whether the National Firearms Act was unconstitutional. While Frederick expressed general opposition to federal gun restrictions, he did not question the government's ability to enact them. He said states were certainly free to regulate guns, and Congress could do so also through its taxing power.

"I am personally of the opinion, as a lawyer, that Congress may legislate in the way of taxing certain transactions with respect to firearms," Frederick said. "That, I think, is clear."

Within three decades, the NRA would launch a campaign to make sure that settled view was anything but clear.

POWER

DROP BY DROP UPON THE HEART

AS A YOUNG civil engineer in the late 1920s, Albert Leslie Hertz left the confines of small-town Iowa and took a job in the Panama Canal Zone, helping build dry docks, highways, even a townsite for two thousand employees of the canal's dredging division.

Soon he joined the US Army Corps of Engineers and moved to Pennsylvania to work on a massive flood-control project in Johnstown, the site of several flooding disasters that killed thousands of people. When World War II began, Hertz's skills were put to use designing military facilities for the war effort, and he was later sent to the Philippines to help with rebuilding a harbor. He eventually achieved the rank of lieutenant colonel.

He was in South Korea in the late 1950s consulting on postwar reconstruction projects when he began downshifting into retirement. By 1965, the sixty-seven-year-old Hertz was living quietly in the Los Angeles suburb of Alhambra, which arose on land once part of the San Gabriel Mission built during the eighteenth-century Spanish occupation. It was a solidly upper-middle-class community where residents generally felt safe in their mid-century modern bungalows and Victorians.

That is, until the summer of '65.

Rising crime, along with the simmering cauldron of racial segregation and abusive policing practices in Los Angeles, had created a sense of foreboding. It came to a head in August in the Watts district of LA, when police pulled over a twenty-one-year-old Black man suspected of drunk driving, leading to a physical confrontation in front of a crowd. Watts exploded in days of rioting, arson, and looting, quelled only after thousands of National Guard troops were called in and more than thirty people were dead.

In Alhambra, a half-hour drive away, residents had already been taking steps to defend against what they saw as encroaching chaos. The day before the riots started, Hertz went to the Pasadena Gun Shop and spoke with an employee there about getting a firearm for protection. Despite his long experience in the military, guns had never figured prominently in his civilian life. He settled on a .22-caliber snub-nosed Iver Johnson revolver.

This particular model, called the Cadet, was somewhat unusual in that it could chamber eight bullets, instead of the more common six. The small, easily concealable pistols were named after their nineteenth-century Norwegian inventor, who also manufactured bikes and motorcycles. Johnson's guns had the ignominious distinction of having been used to assassinate Pres. William McKinley in 1901 and Chicago Mayor Anton Cermak in 1933.

Hertz and the salesclerk, James Pineda, filled out and signed the required California State "Dealer's Record of Sale of Revolver or Pistol" in triplicate. Boxes were checked: *Yes* to being an American citizen, *No* to having been convicted of a felony or being addicted to drugs. The gun's serial number, H53725, was recorded.

When they were finished, it was 9:30 a.m. on August 10, 1965. Per state law, Hertz had to wait five days before receiving the handgun. He then brought it back to the apartment he shared with his wife and put it in the bottom drawer of a filing cabinet. Fortunately for Hertz, he would never need to use it.

Unfortunately for the country, the gun would prove useful for someone else, who was looking to assassinate a candidate for president.

Political violence is often cited as a barometer of a society's health and stability. Many scholars have raised an alarm about the rising number of attacks in recent years on politicians and public figures in the United States: the attempted assassination of Donald Trump, the murder of Charlie Kirk, the shooting deaths of Minnesota lawmakers, pipe bombs mailed to prominent Democrats, political donors, and journalists—the list goes on.

It is bad. But it's also nothing new. Nor is it unique to the United States, though the numbers suggest that, for a relatively young nation, America has seen more assassinations of its leaders, successful or attempted, than almost any other country since the nineteenth century. Only Spain and the Dominican Republic had a comparable number between 1875 and 2004, according to one study.

Guns were used in 55 percent of the roughly three hundred cases around the world during that period. Heads of state have been the target of stabbings, poisonings, and bombings in almost equal numbers to shootings. Except in the United States.

Here in America, every one of the seventeen direct attacks on a president since the country's founding has been with a firearm. Almost all of them were handguns. Lee Harvey Oswald, an outlier, relied on a bolt-action rifle. Only in recent years have semiautomatic rifles become the weapon of choice, used by would-be assassins of Presidents Clinton, Obama, and Trump. One of those attacks was by the youngest person ever to try to kill an American president.

Thomas Crooks was twenty when, using an AR-15 sold to him by his father, he shot at Donald Trump at a campaign event in Pennsylvania in July 2024. Socially awkward and struggling with mental health issues, Crooks lived with his parents, whose home had fourteen guns. On the day of the assassination attempt, he wore a T-shirt with the logo of a popular Texas-based gun influencer on YouTube.

Andrew Jackson has the distinction of inspiring the earliest assassination attempt of an American president, in 1835. The attacker, a mentally ill house painter, used two small single-shot pistols that each misfired, probably because of dampness in the air (Jackson went with divine intervention as the cause).

Assassination attempts in the United States reached a sort of ugly crescendo during the two decades between 1963 and 1981, which saw six attacks on presidents—as many as in all of the previous one hundred years. And that's not counting the assaults on other high-profile public figures. As a member of the television generation who came of age in the 1970s, I had a front-row seat to the carnage.

Lolling at the foot of my parents' bed and watching an after-school special on a black-and-white TV set in May 1972, my nine-year-old brain was forever imprinted with the news flash of Democratic presidential candidate George Wallace being shot with a .38-caliber revolver. They showed the whole thing right there on afternoon television.

A few years later, I found myself bending the rabbit-ear antenna on our living room television for a better view of the person who tried to shoot President Ford outside the California capitol. The would-be assassin used a government-surplus M1911 pistol but forgot to chamber a round first, so nothing happened when she pulled the trigger.

And in March 1981, I had called in sick from school when I was, of course, watching TV at home as news broke that President Reagan had been shot in Washington, DC. I gawked at the screen as they replayed the chaotic scene, with the *pop-pop-pop* sound of gunfire and people falling wounded as the presidential limo sped away.

Assassination attempts became so routine they seeped into popular culture. They provided plotlines for movies and books such as *The Parallax View*, *Taxi Driver*, and *Three Days of the Condor*. They were mentioned in songs you heard on the radio by Smokey Robinson and Neil Diamond. Kids in my middle school actually played a game we called Assassin, where we'd carry around toy dart guns, sometimes inside hollowed-out books, and try to shoot each other.

For all their seeming ubiquity throughout American history, political assassinations really only catalyzed a successful movement for greater gun control once. It was at the end of the 1960s, when public sentiment finally boiled over as successive shootings cruelly extinguished important voices on the national stage. One of those shootings, in particular, proved to be a crucial tipping point.

As is often the case, the gun that was used traveled like a pathogen through the population—ricocheting, if you will—passed around by people who served as carriers, immune to its destructive capabilities, before finding an eager host far removed from Albert Hertz and his worries about personal safety.

Long after the Watts riots had subsided and some semblance of calm had returned to the Los Angeles region, Hertz's wife, Sarah, stumbled upon the Iver Johnson revolver he had stashed in their Alhambra apartment. She immediately decided she did not want it in the house.

The next time their daughter, Dana Westlake, was visiting, Sarah Hertz asked her to dispose of it, along with some boxes of other stuff that was no longer wanted.

"Throw it in the dump," Sarah said.

Westlake, who lived in nearby Pasadena, didn't throw the gun away, but instead hid it in the attic of her house. In the fall of 1967 she and her husband, Robert, were having their home remodeled when she remembered the gun in the attic. Concerned that their children might find it if she moved it somewhere else, she concluded she would need to get rid of it.

She knew that her neighbors had a nineteen-year-old son, George Erhard, who might be interested. She gave it to him.

"He was a collector," Westlake later recalled, "and I didn't want the darn thing around."

As the Hertz family grappled with how to rid itself of the unwanted gun, the nation was dealing with essentially the same problem writ large. One of those at the forefront of renewed efforts to regulate firearms was Ted Kennedy. In the spring of 1967, the liberal Democratic senator from Massachusetts asked for the chance to address a private meeting of the National Rifle Association's leadership, and the group warily agreed.

Kennedy's appearance followed impassioned debate inside the organization on whether to hear from him. Some regarded his request as a publicity stunt. Even though the meeting was not open to the public, Kennedy's people were spinning his overture as an act of political courage—the mere image of him taking on the NRA would be a win for the pro-gun-control side.

The NRA by the mid-1960s was on the defensive. The assassination of Pres. John F. Kennedy in 1963 had given a sense of urgency to existing efforts, pushed mostly by Sen. Thomas J. Dodd, the Connecticut Democrat, to tighten gun laws already on the books. Initially, the NRA had worked with Dodd on his bill, which would have required mail-order handgun buyers to provide notarized proof that they were at least eighteen years old.

But after the president was murdered—with a mail-order rifle purchased, under a fake name, through an ad in an NRA magazine—Dodd and the Johnson administration rewrote the proposed legislation to include stronger restrictions. Among other things, it would ban interstate gun sales through the mail and tighten federal licensing requirements for dealers.

Speaking to the Senate Commerce Committee in December 1963, Dodd made the point that even with the limits he proposed, the nation's gun laws would still impose "no real obstacle to any law-abiding citizen who wishes to purchase a weapon, no more an obstacle than that to operate a bicycle, far less than that required to operate an automobile." But the committee also heard from another lawmaker with a very different point of view: Rep. John D. Dingell Jr.

The Michigan Democrat warned there was "a growing prejudice against firearms in many segments of our society" that was threatening basic freedoms. He suggested that President Kennedy's assassination had prompted an overreaction and that it would be wrong to deprive Americans of the ability to buy guns through the mail just because that's how Lee Harvey Oswald did it.

"Present-day firearms legislation is pointed in the wrong direction," he said. "It disarms the law-abiding citizen while it fails miserably in its avowed purpose of disarming the criminal. It is aimed at outlawing the gun, which is incapable by itself of doing evil, rather than at punishing criminals who use a gun for illegal purposes."

Dingell was expressing a view not unfamiliar to anyone who had heard NRA leaders testify on the subject going back to the 1934 hearings on the National Firearms Act. But Dingell was not an NRA official. He was a sitting member of Congress offering his help, and doing so with an aggression and bluntness that executives of the organization had never utilized. The NRA took notice.

With assistance from Dingell and a few other sympathetic legislators, the organization successfully stiff-armed new gun control bills for the next several years, as heated disagreement arose in Washington and across the country between the vast majority of Americans—polling suggested 80 percent—who favored stronger laws versus what was becoming known, pejoratively, as the "gun lobby." By the time Senator Kennedy arrived at the NRA meeting in 1967, battle lines had been drawn.

Kennedy stood before the room and spoke briefly about the need for reasonable limits on firearms. The atmosphere was tense. He made a pitch for cooperation on the legislation being considered, an updated version of the original Dodd proposal that would create national age minimums for rifle and handgun purchases and increase fees for licensed dealers.

But he also did not hide his contempt for what gun control advocates had taken to calling "the lunatic fringe" that opposed virtually any gun laws. Kennedy, at times, appeared to equate that to the "gun lobby," another term that irked the NRA men, who assumed he was implicitly referring to them.

When Kennedy was finished, to a smattering of polite applause, he thanked the group and excused himself, saying he had to get back to the Senate. Before he made good his escape, however, a tall, imposing man with a crew cut and glasses stood and began speaking. It was Dingell, who had also been invited to the closed-door meeting.

"I hope that Senator Kennedy will stay around just a minute or two," he said, "because I have a couple of things that I want to say to him."

"I wish I could," Kennedy replied, continuing to move to the door.

Turning to the audience, Dingell issued a pointed barb: "I think if he listened to me he might learn a little something on the subject." The NRA men clapped.

"While you are walking out, Senator," Dingell continued, "I would like to say I don't think we will get a gun bill like you are talking about this year. Second, these are honest law-abiding American citizens, they are not a gun lobby."

As Dingell defended the NRA leaders, saying they were merely exercising their right to oppose legislation they disagreed with, Kennedy paused on his way out.

"You don't have to convince me of any of that," he said, offering an olive branch.

But Dingell wasn't finished. "I have one more thought for you as you walk out the door. I think you ought to bear in mind that if you work with the National Rifle Association, we will be able to get some decent legislation that will not unduly cripple the right to have a firearm and will not—"

Kennedy had turned again to leave, and Dingell's well-known temper was rising.

"Incidentally," he fumed, "I listened to you quite a while, I was not running for the door while you were talking, but you go ahead. I do want you to know this."

"I will read about it," Kennedy replied, and then he was gone.

"I doubt seriously you will!" Dingell called after him.

Collecting himself, Dingell turned his attention back to the NRA men. "You know, education comes hard in this country, and sometimes we have got to seize on whatever opportunities we can to dispense it."

The room burst into applause.

Ted Kennedy was not the only member of his family working to reform gun laws following the assassination of his brother. Robert F. Kennedy had also taken up the cause.

By then a freshman senator from New York, RFK in 1968 had a big agenda of liberal social causes that would help propel him into the Democratic presidential nomination contest. Gun control did not top the list. Yet, as with so many things that Kennedy put his mind to, when he did choose to speak on the topic, it was with an elegance and directness that made people sit up and listen.

During hearings on Congress's increasingly quixotic quest to pass the first major gun legislation in thirty years, Kennedy made a brief but impassioned plea for common sense and reason:

"For too long, we have dealt with these deadly weapons as if they were harmless toys. Yet their very presence, the ease of their acquisition, and the familiarity of their appearance have led to thousands of deaths each year—and to countless other crimes of violence as well.... It is past time that we wipe this stain of violence from our land."

Kennedy was getting at something that few other gun control proponents seemed to have the words for. He was calling out a selfishness and lack of responsibility that undergird much of the opposition to tighter gun laws.

To all those complaining it would be harder to order guns through the mail or buy cheap foreign imports, the man whose brother was killed with a cheap imported mail-order rifle was saying, essentially, *So what? Can't you accept a little inconvenience for the safety of the community?*

That appeal to Americans' sense of civic duty was again foremost on Kennedy's mind when, on the night of April 4, 1968, he interrupted a campaign speech in Indianapolis to break the news of Martin Luther King Jr.'s assassination to a mostly Black crowd. He reminded them that his brother also was shot down, and he understood the anger and urge for retribution they might be feeling.

But what was needed, he continued, was "not violence and lawlessness, but is love and wisdom and compassion towards one another." They must put aside their hurt for the greater good of the country.

"My favorite poet was Aeschylus," Kennedy told his audience, many of whom were now weeping. "He wrote, 'In our sleep, pain which cannot forget falls drop by drop upon the heart until, in our own despair, against our will, comes wisdom through the awful grace of God.'"

About a month later, in an interview with the French writer Romain Gary, Kennedy returned more directly to the issue of gun violence. Discussing the work of Ernest Hemingway, Kennedy had some thoughts:

"I like Hemingway very much as a writer. But he was the founder of a ridiculous and dangerous myth: that of the firearm and the virile beauty of the act of killing."

George Erhard didn't keep the gun that Dana Westlake had given him for long. He soon decided he would rather have some cash. At the F. C. Nash department store where he worked, the subject of firearms came up in a conversation he had with a fellow employee. The coworker, whom Erhard knew only as Joe, said he was in the market for a cheap handgun, and Erhard agreed to sell him the snub-nosed Iver Johnson.

In early February 1968, Erhard and a friend drove to a low-slung modest dwelling on East Howard Street in Pasadena to meet Joe and parked by the curb. Erhard showed the pistol to Joe and another young man, whom Joe introduced as his brother. They dickered over the price for a bit before settling on $25 for the gun. Joe only had $19 on him and had to get $6 from his brother to complete the purchase. As far as anyone knew, the pistol had never been fired.

A few months later, when Joe reported to work at F. C. Nash early on the morning of June 5, he learned some shocking news: Someone had shot Robert F. Kennedy shortly after midnight at the Ambassador Hotel in Los Angeles. It was unclear if Kennedy, who had just won California's Democratic presidential primary, would survive.

Then, on a television screen, Joe—whose real name was Munir Sirhan—saw a picture of the would-be assassin. He recognized him immediately. It was his brother, Sirhan Sirhan.

Meanwhile, in Alhambra, someone knocked on the door of Albert and Sarah Hertz's apartment. A Los Angeles police officer was there, asking about the Iver Johnson Cadet revolver Albert had bought for protection back in 1965.

A short time later, there was a knock on the door of Dana Westlake's home north of Los Angeles. It was investigators from the Marin County Sheriff's Office inquiring about the gun that her mother, Sarah Hertz, said she had given her to throw away.

Not long after that, an LAPD officer was in touch with George Erhard, wanting to know about the pistol his former neighbor, Dana Westlake, said she had given him six months earlier.

Soon, police arrived at the F. C. Nash department store with a question for the manager: Did he have an employee named Joe? While they were talking, Joe walked into the room. He was arrested and taken to police headquarters.

The shooting death of Robert Kennedy, coming in the wake of King's assassination two months earlier, upended the calculus of gun legislation in Congress.

Suddenly, it was not a matter of whether something would pass, but how soon and what it would contain. The national mood had shifted, if only for a time, and there was a sense that Americans had finally had enough.

"All too widely," intoned *Time* magazine, "the country is regarded as a blood-drenched, continent-wide shooting range where toddlers blast off with real rifles, housewives pack pearl-handled revolvers, and political assassins stalk their victims at will."

Sen. Joseph Tydings, a Maryland Democrat who had taken the lead on gun control after Dodd was censured for misappropriating campaign funds, declared, "It is just tragic that in all of Western civilization the US is the one country with an insane gun policy."

Even the NRA was knocked back on its heels. Whereas in the past the group activated its members to pepper lawmakers with letters, phone calls, and telegrams whenever a new gun law was proposed, it was largely silent this time—at least at first. A top NRA executive said while there were parts of the proposed bill, known as the Gun Control Act, that were unappealing, on the whole it was something "the sportsmen of America can live with."

John Dingell, however, was not one of them. He continued to work from the inside to undermine both the legislation that was advancing through the House, and the administration's efforts to tighten existing firearms limits.

A few weeks after Kennedy's killing, Dingell placed a call to the Library of Congress's legislative reference service to research gun control laws in Nazi Germany, part of his effort to show that the new firearms restrictions would be a slippery slope toward outright confiscation. Dingell also wrote to the US Postal Service demanding it justify its authority to escalate enforcement of regulations on guns shipped through the mail.

His staff, meanwhile, was carefully tracking public sentiment back home in Michigan. By July 24, 1968, the day that the gun bill was coming up for a vote in the House, the number of letters sent in by constituents in Dingell's district was evenly split on whether he should support the legislation. Letters and petitions coming from outside Michigan, however, were overwhelmingly in favor, as were those from inside the city of Detroit, most of which was not in Dingell's district.

It was largely a reflection of Americans' divergent views on guns depending on geography and demographics. Rural areas continued to oppose new restrictions. But eventually, public pressure was enough to push the Gun Control Act through by comfortable margins in the House and Senate. Of Michigan's nineteen representatives, Dingell was the only one who voted no (another Democrat, John Conyers, abstained).

The new law was the first substantive gun legislation in decades. It restricted interstate mail-order purchases, imports of guns not "suitable for sporting purposes," and sales to the dangerously mentally ill or substance abusers. It also required that all guns have serial numbers. The usefulness of serialization was made clear after Kennedy's shooting, when police turned to California's Bureau of Criminal Identification and Investigation and quickly traced Sirhan's gun to its original purchaser.

But as the state's deputy attorney general, Charles O'Brien, pointed out, that did little to prevent gun violence from happening in the first place.

"Post facto—after the crime—California has one of the best systems in existence," he said, adding, "But before the fact—before the crime—when it comes to limiting gun traffic or effective registration of gun ownership, California laws are pathetically weak."

President Johnson had wanted the Gun Control Act to be tougher. Among other things, he favored mandatory gun registration and licensing for purchases, but the NRA had worked hard to beat back those provisions. Never one to roll over, Johnson publicly attacked the gun group. His administration cut the army's support for its marksmanship contests and opened an FBI investigation into whether it had illegally lobbied by not registering.

The lobbying charge, in particular, stung. Despite its reputation for getting its way on Capitol Hill, the NRA did not see itself as a lobbyist. Its top executive, Franklin Orth, seemed genuinely offended by a 1964 magazine article that called the NRA a "high-powered pressure group," dismissing it as "scurrilous and unaccurate."

In interviews with FBI agents in 1968, NRA officials continued to insist they did not lobby Congress and served only to provide information when asked. But a curious detail emerged in their responses to the agents.

When Louis Lucas, the NRA's executive director and treasurer, was questioned about the organization's dealings with congressmen, he said, "Two of them are members of the board of directors" of the NRA, according to the FBI's report of the interview. Similarly, Frank Daniel, the NRA's secretary, "pointed out that there are several members of Congress listed as members of the board of directors."

The implication seemed to be that the NRA did not need to hire lobbyists to pressure lawmakers—it already had members of its own board occupying seats in Congress. Lawmakers are permitted to serve as directors of nonprofits so long as they are not paid. And for many years prior to the 1960s, when the NRA concerned itself mostly with hunting, sports shooting, and conservation, nobody thought much of it.

But by 1968, things had changed. America had reached a crossroads in the formation of gun culture. Following the political assassinations, the country could have gone purposefully in the direction of a more balanced relationship with firearms. Instead, the efforts of reformers were met with an upswell of opposition that never slowed. This opposition would continue to grow in the ensuing decades, gain power and influence, and ultimately triumph in ways unimaginable from the fraught vantage point of the sixties.

In that transition, the NRA's lawmaker-directors became far more influential and important to the group. None more so than Dingell.

The precise origins of Dingell's passionate embrace of the Second Amendment were always a little murky. He followed the path of his father, John D. Dingell Sr., into Congress, representing a working-class suburb of Detroit. Hailing from blue-collar Michigan, the elder Dingell was known to appreciate hunting and sport shooting, and he got junior enrolled as an NRA member while still in his youth.

The younger Dingell sometimes claimed that, before his father passed away in 1955, he made his son promise to defend the Second

Amendment. It was a rationale the younger Dingell offered to explain what even he recognized as an unusually aggressive, often uncompromising, embrace of gun rights. Whatever its roots, Dingell's attitude was painfully on display in his 1967 colloquy with Sen. Ted Kennedy at the NRA meeting.

There Dingell was, taunting a fellow Democrat who had seen his brother assassinated and was, understandably, now campaigning in favor of stronger gun laws. Rather than do Kennedy the favor of gracefully agreeing to disagree, Dingell couldn't help but default to attack mode and grandstand in front of a friendly audience.

It did get him something of value: the enduring appreciation of the NRA.

"Let me say," a top NRA official wrote to Dingell afterward, "that the 'marching fire' with which you pursued a retreating member of another legislative body was one of the most accurate and cheering things in a long time."

"It was great, just real great," another official wrote.

Within a year, the NRA had invited Dingell to join its board of directors.

THE PRICE WE PAY FOR FREEDOM

TRADITIONALLY, IF YOU were a journalist trying to gain insights into the inner workings of the NRA, it was like peering into a coal mine without a headlamp. You can sense deep tunnels and objects in the darkness, but you can't see them. You don't get far before having to turn back.

Because the NRA is a private organization, it has no obligation to open up its files to anyone outside the group. It has, over the years, shared details of its decision-making through articles in its magazine, *American Rifleman*. Some of them are interesting, and as the only written record that comes close to documenting the NRA's evolution during the past century, historians and writers have tended to rely on them as source material. That's fine. But *American Rifleman* only publishes what the NRA is comfortable releasing to the public.

That wasn't good enough for me. I decided in 2023 to try to figure out how to turn some lights on inside the coal mine.

Of the two main wellsprings of information for investigative reporters—documents and people—I assumed the latter is where I might have some success. Documents seemed out of reach, but finding people to provide an inside view of the NRA was a possibility. Its board of directors is unusually large, with some seventy-five members, so I tried reaching out to some who had served in the past. None were interested in talking to me. This wasn't completely surprising, since NRA directors tended to be true believers, who often regarded *The New York Times* as some sort of communist politburo.

As I was researching names of previous directors, a realization dawned on me. I had not known that active members of Congress simultaneously served on the NRA's board. I identified at least nine senators and representatives who had doubled as NRA directors over the past half century. This sparked an idea.

If I had learned anything from covering politicians, it's that most are desperately concerned with their legacy and being seen as important historical figures. To that end, it's common for retired members of Congress to donate their papers for posterity to a university or some other august institution. I wondered if any of those former lawmakers who were also NRA directors did that and left internal NRA documents mixed in with their own materials. I started checking.

There was the late Zell Miller, a former senator from Georgia, who had served on the NRA's board in the early 2000s and gave his papers to the University of Georgia. As I reviewed the website for the school's archives, it was unclear if the papers contained anything useful.

Then there was Bob Barr, another Georgia politico. He had sat on the NRA's board while also serving in the House in the 1990s and early 2000s, and his files were at the University of West Georgia. Unlike Miller, the index for Barr's papers looked promising: I counted thirteen boxes described as containing NRA materials of some kind, though exactly what was unclear. I started making arrangements to visit Georgia to find out.

A couple of other congressmen, long dead, had been on the NRA's board in the 1960s, and their papers seemed to be available. But the papers I really wanted were from John Dingell.

Dingell, the longest-serving member of Congress before his death in 2019, had been on the NRA board for decades and bragged about creating its lobbying arm. Googling around, I found a story posted on the University of Michigan's website from May 2015 announcing the donation of all of his papers to the school's Bentley Historical Library. The 550 boxes contained hundreds of thousands of documents, and Dingell had proudly said he wasn't "culling what is in there"—he had nothing to hide.

"Bentley has officially received the materials and will begin processing the collection to prepare for public use, which may take up to one year," the story said.

Great! There was just one problem: I couldn't find any reference to Dingell's papers in the Bentley Library's index of collections. Confused, I emailed a librarian in January 2023 and was told that the congressman's papers "are not open for research." In my reply, I pointed out that the library director had boasted eight years earlier that Dingell's files were so important that "anyone wishing to write the history of national politics in the twentieth century will need to consult them." I asked for an explanation.

Days went by before I got an answer: "I can confirm that although the Bentley did physically receive the records, the library is not authorized to make the collection accessible at this time." I then noticed that the May 2015 story announcing Dingell's donation had suddenly disappeared from the university website. Through weeks of back-and-forth with library representatives, I grew increasingly frustrated at their inability or refusal to provide straight answers. I also learned that at least one other author researching gun issues had run into the same problem and gave up trying to access Dingell's files.

This is where the power of *The New York Times* is useful. I got our lawyers involved, and I then moved up the food chain at the university, demanding copies of the transfer agreement for Dingell's files and all communications between university officials and representatives of the congressman's estate.

Eventually I discovered the sticking point: Dingell's wife, Debbie—who had succeeded him in Congress—never signed off on the agreement transferring his files to Bentley. So I called her office, spoke to an aide, and soon the congresswoman called me back.

Debbie Dingell, whose favorable view of gun control is widely known to be the polar opposite of John's, explained that she had intended to sign it, but simply never got around to it. Now that she knew the *Times* wanted access to the files, she said, she would put her lawyers on the task and complete the transfer as soon as possible. And she did.

I give the congresswoman credit for helping me. I'll accept her word that failing to authorize release of her husband's papers was just an oversight. At the same time, the university's strangely anxious response to the whole thing was troubling, and I came away from the experience feeling like I never fully understood what was going on there.

At any rate, in May 2023, five months after I had first contacted the University of Michigan, I traveled to Ann Arbor and pulled up a chair in the Bentley Library to begin going through Congressman Dingell's files. I lifted the lid on a heavy cardboard file box labeled NO. 233, and there on top of the papers was his black leather ID wallet stamped with the gold seal of the NRA.

This was going to be good.

The reply note that was dashed off to a critic back home in Michigan was vintage John Dingell: acerbic, blunt, and self-assured.

"It would appear that before you write the kind of insulting and offensive letter signed by you on July 24, 1968," Dingell huffed, "you should take the trouble to learn more of the facts of the matter."

The House that day had approved the Gun Control Act, and Michiganders had taken notice of their congressman's "no" vote. Many applauded it. But a good number of them did not and told him so in angry letters.

Dingell was a rare species of politician. He was exalted by the Democratic establishment as one of the party's great liberal warriors on issues such as labor, the environment, and health care, all the while occupying an increasingly isolated perch as an extreme defender of gun rights. Elasticity is a common asset among successful politicos, but the Dingell dichotomy was jarring—and largely ignored by party faithful throughout his fifty-nine years in the House.

Nicknamed "the truck" because of his intimidating size, along with his tendency to run roughshod over political adversaries, Dingell was a masterful legislative technician skilled at manipulating the machinery of Congress. He was also unafraid to speak his mind and press his case. So long as he was directing his formidable powers at their favored causes, liberals seemed content to look the other way when he started talking about guns.

Dingell could be jarringly blunt in his attacks on legislative opponents, even those within his own party. He derided Senator Dodd's gun control bill, dismissing supportive remarks by President Johnson as "a speech written for him by someone else" and calling gun control advocates "high-handed, arrogant and careless of the public interest."

He thundered, "The citizenry at large will not sacrifice an ancient right and privilege for the falsehoods and misrepresentations of the proponents of this legislation."

In his correspondence with critics over the years, Dingell would defend his record at length and attempt to explain his philosophy. He asserted he was neither "pro-gun nor anti-gun," but simply an "old style civil libertarian who does not believe that the innocent should be punished for the criminal wrongdoings of others." He painted a dystopian image of the justice system that rationalized an armed response:

"I observe criminals being released immediately to the streets to continue rapes, holdups, muggings and other actions against innocent and inoffensive citizens in their homes and on the streets of America. Juries do not convict, judges do not sentence, probation and parole officers do not supervise and the citizens are denied the simple pleasure of enjoying life in the cities of America because they remain home in fear."

Dingell's letters revealed a guiding philosophy that underpinned his disdain for firearm restrictions. As he had testified back in 1963 in opposition to attempts to ban mail-order gun purchases, his fundamental view was that "no legislation" could prevent criminals from getting guns, therefore firearm restrictions are mostly pointless.

To counterbalance the dead-end logic of the argument, Dingell always advocated stronger enforcement of existing laws and after-the-fact punishment of perpetrators. This was usually presented as having a deterrent effect, though rarely was any effort made to put forward research supporting that idea.

Over time, this curiously defeatist construct, which seemed to concede a level of violence as a fair price for being able to easily buy a gun at your local hardware store, was refined and polished until a mantra emerged for the gun rights movement. The gist of it was this: Gun control not only failed to prevent crime, it actually *increased* crime by disarming law-abiding citizens (which echoes NRA leader Wayne LaPierre's "good guy with a gun" argument decades later).

Certainly, this view existed before Dingell, and others espoused it contemporaneously to his own expositions on the subject. But no one delivered it with as much force, repetition, and—most important—position of authority as Dingell did at just the right moment in the great American gun debate.

The history of the NRA can essentially be divided into two eras: Before Dingell and After Dingell. Prior to his arrival, the NRA was not even registered as a lobbying organization. It was founded in 1871 by two veterans of the Union Army—one of them a former *New York Times* correspondent—with the goal of improving civilian marksmanship through rifle training. Over the next century, it mostly occupied itself with shooting sports, hunting, and conservation.

Certainly, the NRA chafed at gun regulations—it worked to water down the National Firearms Act and Gun Control Act. But its exertions only went so far before it accepted, albeit reluctantly, the demand for limits. Its views were tempered. Dingell's were not.

Agitated by the success of pro-gun-control forces in 1968, he wrote a letter that September to an NRA official warning that "many of the irresponsible people involved in this fight will never rest until they have disarmed all of us." He urged action.

"I believe it is highly important that the NRA begin moving toward a legislative program in the field of firearms ownership and sales which will protect the rights of sportsmen and law-abiding citizens to own firearms for legitimate sporting and defense purposes," he wrote.

This strategy, he continued, "should be bottomed upon several constitutional powers of the Federal Government. First, the provisions dealing with the right to bear arms; second, the interstate and foreign commerce powers and, perhaps third, the general welfare clause." Doing this at the federal level, Dingell wrote, would effectively neutralize state and local gun restrictions.

The lawyerly prose belied a bold objective: Expand the constitutional protection of a *collective right* to bear arms as a militia to include an *individual right* for "sporting and defense" as well. Looking back, as we are, from the twenty-first century, what Dingell was saying might seem unexceptional. For that time period, however, it was radical.

The Supreme Court had never directly taken up the question of the Second Amendment's scope and intent in a forceful way, and its utterances on the matter tended to be tangential to other legal issues that came before it. Part of the reason was that justices through the centuries seemed to take for granted the reference to militia service—the high court's 1939 *Miller* ruling offhandedly referred to it as the "obvious purpose" of the Second Amendment.

But now Dingell was suggesting that the NRA launch a campaign to upend that largely settled view of what the founders had in mind when they spoke of a right to bear arms as "a well regulated militia." The NRA would seek to reframe it by asserting that what James Madison et al. really intended was to allow every Tom, Dick, and Harriet to also arm themselves just for fun or out of fear.

Achieving his objective would require building a machine.

Dingell was aware that his dual position as a member of both Congress and the NRA's board of directors could be seen as problematic. He once wrote to a constituent that he tried to keep his "responsibilities in the two capacities separate so that there is no basic conflict."

That did not stop him, however, from using the resources of the House of Representatives to advance his NRA goals.

In March 1973, he placed a call to the Congressional Research Service to order up an overview of lobbying regulations and tax-exempt special interest groups that were registered in Washington. He also put one of his congressional aides to work helping draft a proposal for a new such tax-exempt entity that would become the lobbying arm of the NRA.

An early version of it, sketched out in a one-page typed outline, was called the Firearms Rights Institute. Dingell sought to replicate the success of progressive groups such as those run by Ralph Nader, the consumer rights activist—one of the institute's goals would be to create a "Nader-type legal challenge program" for "developing and executing strategy for attack on anti-gun legislation or administration."

His proposal borrowed heavily from the playbook of left-leaning organizations that he was familiar with as a liberal Democratic politician. The new institute, Dingell wrote, would be "affiliated with NRA in the same fashion that COPE is affiliated with AFL-CIO," a reference to the labor union's tax-exempt political arm. Elsewhere he cited the American Civil Liberties Union as a model for how the new institute should defend gun rights.

Undergirding Dingell's desire for more aggressive action was his belief that the NRA did not take the threat of gun control seriously. From his perch on Capitol Hill, he saw enemies everywhere, mostly from within his own party. He was constantly warning the NRA about what his legislative colleagues were up to.

When he got wind of new legislation a fellow Democrat was considering, Dingell would dash off a note to an assistant: "Notify NRA." He would attend NRA meetings and brief the board on the gun control agenda in Congress and what they needed to do to get ahead of it. The NRA leadership was deeply appreciative.

"His insights and guidance on the details of any gun-related matter pending in the Congress, and of the choice of tactics for success in the situation, are continually provided and have been uniformly successful," NRA director Lloyd Mustin wrote to an associate.

He explained that Dingell would also take action himself, sometimes in stealthy ways, to undermine attempts to regulate guns.

"As matters of strategy and tactics," Mustin continued, "these actions by him are often carefully obscured, for obvious reasons, so may not be recognized or understood by the uninitiated observer. But those who know what's going on are fully aware of them."

Examples abound. When the Consumer Product Safety Commission was being set up in 1972, Dingell slipped in an amendment, largely unnoticed, exempting firearms and ammunition from regulatory oversight. Extending the law to guns might have forced development of safe-storage standards and "smart gun" technology to minimize accidental shootings and thefts.

On another occasion, he boasted to constituents back home that he had proposed a bill cracking down on cheap handguns known as Saturday night specials. But, as another NRA president, C. R. Gutermuth, explained privately in a letter in 1974, Dingell only "did so with the thought of slowing the efforts by others to pass more damaging legislation."

"Obviously," he wrote, "this comes under the heading of legislative maneuvering and strategy."

Still, the NRA's old guard was willing to go only so far to accommodate Dingell's increasingly strident calls for change. Gutermuth, while expressing gratitude for the congressman's help, bristled at his "unfair" attacks, saying Dingell would "always talk about what the NRA has not done and damn little about what it is doing." Dingell was demanding too much, Gutermuth complained.

"John wants an all out action program that goes way beyond what we think we dare sponsor or could finance," Gutermuth wrote to an NRA executive, adding that Dingell "seems to think that we should become involved in partisan politics. He obviously wants us to help knock off members of Congress that do not perform right."

Gutermuth, a naturalist and conservationist uncomfortable with the rough-and-tumble of politics, represented the traditionalist leadership of the NRA, which was under mounting pressure, not just from Dingell but from younger board members who also favored a more combative approach. Dingell was working these men hard to line up support.

In the fall of 1974, he had breakfast with one of them, Robert Lindahl, an acoustical engineer also from Michigan. Over pancakes, they plotted how to get the "old goats" who ran the organization to allow Dingell to formally present a resolution creating what he was now calling the Institute for Legislative Action.

Lindahl felt out other sympathetic directors. He quietly circulated a letter urging them to support a motion to allow Dingell to appear before the executive committee in January 1975, citing the congressman's warnings about a looming legislative threat.

"He is disturbed about our ability to combat the expected number of Gun Control bills which will be introduced now that Watergate is over and Congress has time to think of other problems," Lindahl wrote.

Dingell got his wish. At a two-day meeting at NRA headquarters in Washington, DC, the executive committee heard from him—sandwiched between discussions of the Intercollegiate Skeet and Clay Pigeon Championships and the Amateur Trapshooting Association—and voted to adopt his plan. Despite how little fanfare it received at the time, the proposal was breathtaking in its ambition and scope.

A more detailed thirty-three-page blueprint, prepared several months later by Dingell and his compatriots, said the institute would develop a lobbying, legal, and communications operation in Washington and across fifty states, using "all available resources at every level" to defeat gun control measures and expand gun rights. Among other things, the institute would:

> Maintain files for each member of Congress and key members of the Executive Branch.
>
> Develop contacts in each Congressional office, majority and minority counsels on key committees, and key persons at the White House, Executive Departments and Independent Agencies.
>
> Using computerized data, bring influence to bear on elected officials, and, through them, to appointed officials by effective lobbying supported by active 'grass roots' pressures from constituents and other influential persons in affected states and districts.
>
> For greatest effectiveness and economy, whenever possible, influence legislation at the lowest level of the legislative structure and at the earliest time, by the monitoring of trends, close contact with decision makers and the mustering of 'grass roots' supportive influence.

There would also be a legal action program to "utilize the nation's judicial machinery" to advance the NRA's mission. Here, Dingell was particularly explicit in laying out a plan for achieving his ultimate goal, first described in his September 1968 letter, to reframe the Constitution's protection of gun rights. He wanted to not only wage court battles against specific laws, but to win the wider legal and ideological conflict over gun rights in America.

First, he called for a strong in-house legal team. It would be augmented by "a nationwide corps of volunteer lawyers" to file challenges to gun restrictions, defend "meritorious cases" of citizens accused of violating gun laws, and launch lawsuits "against anti-gun groups, designed to harass or impede their operations, and consume their time and resources."

But perhaps most important, Dingell saw the need to fund legal research and scholarship "designed to implant in the consciousness of the legal community an attitude of resistance [to] certain forms of gun control. The objective is to develop a legal climate that would preclude, or at least inhibit, serious consideration of many anti-gun proposals."

Specifically, "constitutional study" was required to establish "affirmative foundations for firearms rights" not only using the Second Amendment but also other federal laws. And to accomplish such a sweeping conversion of public attitudes, Dingell proposed employing the sort of sleight of hand that he used to such great effect in Congress: seeding pro-gun legal writings in ways that could not be connected to the NRA.

"For example, the services of firearms-oriented lawyers and others could be utilized to produce and publish articles for law reviews and other opinion-making journals from 'sterile,' e.g., non-firearms-connected, sources."

It would take time for the institute to get off the ground. In the coming months there was bureaucratic wrangling over its funding and internecine fights with establishment NRA figures who resisted the new approach. But the die had been cast. Dingell's vision had prevailed.

No one could quite see it yet, but the NRA had declared war and there would be no turning back.

To run his new creation, Dingell sought a leadership structure for the institute that would operate with its own budget and have, at the top, an executive director separate from NRA's in-house management. Harlon Carter was his preferred candidate.

Carter was a familiar, if pugnacious, presence at the NRA, having joined the board in the 1950s and serving as its president for two years in the mid-1960s. He had been an NRA member most of his adult life and had won awards for marksmanship in his youth.

Blue-eyed and bald (*bullet-headed* seems too apropos), Carter cut an imposing figure that he enjoyed using to intimidating effect, though many people who knew him assured me that, in private, he could be warm and bighearted. Like many professional men of his generation, he had a somewhat formal manner of speaking, if roughened around the edges by his south-Texas upbringing. His lower lip and jaw tended to jut outward when he talked. In making a point during debate, he often accompanied it with a self-satisfied squint and toothy grin.

Going to work for the US Border Patrol was an unsurprising choice for Carter, given that his father had been a border agent. But unlike the elder Carter, the son propelled quickly up the ranks to become the youngest chief of the agency ever. He was just thirty-seven when he assumed command in 1950 and began implementing military-like operations designed to instill fear in immigrant communities. Among other initiatives, he led a controversial program called Operation Wetback, to expel hundreds of thousands of Mexican immigrants, some of them American citizens, from the country.

A few years after he retired in 1970, Carter was investigated in connection with several allegations of wrongdoing, including the disappearance of about fifty thousand rounds of ammunition from the agency's stores. He testified before a grand jury but was never charged. It is unclear whether this was known to Dingell, who took a dim view of government corruption, as he pushed the NRA to hire Carter for the lobbying job.

Carter shared Dingell's view that the NRA was not meeting the demands of the moment. In a remarkably biting address to his colleagues on the NRA's executive committee in July 1972, Carter positioned himself as a crusader bent on conquest. Right from his opening line, he made clear they had better buckle up for what he was going to say:

"I have a feeling, a strong feeling, that when a man leans into a situation and if he does not draw a little blood, he is not leaning hard enough and may not actually indicate where he stands and might produce uncertainties as a consequence of his failure to indicate who he is and what he is and what he intends to do."

He went on to speak almost in religious terms, saying the group had to "cleanse" and "purify" itself of its past sins of endorsing some gun restrictions. An unnamed top official of the NRA, Carter said, had recently told him "that he has registered his guns and he didn't see anything wrong with registration, and he wanted to know why I was opposed to registration." Carter was aghast.

"Now this is the sort of thing we are getting ourselves into, gentlemen," he seethed. "We no longer have in our ranks a purification of dedication, and that is a serious charge for a man in my position to stand up here and make. I would not make it unless I can prove it, and don't any of you dare make me prove it because I damn well guarantee you I can prove it."

For his part, Dingell thought Carter was exactly the sort of aggressive point man the NRA needed. Dingell's like-minded approach was captured in a two-page, single-spaced screed he fired off to the NRA leadership lambasting them for "imbecilic" cowardice in the face of attempts to regulate Saturday night specials.

"NRA should not concede, even in principle, the necessity for any new 'anti-crime' legislation imposing further restrictions on the manufacture or sale of certain kinds of handguns," he wrote, adding, "Lending any support even to the general idea of fighting crime by outlawing certain kinds of guns sets a horrible precedent, and completely undermines our most powerful argument: that criminals, not guns, cause crime."

Heading into a decisive annual board meeting in San Diego in April 1975, Dingell was also fuming at what he saw as backsliding by Gutermuth and his ilk on implementing the lobbying institute. After it received unanimous approval from the board's executive committee the previous January, there had been nothing but roadblocks thrown in its way, and Dingell had grown tired of trying to work, diplomatically, behind the scenes. He decided to take a more direct approach.

Weeks before the meeting, Dingell huddled with a close aide, a lawyer named Michael Parker, to prepare a scalding letter to send to all seventy-five members of the NRA's board. It was a risky move. The wide distribution meant it could leak and become public. He could also offend people whose support he needed.

But Dingell knew that his status as an elected official carried weight. Editing a draft of the four-page letter, he scribbled in the margin questions about "what stationery" to use and how to deliver it to board members. He decided to go with his official congressional letterhead, and Parker recommended not leaving it in directors' mailboxes at the meeting "because they will be bombarded with garbage to read there" and said in a note to Dingell, "It won't have the same effect as a personal letter at home from a Congressman."

Parker, who was Dingell's right-hand man for NRA and gun-related matters, encouraged a frontal assault against Gutermuth, whom Parker accused of "poisoning the well" with "lamebrain propaganda" against the institute. Dingell agreed.

His April 11, 1975, letter began with a grave warning about the "great legislative and legal battles that are now upon us—battles that surely will decide within the next few years whether Americans retain the right to keep and bear arms." He described the internal disputes that were holding up implementation of the lobbying institute, blasting the "leisurely response to the legislative threat" that hobbled his efforts. And he named names, apologizing "in advance for any personal offense that some might take."

The top officers, Dingell thundered, lacked a "vigorous, competent, imaginative, and aggressive command" and "have together failed to manage the NRA's legislative affairs in an adequate fashion." They didn't have "any idea at all how to go about reversing the national anti-gun trend and taking a pro-gun offensive," and their meager commitment of resources to setting up the institute was a "bad joke were it not so pathetic."

He continued, "We must not waste any more precious time. Let me urge you as earnestly as I am able to reject any efforts to cut back the Institute resolution and shackle it to the same obstructionism and foot-dragging that has stunted our efforts so far.

"In sum, I am imploring you to decisively ratify the committee's selection of Harlon Carter as Director of the Institute, and to make sure before you leave San Diego that he is armed with any additional authority he needs to harness whatever NRA resources are necessary to get the job done. No matter how important the NRA's other activities might seem, survival must be our number one priority."

Dingell's campaign worked.

Six months later, Carter pulled up a chair at the witness table inside a Congressional hearing room where a House subcommittee on crime was discussing gun control proposals. He was there as the newly appointed executive director of the NRA Institute for Legislative Action. Beside him was Parker, the onetime Dingell aide now serving as the institute's general counsel.

The two men came loaded for bear. By the mid-1970s, the battle between gun control and gun rights forces was fully engaged, largely over the rampant criminal use of cheap handguns called Saturday night specials. The 1968 Gun Control Act had tried, and failed, to address it by banning imports of nonsporting guns, but that did not stop foreign handgun parts from being imported and assembled. Now, there were roughly 170 bills before Congress with proposals ranging from background-check requirements to outright bans on handguns.

The NRA—due largely to the efforts of Dingell—was squarely at the forefront of the fight, carrying the banner of "freedom." Variants of that word were spoken more than a hundred times at the hearing, usually by opponents of new gun laws.

Congressman John Ashbrook, a Republican from Ohio who would soon join the NRA's board, railed against "the punks and the criminals" running amok with guns and claimed new laws would target the wrong people.

"The law-abiding citizen is not the problem," he said, "and I think it is going to evolve in this Congress whether or not we are going to give in and let the criminals and the radical elements run our country or whether the law-abiding citizen is going to be able to keep his freedom."

When it was his turn to speak, Carter hewed to the same theme of freedom—but with a twist. After first laying out in detail the NRA's opposition to the various gun controls being considered, he suddenly pivoted, saying, "Let me put it in personal terms because to me it is a very personal issue."

If the other people at the hearing knew just how personal, they would've been shocked. Because Harlon Carter was not the man everyone thought he was.

Twelve-year-old Salvatore Pena was hanging around with some friends near a creek in Laredo, Texas, one spring evening in 1931 when he saw a tall teenager approaching carrying a 12-gauge shotgun.

Pena and his friends, all Hispanic residents of the border town, had just left a local swimming pool and had crossed through someone's cow lot before heading down to the creek. A little while earlier, an older white woman had come to the rise above the creek and called down to them, demanding to know "What were you doing in my back lot?" The boys had gotten sassy in response, yelling back that it was "none of your business!"

Now, the white teenager with the shotgun was standing before the group. He was seventeen-year-old Harlan Bronson Carter. It was his mother who had confronted the boys earlier about passing through her cow lot. Carter, who was nearly six feet tall and about 150 pounds, rested the butt of his gun on the ground and demanded the boys come with him to his house to be questioned by his mother.

"We asked him why," recalled Salvatore. "And he said, 'Oh, go to my house.'"

That's when Salvatore's sixteen-year-old friend Ramón Casiano, the oldest and largest of the group, stepped forward.

"Hell, no, we won't go to your house and you can't make us," he said.

An argument ensued between Carter and Casiano, who angrily threw off his jacket and pulled out a small Scout knife. It had a three-inch blade and other tools folded into its handle, a type that boys commonly carried. He asked Carter, who was by now pointing his shotgun at Casiano, if he wanted to fight. As Salvatore remembered it,

Casiano dismissively pushed the barrel of Carter's shotgun away and laughed at him.

"You think I won't use this?" Carter said. Then he fired, hitting Casiano in the right side of his chest. The teenager fell to the ground.

As he lay bleeding and in shock, Casiano reached a hand up toward Carter and said, "You're my friend."

Carter knocked the boy's hand away, replying, "You're my friend nothing."

Carter's mother, who had heard the commotion, came running over.

"Son, you hurt that boy!" she exclaimed. She and others flagged down a passing car to take Casiano to the hospital, where he later died.

Carter was charged with murder. At his trial, he insisted that Casiano had tried to stab him and that he only intended to shoot the teen in the shoulder. He said he had brought the shotgun with him because his mother claimed the boys had told her they had a gun.

But after hearing testimony from Salvatore and others, the judge instructed the jury that the circumstances of the killing did not justify a self-defense claim.

"There is no evidence that defendant had any lawful authority to require deceased to go to his house for questioning," said Judge J. F. Mullally, "and if defendant was trying to make deceased go there for that purpose at the time of the killing, he was acting without the authority of law, and the law of self-defense does not apply."

The jury convicted Carter and he was sentenced to three years in prison. He appealed, and in December 1931, a Texas appellate court reversed the conviction, ruling that the trial judge erred by not allowing the jury to consider self-defense. The case was sent back to the lower court, but a retrial never happened because several of the witnesses had since had their own run-ins with the law—Salvatore had been caught stealing and was sent to reform school.

Carter moved on. But not before doing something that would effectively obscure the chances of someone later stumbling across his murder case. When he enrolled at the University of Texas in 1933, the spelling of his first name was changed from *Harlan* to *Harlon*. After college, the newly christened Harlon-with-an-*o* joined the Border Patrol and later the leadership of the NRA—all the while concealing his troubled past.

Now here he was, some forty years later, poised to address a congressional committee on the issue of firearms regulation. It was a fascinating moment. What would Carter say that was so personal? Would he open up about the tragic experience in his youth and use it to draw lessons about the rights and responsibilities of gun ownership, perhaps even find a way to turn it to his rhetorical advantage?

Not a chance.

"I cherish the freedom to be able to own guns," he said. "I have never abused that freedom. I have never robbed or murdered anybody and never in any way abused that right to own a gun. So, why should I have to give up my gun? How does my gun relate to the crime problem? Why should any burdens, any requirements, be imposed upon me at all?"

What Carter was articulating would become a familiar NRA refrain: aggrieved opposition singularly focused on the personal wants and needs of gun owners. Plus, there was a blatant falsehood thrown in for good measure.

The approach was also tinged with a paranoia that would continue to grow in the ensuing decades and become a defining feature. For his part, Parker spoke darkly about the threat of gun registration leading to nationwide data collection on Americans, who "fear the idea of Big Brother" misusing the information "to harm them in some way, if only to take away their firearms."

He also came prepared with a catchy analogy. Objecting to a proposed fourteen-day background-check requirement for gun purchases, he referred to an old television commercial for potato chips whose punch line was "I'll bet you can't eat just one."

"And I have no doubt at all that if it is a good thing to be in favor of a fourteen-day waiting period, next year ATF is going to be back and say we cannot do it in fourteen days, we will have to do it in ninety," Parker said. "Frankly, I can see where that leads, knowing how bureaucracies work. . . . It is a little nibble first, and I'll bet you can't eat just one. So that is how I envision the objection to the fourteen-day waiting period."

Over the hours of testimony, the NRA men constructed a three-legged stool to support their guiding philosophy: (1) Gun violence is not our fault; (2) restrictions are ineffective; and (3) any new laws are a slippery slope. Resting upon the stool was the argument that no gun law is acceptable if it makes it harder for a noncriminal to exercise their Second Amendment right to obtain a gun. But because every criminal starts out as a noncriminal, it meant that some degree of gun violence simply had to be accepted as inevitable.

They didn't come out and say that directly. Instead, that cynical central premise remained in shadow.

Eventually, Congressman George E. Danielson had heard enough. The Democrat from California, a former FBI agent and prosecutor, attempted to bore down to the nihilistic root of the NRA's viewpoint. How, Danielson asked, can society prevent dangerous people from getting a gun "if there is not some way of having an application and a screening operation"?

Parker attempted a lawyerly response: "What you are really talking about is prior restraint, and we have always had, and one of the very fundamental things, precepts, that this country was founded on two hundred years ago was the idea that each individual would be judged as an individual. He had the presumption of innocence. He was not punished in advance for things he might do."

Danielson wasn't having it: "I will accept that. Now, will you answer my question?"

Pushed by the congressman, Parker edged closer into a trap: "I am trying. I do not know of any way that you can make a predetermination that someone is going to misuse a firearm. . . . I do not know of any practical way to do it, sir, without causing a great deal of difficulty for the people who are not causing the problem."

Danielson moved in for the kill: "So therefore you would rather allow those convicted violent felons, mentally deranged people, violently addicted-to-narcotics people to have guns, rather than to have the screening process for the honest people like yourselves. Is that correct?"

Carter had been stewing at the witness table as the California Democrat pressed his case. Now he couldn't take it anymore. Before Parker could respond, Carter piped up:

"A price we pay for freedom."

There it was.

SCORNED AND DENIGRATED

On October 8, 1980, as Pres. Jimmy Carter was visiting Nashville, a strange young man was stopped at the local airport by security officers, who found three unloaded handguns and a pair of handcuffs in his luggage. He was turned over to city police, who took his guns, fined him $62.50, and sent him on his way.

That did not deter the young man, however. A few days later, he traveled to Dallas and bought more guns at a pawnshop. He started seeing a psychiatrist, but it didn't seem to help his agitated mental state. He restlessly crisscrossed the country. He tried writing poetry to express his feelings, including a poem called "Guns are fun!"—about shooting the president.

Five months after he was detained at the Nashville airport, the strange young man, John W. Hinckley Jr., finally used one of his cheap pawnshop revolvers, along with exploding Devastator bullets, which could be legally purchased, to shoot Pres. Ronald Reagan and three others outside a hotel in Washington, DC. In Hinckley's wallet, police found $129, a photo of Jodie Foster, and a small card printed with the Second Amendment.

A few months earlier, another deranged man, armed with a revolver and hollow-point bullets, had shot and killed John Lennon outside his apartment building in New York City; the killer, Mark David Chapman, managed to buy the pistol despite having previously been committed to a psychiatric hospital. A couple of months later, Mehmet Ali Agca would shoot Pope John Paul II in Vatican City.

The year 1981 was shaping up to be a really bad one for the gun lobby.

The momentum that had been building in the United States throughout the 1970s to do something about the proliferation of handguns was nearing a crescendo. To be sure, the NRA had successfully stiff-armed gun control attempts in Congress since 1968, and the group's membership was rising as its newly aggressive posture attracted like-minded gun owners. But by the end of the decade, with more than 30 million handguns circulating and about ten thousand deaths a year attributed to them, public opinion overall was not in the NRA's favor. Polls showed that as many as three-quarters of Americans favored tighter limits.

Growing up during that time, I personally experienced the seeming ubiquity of these cheap weapons. My parents and I lived in a trailer park in a sketchy area not far from a navy base, and the residents—a mix of factory workers, teachers, tradesmen, and retirees—grappled with break-ins and domestic problems. There were occasional gunshots. My friend's father, who drove a dump truck, was assaulted one night and threatened with a gun. Every home seemed to have a firearm in it, including my own.

Once, when my mother came home late and had forgotten her front-door key, she tried to get in the back door to our trailer, which we never used because it opened directly into my parents' bedroom. My father, awakened by the sound of someone fiddling with the lock, kicked the door open and pointed his pistol before realizing it was my mom, who screamed and cried. I was only about seven at the time and I never forgot it. A few trailers down the road, it was well-known among us kids that someone's father, a plumber, kept a pistol in a living room end table that usually had *Playboy* magazines on top. Looking back now, I wonder if he left the magazines there to distract boys from the gun; if so, it didn't work, because we found it anyway and used to play with it.

The trailer park backed up against a sprawling junkyard, where the kids from my neighborhood would catch bullfrogs, tinted orange from rusty pools of rainwater, and explore the wrecked cars. Once we stumbled across an old revolver stashed inside a burned-out automobile, evidently forgotten under the driver's seat. None of us took it home because we knew that would mean the end of our junkyard privileges.

Then there was the time when I was about thirteen years old and I encountered one of my relatives sitting alone with a handgun on their lap. They told me they didn't feel like living anymore and asked me if I knew how to use the gun. I went and found help. Thankfully nothing happened, and it was never spoken of again.

Concerns about handguns, specifically, led to the creation of the first organized gun control groups, beginning in 1971 with the Civic Disarmament Committee for Handgun Control, formed by Laura Fermi, an environmental activist and widow of the atomic scientist Enrico Fermi. Her interest in restricting firearms seemed a natural progression from her involvement in the nuclear peace movement, and Fermi brought an abolitionist's zeal to the crusade. It was a reminder that, as far back as the National Firearms Act, women were among the most vocal proponents of stronger gun laws.

Wives and mothers are often on the receiving end of domestic violence, as well as street crimes that take the lives of their children, which is why the General Federation of Women's Clubs had protested the exclusion of handguns from the 1934 law. The telegram the federation had sent to Congress that year asserted that "the security and safety of the homes and families of all the people of this country . . . transcends the selfish interests of any organized small minority."

Fermi was taking up and renewing that cause. As her committee noted in a 1974 newsletter, "It is clear the women have a weapon in 'expending their might': it is their heart.

"Let us see who will win in the conflict that will ensue: the women with their hearts or the gun advocates with their guns!"

Fermi's efforts—which generated hate mail threatening rape and murder for her and the women she worked with—inspired other activists. Groups such as Handgun Control Inc. and the National Coalition to Ban Handguns soon followed, gaining money and supporters with each high-profile shooting. Meanwhile, at the opposite end of the ideological spectrum, new gun rights groups were also forming.

In the mid-1970s, the Second Amendment Foundation and Gun Owners of America emerged to challenge and prod the NRA to become more aggressive. Both were founded by Republican political activists with a broader conservative agenda. The Second Amendment Foundation was the brainchild of Alan Gottlieb, a young nuclear engineer who was turned off by antiwar protests roiling college campuses and had instead joined Young Americans for Freedom, a right-wing organization that supported the Vietnam War. Later, he became a leader of the American Conservative Union and was a pioneer in the use of direct mail to raise money for Republican campaigns.

Similarly, the founder of Gun Owners of America was a Republican state senator from California, H. L. Richardson, who once belonged to the far-right John Birch Society, ran his own conservative fundraising operation, and formed the pro-business Free Market PAC. His preference, he said, was to "carve this government up like you wouldn't believe, into much, much smaller pieces than are out there now."

These competing forces, for and against limits on guns, resulted in a kind of stalemate on the issue. They also reflected a widening cultural and political gulf in America. The battle over firearms became a proxy for other arguments about evolving social mores and values, race and urban crime, and the role of government in people's lives. As is often the case, extremists from both sides, demanding either no guns or no gun laws, tended to dominate the national discussion. At its worst, it could seem like *All in the Family*'s Archie Bunker versus Meathead writ large—prejudiced blue-collar Neanderthals on one side, overeducated moralizing elites on the other.

This fracture was captured vividly in a July 1980 episode of *Firing Line*, the television talk show hosted by conservative firebrand William F. Buckley Jr., who invited two guests to debate the gun issue.

Defending gun rights was the NRA's Harlon Carter, who had by then risen to the top of the organization—and in dramatic fashion. He had emerged as the victor during an infamous NRA annual meeting in May 1977 that became known as "the revolt at Cincinnati," in which hard-liners rallied a majority of the two thousand members present to take the NRA in a new, uncompromising direction. The old guard was toppled and Carter installed as chief executive following a tumultuous eight-hour meeting that ended at 4:00 a.m.

Facing off with Carter in the hour-long TV segment was John J. Buckley (no relation to William F.), a liberal sheriff from the Boston suburbs who championed inmate rights, opposed the death penalty, and advocated a ban on civilian purchases of handguns. A Boston College grad, he spoke with a Bay State accent that screamed "Hahvahd Yahd."

Buckley, the host, began by alluding to the murder a few months earlier of Allard Lowenstein, a well-known progressive activist and former congressman who was shot in his Manhattan office by a mentally ill stalker. The killer had obtained the gun, Buckley noted, with "only a little more difficulty than he'd have had ordering a McDonald's hamburger."

Sheriff Buckley rattled off additional examples of mayhem, including accidental shootings, suicides, and increased fear of assassinations. He cited statistics showing a reduction in handgun crimes following passage of stricter laws in Washington, DC, and Massachusetts, adding that unless a national ban was enacted, "the next generation will look back upon us as if it were the Wild West."

He said, "This is a public health problem, We can talk about the umpire in a softball game last week who was shot and killed in an argument, or the father in Massachusetts who shot his sixteen-year-old son for using too much hot water in the shower. We can do something about that. We can't stop all crime or all murders, but we can do better than this!"

Carter responded with the standard line that people, not guns, were the problem. He quoted an ancient Roman poet, Juvenal, to make the point that even before firearms were invented, citizens during the reign of Augustus faced rampant crime and violence:

"He wrote that the rich went out at night only when surrounded by their armed guards and torchbearers, and that the poor went out not at all, except at grave risk to their lives."

The not-so-subtle subtext to Carter's analogy was that many of those arguing for gun control were elites, living in the relative safety of wealthy suburbs and Manhattan high-rises, who did not have to deal with everyday dangers faced by inner-city shopkeepers and homemakers. He espoused an essentially Hobbesian view that humanity, left to its own devices, cannot be trusted without strict law and order, including the ability of people to arm themselves.

Toward the end of the show, the young commentator Jeff Greenfield, who played the role of Robin to Buckley's Batman, took over and pressed Carter to acknowledge a growing sense that toxic male psychology was getting in the way of sensible gun policy. Greenfield pointed to bumper stickers saying YOU'LL HAVE GUN CONTROL WHEN YOU PRY MY RIFLE FROM MY COLD, DEAD FINGERS as evidence of misplaced passions.

"Some of what we're talking about here is a psychological identity between the holding of a gun and the possession of masculinity," Greenfield said. "In fact, if it were just an issue of protection, it wouldn't be a ninety-six percent male organization that you represent."

Carter at first appeared to concede some of Greenfield's point, adding, "I personally reject the bumper-sticker psychology." But then Carter, who could be crafty in public interviews at telegraphing the NRA's more unsettling viewpoints in deceptively mild terms, cited another bumper-sticker message that he said is "beginning to be prevalent and seems to be interesting.

"It says, 'what do you have in mind for me, mr. politician, that my possession of a gun makes you so nervous?'"

"That's a bumper sticker?" Greenfield replied. "What's the size of the bumper?"

"Well, the people out in Arizona put it on the endgate of their pickup trucks."

"Oh, I see. It doesn't fit on the Volkswagens, I guess."

There had always been a strain of paranoia coursing through the gun rights movement. Its roots stretched back to the founding.

During debates over ratification of the Bill of Rights, Anti-Federalists had raised the specter of a despotic central government disarming the populace to control it. Federalists may have waved off such talk as the product of "a counterfeit zeal," but those who took it seriously saw the Second Amendment as protection against such a worst-case scenario.

The sentiment reflected in Carter's Arizona pickup truck sign would have been right at home in an Anti-Federalist pamphlet in 1791. But to say that things had changed over two centuries was an understatement, and the idea that average Americans in 1980 needed to be able to arm themselves against their own democratically elected government was lunacy to most people—especially if doing so meant tolerating everyday bloodshed.

By the time the NRA's board of directors convened in Denver for its annual meeting in May 1981, the political consequences of that everyday bloodshed were tangible.

It was the first time the full board had met since the murder of John Lennon and the attempted assassination of President Reagan, and public reaction had, for the moment at least, derailed the NRA's agenda. Neal Knox, one of the hard-liners who had wrested control of the group in 1977 and succeeded Carter as head of its lobbying institute, grumbled that the shootings "bring to mind that phrase about 'the best-laid plans of mice and men.'"

He reported to the group, "Our priorities, plans, and activities have necessarily been altered somewhat."

Brush fires were flaring across the country in the form of state referendums to ban handguns, and restrictive bills were being introduced in Washington. Harlon Carter himself had warned of this moment back in 1972 in his fiery, and prescient, speech to the NRA's executive committee: "We must prepare now, and I know the gentlemen will cringe a bit, but we must prepare now for the next assassination. What is going to be your answer? How are you going to blunt the effort to control? What are you going to say and what are we going to do?"

The moment had arrived, and it was Carter who was in charge. As if the cascading crises of gun violence and legislative responses were not enough, the NRA was soon hit with a curveball. A *New York Times* reporter interviewing Carter during a break at the Denver meeting posed an unexpected question: Is it true that you shot and killed a Mexican teenager in 1931?

Carter had worked his entire adult life to keep this dirty secret hidden. Thrown off-balance by its sudden reappearance, he at first denied knowing anything about it. He insisted he had never changed the spelling of his name and had actually been in college in Austin at the time of the incident. But as the interview wore on, it was clear that the reporter had the goods. When the *Times* story appeared, it laid out the case against Carter in damning detail, quoting records from courthouses, county clerks, and the college to show that he was lying.

Eventually, Carter was forced to admit his involvement in the killing and said he regretted it, though he took a swipe at the *Times*: "The motivation behind any story which reaches back fifty years is truly outrageous." In the long run, the unmasking of Carter's criminal history had little effect on his tenure at the top of the NRA—he would continue to lead the organization for four more years, until his retirement.

But in 1981, it appeared to be a devastating revelation at a time when the NRA could least afford another public relations crisis. The immediate outlook for the group's grand plans was grim, and it was unclear if even the hard-charging Carter was capable of turning things around anytime soon.

That is, until a white hat emerged from a hail of gunfire and came riding to the rescue.

The lights dimmed and the crowd hushed inside the cavernous banquet hall in Phoenix as the first stirring notes of "Hail to the Chief" sounded. An announcer made the introduction:

"Ladies and gentlemen. The president of the United States and Mr. Harlon Carter."

President Reagan, looking polished and relaxed in a sharp tan suit, strode onto the dais, trailed by Carter, who lumbered along in a dark suit with a name tag dangling from the lapel. The audience rose and cheered loudly—as much for Carter as for Reagan.

Exactly two years had passed since the dark days of 1981, and now the NRA's board was meeting again, this time with none other than the president of the United States as its honored guest. And the venue spoke volumes: Arizona.

This was where Carter had spoken approvingly of seeing those verbose signs on pickup truck tailgates. It was a message of fear, insecurity, and resentment that had taken hold in a significant swath of America—and within the NRA itself.

A month before Reagan's appearance at its annual meeting, several leaders of the group drafted a twenty-five-page internal report entitled "Committee for the Year 2000." It laid out a vision for what the NRA should seek to accomplish in the decades ahead and, in so doing, produced an almost primal scream echoing the frustrations of a society cleaving itself in two. The document complained bitterly that NRA members and American gun owners in general were victims of "a distinct metropolitan upper-middle-class snobbery, where the familiar pursuits of small-town and rural America are scorned and denigrated." "Powerful tides in the cultural ocean" were working against them, propelled by elites, defined as the "college educated, intellectual, political, educational, legal, religious and also to some extent the business and financial leadership of the country."

It further opined that this cabal of snobs, located mostly in big cities and on university campuses, "dominates the flow of information and profoundly influences the formation of public opinion in the United States" against gun culture. And it blamed them for overreacting to the assassinations of Pres. John F. Kennedy, Robert F. Kennedy, and Martin Luther King:

"The repeated traumas of these shooting deaths of men they admired fixed and reinforced in the minds of this powerful group, unfamiliar with the legitimate uses of firearms, a vision of guns as nasty, dangerous and undesirable, and of gun owners as disreputable and violent."

It was a breathtakingly crass statement. To the extent that it reflected a dominant view within the NRA and its 2 million members, it was hard to imagine the opposing forces of gun rights and gun control ever finding common ground.

The balance of the report actually proposed a positive plan of action. It focused on ways of rallying public opinion in favor of firearms ownership and presenting the NRA as more than just a bastion of white gun guys and suggested enlisting Black, Jewish, and "left-wing liberal" gun owners to offer testimonials.

But these more optimistic prescriptions for expanding the tent and winning hearts and minds ran in parallel to a darker, more fatalistic view of gun rights as a shield against some ill-defined menace of government control. The "cold, dead fingers" mentality that started appearing on pro-gun bumper stickers in the 1970s was not just a sociological manifestation of anger and suspicion, it was fast becoming a political tool.

Few elected leaders wielded this tool better than Ronald Reagan. His views on guns tended to track those of the NRA and, in that way, reflected a growing radicalism in the Republican Party on the issue. Certainly, his commitment to gun rights was genuine and personal. As head of the Screen Actors Guild in the 1940s, amid violent union strikes and controversy over communist influence in Hollywood, he sometimes wore a pistol in a shoulder holster.

At the same time, Reagan had supported California's fifteen-day waiting period for purchase of a handgun. And as governor in 1967, he had signed into law a ban, favored by the NRA, on public carrying of firearms, the impetus for which was armed patrols in minority neighborhoods by the Black Panthers (the state GOP and NRA would insist that race played no role in their sudden, and fleeting, appreciation for gun control).

Still, Reagan held to a basic belief that any firearms laws should focus on "the illegal use of and not the ownership of guns," consistent with the NRA's long-stated emphasis on criminals and not guns themselves as the cause of gun violence. This set him apart in some ways from others in the Republican establishment, including Pres. Richard Nixon, who supported banning Saturday night specials, and Pres. Gerald Ford, whose administration favored restricting the carrying of handguns in high-crime areas.

By the time he unsuccessfully sought the Republican presidential nomination in 1976, Reagan's comments on gun rights had become increasingly extreme. An extraordinary column that appeared under his name in *Guns & Ammo* magazine in September 1975—most likely red meat to appeal to GOP primary voters—could have been written by Harlon Carter himself. Filled with simplistic, if misleading, aphorisms such as that cars kill more people than guns yet "there is no talk of banning the auto," it also struck a paranoid note on the subject of the Second Amendment:

"We may not have a well-regulated militia, but it does not necessarily follow that we should not be prepared to have one. The day could easily come when we need one."

Yes, in Reagan the gun lobby had finally found its avatar. He could not have fit the role better, having literally played gun-slinging heroes in Hollywood westerns, earning him the Secret Service code name Rawhide. The NRA couldn't believe its luck.

"I've always felt a special bond with members of your group," he told the adoring crowd at the May 1983 Phoenix meeting. "You live by Lincoln's words: Important principles may and must be inflexible."

In his speech that day, Reagan boasted of increasing government sales of surplus M1 rifles to civilian marksmanship programs and eliminating paperwork for purchases of certain ammunition. He praised the NRA for helping defeat a California referendum that would have mandated handgun registration and frozen the number of handguns in legal circulation. And he pledged to sign the Firearm Owners' Protection Act, which, when eventually adopted in 1986, loosened regulations of gun shows, interstate transport of firearms, and mail-order ammunition.

Most important, he rejected the idea that his attempted assassination justified stronger firearms laws, and in so doing he effectively took the wind out of the sails of the gun control movement. One could imagine an alternate universe in which Reagan used his own example to point out that the would-be killer obtained his guns *legally*, and that if there had been more restrictive laws, then perhaps his press secretary, James Brady, wouldn't be confined to a wheelchair with irreversible brain damage.

Instead, Reagan flipped the script: "It's a nasty truth. But those that seek to inflict harm are not fazed by gun control laws. I happen to know this from personal experience."

In October 1997, I found myself standing inside a cavernous expo hall at the Indiana State Fairgrounds. Hundreds of people milled about the rows of booths where one could buy survivalist gear and learn "truths" the government and global elites were hiding from people. I had gone there as a journalist to write about the burgeoning antigovernment "militia" movement.

Two years earlier, the Oklahoma City bombing that killed 168 people had awakened Americans to the simmering threat of domestic extremism. It was carried out by seemingly average white guys from flyover country in retaliation for the government's heavy-handed sieges at Waco and Ruby Ridge, where federal agents enforcing gun laws ended up triggering deadly clashes in which women and children were killed.

The incidents played into a narrative propagated by the gun lobby that the government was the enemy of freedom. The NRA circulated a fundraising letter in May 1995 that labeled federal law enforcement officers "jack-booted thugs" that have "the government's go-ahead to harass, intimidate, even murder law-abiding citizens." The storyline resonates strongly in some quarters.

The history of antigovernment sentiment in the United States has a rich vein of armed extremism running through it, stretching from both ends of the ideological spectrum. A century ago, anarchists conducted bombings and assassinations aimed at toppling the federal government (which led to the creation of the FBI). In the 1960s and '70s, it was the Weather Underground and other left-wing groups. By the 2020s, the most militant activities could be found on the political right, though some left-leaning groups also started arming themselves in response to right-wing attacks on LGBTQ and pro-choice protesters, as well as the shootings of civilians by federal immigration agents that seemed to lend credence to the NRA's earlier warnings about government abuses.

The ideology driving the current crop of right-wing militias, such as the Oath Keepers and Three Percenters, traces in large part to the 1990s, when conservative skepticism of big government seemed to curdle into a paranoia about conspiracy, often coalescing around Second Amendment issues. I was far from alone during that time in feeling that something dangerous was happening in the zeitgeist, a shift of attitudes within a certain overlooked segment of society that needed to be understood.

With me on the 1997 reporting trip was a photographer, Rick Hartford, one of the nicest individuals you will ever meet but who looks kind of scary. Whereas I have the misfortune of being easily mistaken for an FBI agent, Rick dresses all in black with biker boots, wears his hair in a ponytail, and has a craggy face that belies his soft-spoken friendliness.

Our excursion began at a machine-gun shoot in Bullitt County, Kentucky. The event, held a couple of times a year at a "Christian family-owned" gun range in the middle of nowhere, was an exuberant spasm of bullet-riddled pyrotechnics, where guests paid to blast away at old cars and barrels of fuel that would explode into fiery mushroom clouds. It was fascinating, but mainly a sideshow to the real purpose of our visit.

Rick was determined to get access to a private meeting of national militia groups that was convening not far from the machine-gun shoot, and as only he is able to do, he talked his way in. Drinks and snacks were set out on a table. One after another, men who had traveled from around the country to a Veterans of Foreign Wars hall in Kentucky, some dressed in camo with pistols on their hips, stepped to a microphone to relate their fears about the government and the New World Order.

Jim Gillmore, a militia leader from Washington State whose group had formed two years earlier in response to a standoff in Montana between federal agents and antigovernment extremists, spoke of a great battle brewing between good and evil. Globalist bankers were the "head of the monster" and the United Nations was their tool.

"Evil is trying to take away the freedom of mankind," he said.

As this paranoid coffee klatch was going on, similar sentiments were on florid display two hours to the north at the Indiana expo hall, where a survivalist/prepper convention of sorts was happening. I entered with no problems and began wandering the aisles.

A woman was selling VHS tapes of a documentary purporting to reveal secret government plans to build concentration camps to imprison gun-owning patriots who stood up for the Second Amendment. A wild-eyed man presided over a long tabletop covered with laminated photos of Jewish-owned buildings in New York City that had 666—the mark of the devil—in their street address: "Coincidence? I think not." Other vendors were hawking dubious health cures, investments in gold and silver, and plots of land in Idaho where you could build a bunker to survive the end-time.

Walt, a middle-aged insurance salesman wearing a Cleveland Indians sweatshirt, was soaking it all in. I asked him if he really believed some of the crazier-sounding theories he was seeing. He pondered the question for a moment.

"There are pictures of trainloads of tanks, accompanied by Chinese soldiers, traveling at night," he said. "The tanks say UN on them. You tell me: Why doesn't the media report this?"

As I scanned the tabletops of extremist ephemera, something caught my eye: It was a framed copy of Ronald Reagan's *Guns & Ammo* column from 1975. I had never seen it before and paused to take a look. The proprietor of this booth, an older man with a beard and ball cap, was animatedly discussing firearms technology with another visitor.

Reading the words of the future president for the first time, I was taken aback. I had not known then, as I do now, that he had ever expressed such radical views on guns. After all, by 1997, Reagan had famously evolved on the subject of gun control, backing the Brady Handgun Violence Prevention Act in 1991, which would create a national background-check system, and joining other ex-presidents in supporting the 1994 assault weapons ban. And while he had always voiced enthusiasm for the Second Amendment, it was usually to make the point that Americans had a fundamental right to own a gun.

Yet here he was, speaking from behind framed glass, saying something much more militant. He was basically encouraging citizens to arm themselves as "protection from what has always been the chief source of despotism"—their own government and elected leaders.

As I finished reading it, the man with the beard and ball cap had moved on from his conversation and was now hovering before me. He pointed at the framed article.

"Ronald Reagan was the man!" he exclaimed. "He warned us."

A COUNTERFEIT ZEAL

"A WELL REGULATED MILITIA, being necessary to the security of a free State, the right of the people to keep and bear Arms, shall not be infringed."

For more than two hundred years, courts accepted that the right to bear arms was tethered to the desire for a well-regulated militia. Sporadic attempts, starting in the early 1800s, to push the boundaries of that understanding were mostly dismissed.

But by the close of the twentieth century, a movement was in full swing to reinterpret what seemed like a settled view of the Second Amendment. The movement, financed and promoted by the NRA and other pro-gun interests, generated legal research, opinion articles, and, ultimately, court cases tailored to undo our understanding of gun ownership as a *collective* right for the purpose of state security and replace it with an *individual* right.

Such a reframing of the Constitution would have enormous consequences, since the right to bear arms would no longer be connected to the common defense, but thrown open to include self-defense, hunting, sport—virtually any lawful purpose an individual American wished. As the scope of that right expanded, the ability to regulate it contracted.

Even though I'd spent a good part of my four decades as a journalist writing about gun violence, I had not known until recently the full scope of the campaign to achieve this reformulation of history. It wasn't until I had accumulated, over many years, thousands of pages of internal NRA files and confidential firearms-company documents and interviewed key players who were willing to talk that it began to take shape for me.

In hindsight, the NRA's central role should have been obvious. On a visit to the group's headquarters in Fairfax, Virginia, I once noticed the inscription displayed on a wood-paneled wall outside the entrance to its firearms museum: ". . . THE RIGHT OF THE PEOPLE TO KEEP AND BEAR ARMS, SHALL NOT BE INFRINGED."

It quotes only half of the Second Amendment, deleting the reference to a well-regulated militia.

Taking an eraser to history required, among other things, marshaling legal arguments drawn from a highly selective picking over of centuries-old writings and court decisions. Few quotations were more valuable to this project than those of a colonial-era jurist named St. George Tucker, one of the most important figures in the American gun debate whom most people have never heard of. His unlikely role serves as a case study in how modern-day activists excavated voices from the past to create a revisionist chorus.

Tucker was not involved in drafting the Constitution or the Second Amendment. Yet, he tends to be ushered forth by gun rights proponents like Woody Allen's summoning of Marshall McLuhan in *Annie Hall* to deliver a smackdown to elitist eggheads who refuse to find an individual right in the Second Amendment. His views appear in countless law review articles and legal briefs, and they undergird some of the most consequential twenty-first-century Supreme Court decisions expanding access to firearms.

Tucker was cited at length by Justice Antonin Scalia in the hugely important *District of Columbia v. Heller*, the landmark 2008 case that for the first time declared the Second Amendment secured an individual right to bear arms for self-defense. Tucker made an appearance again two years later, this time in Justice Samuel Alito's opinion in *McDonald v. City of Chicago*, limiting the ability of state and local governments to restrict firearms. Both decisions noted, approvingly, that Tucker referred to the Second Amendment as "the true palladium of liberty."

Tucker continued, "The right to self-defence is the first law of nature: in most governments it has been the study of rulers to confine the right within the narrowest limits possible. Wherever standing armies are kept up, and the right of the people to keep and bear arms is, under any colour or pretext whatsoever, prohibited, liberty, if not already annihilated, is on the brink of destruction."

Tucker was a contemporary of James Madison's. (Madison, despite being the author of the Second Amendment, is barely mentioned in the decisions of Scalia and Alito.) Originally from Bermuda, Tucker studied at the College of William & Mary before obtaining a law degree and joined the Virginia militia as an officer during the Revolution. He distinguished himself in the war and was injured at the Battle of Yorktown.

Afterward, he resumed his legal practice and was quickly recognized for his acumen and skill, earning several appointments in Virginia, though he remained on the fringes of the official work of drafting the US Constitution. Later, he joined the William & Mary faculty as a law professor, where he threw himself into research and writing on weighty topics of the day. Tucker was in the habit of incorporating William Blackstone's *Commentaries on the Laws of England* in his lectures on US law, and he eventually produced a five-volume treatise that used Blackstone's foundational work to interpret and analyze America's Constitution and emerging legal system. It was, essentially, an "American Blackstone" that instantly became required reading in law schools and was frequently cited in early-nineteenth-century court cases.

Tucker was an Anti-Federalist, though not in the extreme. His suspicion of federal authority is important to understanding the context of his writings on the Second Amendment. Had he been involved in the ratification debates to the same degree that Madison was, Tucker would almost certainly have been on the opposing side.

In his Blackstone treatise, Tucker makes several comments about the right to bear arms, including a footnote in which he states, "In America we may reasonably hope that the people will never cease to regard the right of keeping and bearing arms as the surest pledge of their liberty."

Elsewhere, he refers to the right of self-defense as the "first law of nature." He points out that, in England, guns were generally denied to commoners "under the specious pretext of preserving the game" when it was actually intended to prevent armed rebellion.

These provide the grist for most of the references to Tucker one finds in gun rights scholarship. For example, David Kopel, a pro-gun lawyer whose work has received financial backing from the NRA, frequently quotes Tucker's footnote to support the claim that the founders had in mind an individual right to bear arms for self-defense when drafting the Second Amendment.

"As Tucker demonstrates," Kopel wrote, "the Second Amendment right is individual, not a state's right; it belongs to everyone, not just militia members; its purposes include collective defense against tyranny, individual defense against lone criminals, and hunting."

Missing from this analysis is that whenever Tucker wrote about self-defense and bearing arms, he tied it to the threat of a standing army—that great bugaboo of the founders. Right after his "palladium of liberty" remarks, Tucker wrote about how the right to keep and bear arms was threatened "wherever standing armies are kept up."

He makes clear that he viewed the Second Amendment essentially as a compromise to assuage the fears of Anti-Federalists that states could lose the right to arm their militias, which, in the worst case, they saw as a bulwark against federal tyranny. Furthermore, Tucker's ruminations on self-defense being a "law of nature" are anchored not in constitutional theory but Blackstonian common law, which was the backdrop for his entire treatise.

The distinction between common and constitutional law is crucially important to the debate over gun regulation. Something governed by common law is more easily subject to legislative oversight than if it was explicitly singled out for protection in the Constitution. If pro-gun advocates can identify an individual right to own firearms in the Second Amendment, then it becomes much harder to legislate limits on their use. And the opposite is true if gun control proponents can establish that there is no individual right.

The significance of this became clear early on, as state courts first began wrestling over the meaning and boundaries of the Second Amendment in the nineteenth century. An influential example was the 1842 case of *State vs. Buzzard*, where the Arkansas Supreme Court ruled that the US Constitution did not prevent the state from regulating the carrying of concealed weapons.

Justice Townsend Dickinson wrote a concurring opinion spelling out how the individual carrying of arms for nonmilitia purposes was not safeguarded by the Second Amendment: "The class of cases to which the constitutional provision applies is widely different from the right of a private citizen to bear, concealed about his person, deadly weapons or arms. In the one, they are kept and carried in conformity with the Constitution and laws of the United States, with a certain specific object in view; in the other, they are kept and carried for private purposes, wholly independent of any constitutional regulation, and to answer private ends, wh[i]ch have no bearing upon the security of the State[.] If this idea be correct, then it follows that when arms are not kept or used for the defense of the State or Federal government, the manner of carrying and mode of using them are subject to the control and authority of the State Legislature."

The Arkansas court was saying, just as most courts would for the next century and a half, that the Second Amendment was born out of a civic commitment to a collective defense (to be replaced later by the modern National Guard), and that there was nothing in its text, or context, about a right to bear arms unrelated to that well-regulated common duty.

That prevailing view would be upended with the US Supreme Court's *Heller* case in 2008.

Gun rights proponents would argue that the Washington, DC, handgun ban at issue in the *Heller* case was a gross overreach of government authority that invited a judicial brushback. Under the District's law, owning a handgun was prohibited and any long guns kept at home, even for self-defense, had to be unloaded and disabled. A Washington resident, Dick Heller, sued after being denied a handgun permit.

A gun-friendly outcome to the case was made likelier given that Justices Scalia and Thomas, who occupied the far-right end of the court's slim conservative majority, had been waiting to take up a Second Amendment case. They sought opportunities to put into practice the theory of "originalism" that calls for navigating present-day legal thickets based on the historical circumstances at the time a law was put on the books.

That has an appealing ring of logic to it. But interpreting historical circumstances can be a zero-sum game, with the winner being whoever can most convincingly filter history through an ideological lens to their liking.

The NRA made a dark art of this. Understanding how the organization pulled it off helps explain why the writings of Tucker came to achieve talismanic importance in promoting a counternarrative to settled history.

Beginning in the 1970s, the NRA formulated a strategy of using gun-friendly academics and lawyers to generate favorable scholarship—often seemingly independent of the NRA—and then invoking it in lower courts, with the long-term goal of locking in gains with Supreme Court rulings.

The internal NRA records from the early 1980s that I obtained show in detail the origins of this effort. A planning memo bluntly explained that the group "must make every effort to reverse" the public's perception of the Second Amendment and change the prevailing view of a collective right to gun ownership.

"When a gun control case finally reaches the Supreme Court," the memo said, "we want Justices' secretaries to find an existing background of law review articles and lower court cases espousing individual rights, when they begin their research."

In another memo, executives of the group's lobbying institute laid out their scheme for "winning hearts and minds." At its core, it was all about cultivating an "ever-growing cadre of researchers and writers" who would develop "new findings, new scholarship and new channels for marketing this material to the general public." The NRA was already initiating that process, they said:

"We are providing editorial and financial support to numerous scholars in building a body of scholarship—the kind of research which will be definitive and useful in court cases, in legislative battles, and in persuading the majority of the American people to the correctness of our position."

The report went on to describe the work of some of the scholars and said it intended to "purchase and distribute these publications to libraries, activists and legislators throughout the country.

"For example, Dr. Joyce Malcolm has completed but not yet published her book, written at Harvard with an NEH grant, on the English 17th and 18th century concepts of weapons rights. David Hardy's and Steve Halbrook's books are also in manuscript. We must see that all are published."

The public connections of these scholars to the NRA over the years have varied.

It's no secret that Halbrook, for instance, a lawyer at a libertarian think tank who has taught at George Mason University, has done extensive legal work with the NRA in gun cases—his résumé is littered with references. In addition to advancing the "individual right" viewpoint, he has also argued against gun control by claiming that Nazi disarmament of Jews contributed to the Holocaust. In 2021, the NRA's board voted to honor Halbrook with an award that came with $10,000 and a commemorative plaque.

Dr. Malcolm's curriculum vitae mentions the NRA only in passing: a presentation she gave at its annual conference. Her 1994 book, *To Keep and Bear Arms: The Origins of an Anglo-American Right*, became a seminal work for Second Amendment advocates. It argued that the founders essentially imported the concept of an individual right to gun ownership from England, where, Malcolm asserted, it had been articulated in the 1689 Declaration of Rights. She later became the Patrick Henry Professor of Constitutional Law and the Second Amendment at George Mason, a position originally endowed by the NRA.

Hardy's online bio doesn't refer to the NRA at all, though his personal website links to it. He is a prolific author of pro–Second Amendment books and articles, including a 1974 paper in the *Chicago-Kent Law Review*, credited as one of the earliest to provide a scholarly underpinning for the "individual right" argument. As recently as 2018, NRA records showed approval of grants to Hardy to underwrite writing projects, part of funds totaling hundreds of thousands of dollars paid to him over the years.

It took a few decades, but when gun control cases finally did reach the Supreme Court, the work of these influential NRA-connected researchers were cited in the pro-gun opinions produced by the conservative majority in *Heller* in 2008, *McDonald* in 2010, and, in 2022, *Bruen*—the Big Three cases that vastly expanded Second Amendment rights. Of these, the most consequential was Justice Scalia's opinion in *Heller* because it cracked open the door for the later rulings to push wide open.

A striking feature of Scalia's decision is the degree to which it drew upon historical voices that were on the losing side of the "bearing arms" debate.

Rather than cite, for instance, the *Buzzard* precedent, which more accurately reflected the judiciary's long-standing consensus, Scalia pointed to, among others, an outlier in *Bliss v. Commonwealth*, an 1822 Kentucky case that did not even involve the Second Amendment. In that case, the Kentucky Court of Appeals determined that a law prohibiting concealed carrying of weapons violated the *state* constitution's protection of "the right of the citizens to bear arms in defense of themselves and the state."

Scalia was trying to show that a sentiment at the time favored an "individual right" interpretation of the law. That may have been true, but it was not what carried the day. The dominant perspective was more accurately captured by the authors of the *Buzzard* decision, twenty years later, who scoffed at the logic of the *Bliss* ruling, saying the threats it posed to social order were "so obvious as to induce the belief that they are present to every intelligent mind, and to render their statement here unnecessary."

An individual right to self-defense was indeed reflected in certain state constitutions, some of which predated the US Constitution. But Madison and Congress had been aware of that when drafting the Second Amendment and saw fit not to include it. Similarly, the US Supreme Court over the centuries had long been aware of the writings of scholars such as Tucker and Joseph Story, an early-nineteenth-century jurist also cited frequently by pro-gun advocates, and did not give them the same weight that Scalia did.

Scalia mentioned Tucker by name eleven times in his *Heller* decision and cited his "palladium of liberty" quote as evidence of founding-era support for the idea that expansive gun rights trumped everything else. But long before Tucker used the phrase in his commentaries on the Second Amendment, it was commonly used to describe guarantees of other freedoms and liberties as well. Tucker himself used it several times elsewhere in his Blackstone treatise when discussing the importance of separation of legislative and executive powers.

The word *palladium* originated in the ancient world as the name given to a sacred object believed by the Trojans and Romans to provide protection and later came to describe anything that affords security. In colonial America, it was frequently used to describe freedom of the press.

As far back as 1734, Andrew Bradford, publisher of Philadelphia's first newspaper, called the free press "the great Palladium of all our other Liberties." During debate over ratification of the Constitution, one of the framers, lawyer James Wilson, spoke of the press as that "sacred palladium for national freedom." Even a conservative critic of newspaper coverage at the turn of the nineteenth century, Benjamin Austin, a Boston politician who published commentaries under the pseudonyms Honestus and Old South, allowed that freedom of the press was "the palladium of public liberty" (elsewhere, he also referred to free elections as the palladium of liberty).

It is important to recognize the era in which the term was so often put into use. The Americans who wielded it to describe one liberty or another were in the crucible of emerging democracy, that radical experiment in self-governance dependent on the proper balancing of freedoms. Reason and argument, religious expression, elective politics, defense of the state, trial by jury—they all needed safeguarding because they were, themselves, safeguards against future threats of demagoguery, authoritarianism, and intolerance.

In this context, *palladium* was meant to describe the equilibrium of power between the people and their government, rather than a right disconnected from its relationship to governmental authority. When Tucker spoke of the right of self-defense, he first quoted the Second Amendment in full, beginning with its qualifier of "a well regulated militia." He specifically referred to the eighteenth-century fear of "standing armies"—the whole rationale for guaranteeing a right to bear arms.

When gun rights expansionists invoke Tucker's "palladium of liberty" phrasing, it is often done with a conveniently blinkered view of this complex history. It is ironic, given how much of their argument relies on theories of originalism and textualism, which have different meanings but are similar in that they attempt to understand the founders' thinking by studying contemporary writings and taking a magnifying glass to language and syntax.

In a blistering dissent in *Heller*, Justice John Paul Stevens accused the majority of invoking scholars who "are for the most part of limited relevance in construing the guarantee of the Second Amendment," adding that the majority "stretches to derive additional support from scattered state-court cases primarily concerned with state constitutional provisions."

But Stevens was now, himself, on the losing side of history. His was a view, increasingly in the minority, that was perhaps best expressed by former Chief Justice Warren Burger, a Republican who called the deliberate reframing of the Second Amendment "one of the greatest pieces of fraud—I repeat the word *fraud*—on the American public by special interest groups that I have ever seen in my lifetime."

He said in 1991, "If I were writing the Bill of Rights now, there wouldn't be any such thing as the Second Amendment."

One of the curious things about the Supreme Court rulings freeing firearms from almost any meaningful regulation is the failure to take seriously the technological advancements that would have made modern guns unrecognizable to the founders.

The court's opinion in *New York State Rifle & Pistol Association v. Bruen*, in 2022, not only established a constitutional right to carry a firearm outside the home, but perhaps more significantly it invalidated any current-day gun law unless it can be traced to some historical antecedent. The majority took the position that, yes, technology has changed lots of things—the mediums of free speech, the manner of searches and seizures, the mechanics of firearms—but the Constitution confers a fixed defense of rights that is at once cognizant of, and yet impervious to, the effects of that technological change.

On a practical level, such ideological rigidity invites problems. By insisting that modern-day gun restrictions pass muster only if a specific historical analog can be found, the court ignored the qualitative differences that technology has wrought. Justice Stephen Breyer, in his dissent, called this approach "unjustifiable and unworkable," adding it is unlikely "future courts will be able to identify historical analogues supporting the validity of regulations that address new technologies."

Adding to the challenge is the *Heller* decision's assertion that only "dangerous and unusual" firearms are exempt from Second Amendment protection. All guns are dangerous, so courts have focused on whether certain kinds are in "common use" and therefore not unusual. But there is an obvious circularity to this logic: If the government successfully restricts a type of firearm (think machine guns), it never becomes commonly used and the restrictions are legal; but if restrictions are never enacted and the gun becomes popular, it cannot later be restricted.

Listening to lawyers for the gun lobby make this argument in June 2023, a federal appeals judge in Illinois said constitutionality does not "wink on and off" depending on popularity and speculated whether hand grenades could not be banned if enough people enjoyed having them. Another judge on the panel dismissed the common-use test as "pretty weird."

The Supreme Court's rulings can seem like an oddly detached response to what has, at times, felt to be an almost-civilizational threat posed by gun violence. With no sense of irony, the court in *Bruen* borrowed a quote from its landmark 1819 decision in *McCulloch v. Maryland*—that the Constitution was intended "to be adapted to the various crises of human affairs" in the future—as justification for hamstringing efforts to address the current crisis with a legal framework tied to the past.

The full *McCulloch* ruling went on to declare that the Constitution should not be treated as something akin to "a legal code" enforced by soulless clerks. The founders, it said, did not intend to establish "immutable rules, for exigencies which, if foreseen at all, must have been seen dimly, and which can be best provided for as they occur."

This crucial understanding was adopted and articulated throughout the centuries, as judges both conservative and liberal saw the Constitution not as a dead instrument that demands absolutist adherence, but a living document whose elements must be balanced against what is necessary to maintain the common good. Justice Robert Jackson, writing in a 1949 opinion, inveighed against a purist view of rights that he said threatened to tip into extremism:

"The choice is not between order and liberty. It is between liberty with order and anarchy without either. There is danger that, if the Court does not temper its doctrine logic with a little practical wisdom, it will convert the constitutional Bill of Rights into a suicide pact."

FREEDOM

OUT OF THE JUNGLE

EUGENE STONER WAS a mild-mannered machinist working for an aircraft manufacturer in the 1950s when he started using the company's equipment in his spare time to pursue a lifelong hobby: building things that go "boom."

As a kid in the late 1920s and early 1930s, Stoner, whose family was relatively poor at times, would occupy himself by blowing up crude pipe bombs in the California desert. He built rockets and small cannons, once accidentally blowing a hole in the wall of his house. When he joined the marines, he naturally gravitated to the ordnance division, where, as he explained later, he had "opportunities, and those jobs, to do a certain amount of experimenting on different types of machine guns.

"And build a prototype here and there."

While working at Fairchild, the aircraft company, the bespectacled, unassuming Stoner, a soft-looking man partial to bow ties, met his opposite in temperament, a big gregarious salesman-type named George Sullivan. The two shared a passion for guns, and Sullivan, a patent attorney for Lockheed Aircraft, was impressed with a lightweight aluminum rifle design Stoner had come up with. Sullivan had created a small firearms-design company called ArmaLite, which soon became a division of Fairchild, and he pegged Stoner as someone with both the creativity and engineering chops to apply new aerospace technologies to the development of small arms.

"We started using some of George's ideas—mainly, he had some foam-filled fiberglass stocks he was putting on some weapons—and then I brought my ideas in on automatic weapon mechanisms, and we kinda started out," Stoner said.

This was the dawn of the atomic age, when technological leaps driven by the military imperatives of World War II were now being repurposed for civilian markets. Everything from satellites and chemical polymers to computerization and lightweight metals were the talk of Wall Street and Madison Avenue. Some of it verged on fantasy: Ford drew up a concept car powered by a trunk-size nuclear reactor (needless to say, it was never pursued).

The US Defense Department, however, saw little downside in taking chances on such pipe dreams. It spent more than $1 billion researching the possibility of long-range nuclear-powered aircraft. The air force eventually abandoned that idea as intercontinental ballistic missiles (ICBMs) lessened the need for strategic bombers. But for a while, in the years immediately following World War II and during the Korean War, manned aircraft was a dominant military focus, which meant ensuring that the crews were properly equipped with the latest technologies.

One item that the air force wanted was a lightweight survival firearm for when crew members were forced to land or parachute in enemy territory. Being in the aircraft business, Fairchild saw an opportunity to put its ArmaLite small-arms division to use developing a weapon design that fit the Air Force's needs.

Stoner and Sullivan came up with a .22-caliber collapsible rifle whose barrel could be detached and stashed inside a hollow fiberglass stock. The whole thing weighed two and a half pounds and, when disassembled, was only fourteen inches long, compact enough to fit inside an airman's pack. And it could float. They called it the AR-5—the *AR* short for "ArmaLite."

Alas, although the air force adopted the AR-5 as its new survival rifle, the need for such equipment soon evaporated as the country's defense posture shifted to ICBMs. Financially, ArmaLite's first weapons contract would be a dud. But that the government chose it gave the fledgling company a boost, and it forged ahead with successive rifle designs with names such as AR-7, AR-10, and so on.

ArmaLite's next big opportunity came when the army announced it was looking for something to replace the M1 rifle, the workhorse firearm used by grunts in World War II and Korea. Also known as the

M1 Garand, it was big and heavy, about ten pounds, all burnished wood and steel. A semiautomatic, it fired .30-caliber rounds.

Named after John Garand, a Canadian-American firearms designer, the M1 was developed following World War I and proved a major advancement in lethality over the bolt-action rifles of that earlier conflict. Its semiauto feeding system allowed eight-round clips to be quickly slapped in, making it capable of forty to fifty shots per minute. The M1 helped win wars.

But with the dawn of the Cold War, and potential theaters of conflict reshaped by technology and geopolitical priorities, battle tactics were changing. Speed and mobility became prized. And having gotten a taste of what machine guns could do during World War II, American military commanders wanted the new combat rifle to be capable of fully automatic firing—hundreds of rounds per minute with a single pull of the trigger.

American firearms designers saw an opportunity to develop lighter-weight, fast-firing weapons for ground forces. Army brass, however, were stubbornly wedded to the large-caliber ammunition that powered the M1, hampering the potential for new designs. In 1957, they decided to go with what became known as the M14, which resembled the M1 in appearance and weight, but with automatic firing capability.

ArmaLite had entered the competition late and with a radical new concept, which, in the end, proved too ahead of its time to make the cut. Stoner's AR-10 was unlike anything yet produced. It utilized a new gas-powered firing system and lightweight materials such as aluminum and fiberglass, later to be replaced with plastic, reducing the weight to about eight pounds.

Most striking, though, was its style—it just looked different. In comparison to the chunky mass of wood that was the M14, the AR-10 had a brutal elegance, a geometry of design that caught the eye. Though the Pentagon had taken a pass on it, the rifle made enough of an impression that more forward-thinking commanders asked ArmaLite to consider reengineering it for smaller-caliber ammunition, making for an even lighter-weight weapon that was also more stable when firing in fully automatic mode.

The M14 had barely been adopted as the standard-issue rifle when already there was grumbling in the ranks that it was worse than the M1—hard to stabilize in fully auto and too cumbersome, especially in jungle environs, where high humidity could warp the wooden stocks. ArmaLite came up with a scaled-down version of the AR-10, weighing in at just over six pounds and firing smaller-size ammo that allowed for larger-capacity magazines, meaning fewer pauses to stop and reload.

It was far superior in almost every way to the M14, yet the infamous inertia of the defense establishment ruled out making a change so quickly after committing to the other design. By 1959, ArmaLite had a decision to make.

What should it do with this new military rifle it called the AR-15?

There are few things that the gun lobby has worked harder at than pushing the myth that the AR-15 was somehow immaculately conceived as a benign sporting accoutrement unsoiled by association with warfare.

"The AR-15 is not a military weapon," said the National Shooting Sports Foundation, the firearm industry's trade group.

This mantra has been chanted so many times that it has become a standard talking point for critics of gun regulations, found in everything from congressional testimony to letters to the editor.

The claim is based mostly on the fact that the AR-15 does not have fully automatic firing capability—it is not a machine gun. To be sure, journalists, politicians, and others have made the mistake of describing it as such, usually as shorthand for talking about assault weapons (a related error is thinking the *AR* stands for "assault rifle"). These technical misnomers are seized upon by pro-gun activists, often in bad faith, as evidence of disqualifying ignorance or worse by "anti-gunners."

I know, because at *The New York Times* we're on the receiving end of such criticisms even when no mistake has been made. After I published a story that accurately referred to a protester holding an assault weapon, it generated the usual flurry of emails mansplaining in forensic detail the mechanics of firearms, insisting that assault weapons can only be fully automatic and demanding a correction. They didn't get one.

In fact, the semiautomatic-versus-fully-automatic argument is largely a semantical dodge to avoid addressing the historical reality that the AR-15 is unquestionably a military weapon. Putting aside the absurdity of claiming that semiautomatic implies nonmilitary—semiautomatic or even bolt-action rifles were standard-issue in every twentieth-century war until Vietnam, and even today soldiers usually prefer semiauto firing for accuracy and stability—the pedigree of the AR-15 is blindingly obvious.

It was specifically designed to meet the requirements of modern combat, part of a series of rifles intended for military use. And it was marketed to the armed forces as early as 1959—just not by ArmaLite.

Frustrated with production problems and its inability to win a US contract, ArmaLite sold its rifle patents to Colt's Manufacturing Company, which promptly made a few design changes and started pitching the gun to foreign governments. One of the first conflict zones where the AR-15 was introduced was Vietnam, courtesy of the Pentagon's Defense Advanced Research Projects Agency, which secretly sent the rifles there as a sort of "tryout" in the early 1960s.

"It was rather a hush-hush thing, they were trying to keep it undercover," recalled Stoner, adding that it "got things underway to start the adoption of the weapon."

Eventually, the US military came around to accepting the AR-15 as its own standard-issue rifle, though they gave it another name: the M16.

While making inroads with the military, Colt also began marketing the AR-15 to law enforcement. Rising public concerns over crime drove an increasing militarization of police agencies, which started acquiring weaponry, vehicles, and other equipment previously found only on battlefields. Colt marketed its line of assault rifles accordingly—although it took some time to catch the right vibe.

An early Colt ad depicted an older officer, who bore a vague resemblance to Andy Griffith's TV sheriff with a six-shooter in his holster, awkwardly brandishing an AR-15 under the heading "Arm Your Men with Confidence." The ad bluntly declared that the rifle was "Colt's answer to the law enforcement agencies' demands for a semi-automatic version of the M-16 automatic rifle purchased by the United States Armed Forces."

It took a decade or so, but Colt eventually found its footing in this new terrain. A 1980s company catalog had a photo of Hollywood-ready SWAT officers, tear-gas canisters hanging from their belts, clambering out of an armored vehicle clutching AR-15s. Accompanying text announced a new, more powerful model in the "family of weapons used by law enforcement and military forces."

The ultimate frontier for Colt's marketing was the general civilian population. And in that realm, the company was far from alone.

Gun dealers, foreign and domestic, had eagerly been eyeing civilians ever since the popular appetite for firearms exploded in the post–World War II era. In the decades after the war, military-surplus weapons flooded into the world market, the vast majority eventually finding their way to American communities. Journalist Carl Bakal, writing about gun culture in 1966, reported that the adoption of new ammunition standards by the North Atlantic Treaty Organization required replacing whole arsenals and contributed to a glut of cheap "foreign military castoffs." US imports of these weapons surged from 14,000 in 1955 to 198,000 in 1958.

"The United States is the dumping ground for about 75 percent and, according to some estimates, for as much as 90 percent, of the world's war-surplus weapons," Bakal wrote. "Why? Because few other nations would have them."

What was happening in American society to create such a demand? For one thing, a generation of men were returning from World War II and the Korean War acclimated to firearms and comfortable with, or even reliant on, having them at home. But that was true in other countries as well.

There was also a perception of burgeoning crime in the United States, which, like mass shootings would do a generation later, created a feedback loop wherein citizens reacted to the fear of gun violence—or fear of restrictive laws that might result—by buying more guns. By the 1960s and 1970s the firearms industry was increasingly using the specter of crime as a marketing device.

But another, less tangible factor was at play. Unique to the United States was an endangered masculine ideal, already evolving for much of the twentieth century and by the 1960s on the verge of coming completely undone. Women had steadily been gaining rights and liberties even before they were called upon to fill men's roles on the domestic front during World War II, and postwar society reflected the new female empowerment. An erosion of cultural dominance, coupled with the encroachment of feminine sensibilities into the traditionally male terrain of gun rights, was upending the American man's self-image.

"Our female-dominated, spastic society has been working overtime for a generation to discredit manhood," bellowed Bill R. Davidson, an editor of the NRA's magazine, following passage of the 1968 Gun Control Act. "People who still like to kill their own snakes bother political leaders in our time. The politicians don't understand and thus vaguely distrust these last traces of self-reliance and do-it-yourself assuredness."

Gun companies understood it quite well. And Colt, looking to expand the market for its AR-15, sought to position it as a hunting and sporting rifle, while at the same time playing up its "manly" military pedigree. It made for a dangerous combination.

The commercial AR-15 was virtually identical to the military M16 but without fully automatic firing capability—a necessary concession to federal restrictions on the sale of machine guns. Still, the lethality of even the civilian version was unlike anything else. The rifle's lightweight design, accuracy, and ability to accommodate magazines with thirty rounds (later expanded to one hundred) made it uniquely capable of inflicting massive damage.

The distinction is more than theoretical. Consider that it took Charles Whitman, a marine sharpshooter armed with a traditional bolt-action rifle, almost two hours to kill fourteen people at the University of Texas in 1966. But in 2012, it took five minutes for Adam Lanza, with no formal training, to kill twenty-six children and adults at Sandy Hook using an AR-15–style rifle and ten thirty-round magazines.

Early advertisements and write-ups for Colt's AR-15 leave little doubt that the company and civilian buyers associated it with military weaponry. A 1960s ad in a gun magazine referred to the rifle as a "military carbine, U.S. Army semi-automatic." Early company literature and ads also unabashedly referred to the AR-15 as an assault rifle, despite later attempts by the gun industry to disown the term.

Popular Science magazine carried a one-page article in 1965 with the headline "Now You Can Buy a Hot Combat Rifle for Sport," saying, "Out of the jungles of Vietnam comes a powerful battle-proven rifle ready for sale to civilians."

Edward Ezell, who curated the firearms collection at the National Museum of American History and wrote a standard reference for small arms, credited the necessities of warfare for birthing what would become known as "America's rifle."

"I suppose if the Vietnam War hadn't come along or hadn't grown hotter," he said, "we wouldn't have seen much of the AR-15 in the long run."

Sociologists have a term for how long it takes for something new to be absorbed into the mainstream: *technology adoption life cycle. Innovators* and *early adopters* are people who take to a new product sooner than most.

By that standard, DeWitt Henry was ahead of the curve.

A troubled, unemployed loser with a background of substance abuse and domestic violence, Henry, twenty-six, showed up at a bar called Uncle Albert's in Klamath Falls, Oregon, late one night in July 1977 looking for a fight. He got kicked out but returned after 2:00 a.m., determined to get revenge. Henry waited in the parking lot with his AR-15 and began shooting at patrons as they left the bar, killing six people, including a woman who was eight months pregnant.

Henry's attack is perhaps the earliest-known spree shooting using an AR-15–type rifle. Sadly, there have long been mass shootings with other kinds of firearms, semiautomatic handguns being the most common. But by the 1980s, there was a noticeable addition to the mix.

Three years after the Klamath Falls attack, a former high school math teacher armed with AR-15 and M1 rifles walked into a church in Texas, announced, "This is war!" and killed four people. In 1982, a former prison guard in Pennsylvania used an AR-15 to shoot to death thirteen people.

The technology adoption life cycle was accelerating.

Crazy people doing terrible things isn't anything new. School shootings aren't even a purely modern phenomenon. Among the items found in Adam Lanza's home after Sandy Hook was a newspaper clipping about a school shooting in Newburgh, New York, that occurred in 1891. In that one, a seventy-year-old man fired a shotgun at a group of elementary school kids. *The New York Times* reported that "none of the children were killed, although several were filled with lead."

In 1914, a fifteen-year-old student in Camden, New Jersey, pulled out a revolver in a classroom and started shooting. No one was seriously injured and he ran out of bullets before being subdued by a school janitor. To be sure, other such incidents in the old days did result in fatalities. In Cleveland in 1933 a deranged man wandered his neighborhood firing indiscriminately with a .22-caliber rifle, killing five people until he was shot to death by police.

But imagine if any of those shooters had been armed with a military-style semiautomatic rifle and thirty-round magazines, or a Glock 9mm pistol that can fire seventeen shots before reloading? The correlation between advancements in firearms technology, the easy commercial availability of it in the United States, and the worsening trajectory of mass shootings is glaring when you consider the historical trends.

Here, it is important to get our definitions straight. What makes an incident a "mass shooting" as opposed to another sort of gun crime with multiple victims? The Justice Department has generally described a mass shooting as one with at least four fatalities. Nonprofit groups that research gun violence use differing parameters, some looser than others. The Gun Violence Archive includes shootings in which the minimum of four victims includes those who were injured but survived.

I'm going with the definition used by the Violence Prevention Project, which defines a mass shooting as having "four or more people shot and killed, excluding the shooter, in a public location, with no connection to underlying criminal activity, such as gangs or drugs." Obviously, this does not capture the full American panorama of gun-related horrors such as domestic violence and gangland killings. But it does highlight the uniquely insidious random-spree shootings that have infected the public consciousness with a sense of resignation and dread.

By this definition, in the 1960s there were five mass shootings with thirty-seven fatalities (almost half attributable to Charles Whitman in Texas), none involving military-style rifles. In the 1970s, the total doubled to ten, with fifty-four fatalities and one (DeWitt Henry) involving an AR-15. And in the 1980s, the numbers more than doubled again, to twenty-three mass shootings with 150 fatalities; seven involved a military-style rifle.

The data show that although assault weapons were increasingly prevalent, other types of firearms, handguns in particular, continued to dominate. That is true even today. But it is the incidents involving military-style rifles, engineered to provide the stability, accuracy, and capacity to quickly maximize kills in combat, where the body count is most terrifying.

It was bad enough when Clemmie Henderson, a troubled Vietnam War vet with a history of violence and drug use, snapped in September 1988 and used a six-shot revolver to kill four people in Chicago. But when Patrick Purdy, a mentally ill twenty-four-year-old with no military training, snapped four months later in Stockton, California, he had an AK-47–style assault rifle with a seventy-five-round drum magazine and an extra thirty-round mag. He fired all 105 shots in less than three minutes into a crowd of schoolchildren, killing five and seriously injuring thirty-one others; had Purdy been more experienced in using the weapon, the toll could've been far worse.

The Stockton school massacre in January 1989 was an ignoble bookend to a transitional decade in the relentless trajectory of American gun violence. As the 1990s approached, there was growing outrage at the easy availability of assault rifles and the bloodshed they could inflict.

In response to the Stockton shooting, California became the first state to ban them. But as an attorney general's report on the incident noted, Purdy had obtained his rifle and magazines outside the state, and there was nothing stopping the next Patrick Purdy from doing the same. To truly lessen the odds of another attack, "national bans should be enacted on assault weapons and high-capacity magazines."

John Dingell was irritated. Again.

His fellow Democrats were in the habit of seeking his support for gun control legislation, knowing it rarely worked but hoping that the famously pro-gun Michigan congressman and NRA man would change his mind. The political benefits could be enormous.

"Leadership always comes to me and says, 'Dingell, you've got to help us on guns,'" he grumbled. "I say, 'Not sure I can help you on guns. I think the only guy who can help you on guns is yourself, and that's to change your damned position.'"

Now here he was, in 1994, being pressured by his party to get behind a massive bill working its way through Congress called the Violent Crime Control and Law Enforcement Act. The $30 billion package of legislation, championed by Pres. Bill Clinton, who wanted Democrats to shake off the "soft on crime" label, would put one hundred thousand new police officers on the streets, create a "three strikes" rule for repeat offenders, broaden the federal death penalty, and add dozens of new criminal categories.

And it would do another big thing: enact a nationwide assault weapons ban.

The ban would prohibit the manufacture, sale, and possession of semiautomatic weapons with features commonly associated with military-style firearms, such as pistol grips, folding stocks, and detachable magazines. It also prohibited large-capacity mags.

The so-called ban had plenty of holes. For one thing, it exempted any assault weapons already purchased before enactment of the new law. It also carved out exceptions for 650 models of guns, including some with similar attributes to those covered under the ban. Most crucially, it had a sunset provision—it would expire in ten years unless renewed by Congress.

But it was seen, rightly so, as the boldest attempt yet to take action against a rising tide of gun violence. The public supported it, as did police organizations, whose members were getting shot with assault weapons. Because its legislative backers had shrewdly woven the ban into the larger bill, it was hard for lawmakers who wished to be seen as tough on crime to vote against the overall legislation. That included Dingell.

The bill's sponsor in the House, Democrat Jack Brooks of Texas, and dozens of other conservative Democrats, mostly from the South and rural states, opposed the assault weapons ban. Brooks tried to have it removed. Using the culture war language of the gun lobby, he called the ban "a vendetta dressed up in fancy clothes" designed to punish law-abiding gun owners.

Dingell also opposed the ban. In the early stages of the legislation, he had voted against it and lobbied hard behind closed doors to have it taken out of the final package. But the ban had narrowly survived, and as a final vote neared in the summer of 1994, Brooks was leaning on Dingell to help in a last-ditch effort to kill it. The two men were pitching NRA-backed "compromise" legislation—in reality, a political fig leaf to cover the absence of meaningful action.

In the weeks before the vote, Brooks and gun industry allies cooked up what they called a "modest revision" of the ban that would, among other things, carve out an exemption for the AR-15 rifle. Brooks sent a letter to Dingell referencing the looming vote and saying "pressure needs to be brought to bear as soon as possible.

"John, I know how you feel on this issue just as I do, and I greatly appreciate your willingness to weigh in at this critical juncture."

But Dingell was also hearing from those on the other side, notably President Clinton, who was calling him at all hours as the crucial vote approached. Clinton had reason to be worried. Just a year before, Dingell had been one of 70 Democrats who had joined 116 Republicans in voting against the Brady Handgun Violence Prevention Act, which created a background-check requirement for firearms purchases from licensed dealers. (Like the assault weapons ban, the successful Brady bill had also received support from former President Reagan, whose late-in-life warming to gun control was dismissed by conspiracists as the hidden hand of First Lady Nancy Reagan at work.)

The 1994 crime bill was a high-stakes gambit by the Democratic Party to win back the confidence of voters, and party leadership was determined to keep it from being picked apart as passage neared. A "yes" vote by Dingell would give precious political cover to anxious swing-state Democrats fearful of blowback from pro-gun constituents.

By Sunday, August 21, 1994, a typically hot, sticky one in Washington, DC, Dingell had made his decision. He had stayed up all night, and as he prepared to go to the House chamber that day for the final vote, he took time to send a fax to the headquarters of the NRA. It was brief:

"After a great deal of thought, I deeply regret that the conflict between my responsibilities as a Member of Congress and my duties as a board member of the National Rifle Association is irreconcilable. Please accept my resignation from the board, effective immediately."

When it was his turn to speak on the House floor, Dingell rose and started by saying, "There are parts of this package with which I violently disagree.

"Most specifically, I find the assault weapons ban to be offensive, obnoxious, and contrary to the rights guaranteed to all Americans under the Second Amendment."

But then he praised the other parts, including money for more police, prison construction, and a stronger border. He cited tougher death-penalty laws for terrorists and cop killers, stricter sentencing guidelines, and funding to combat violence against women.

"As deeply torn as I am, I have concluded that the best interests of the country as a whole on this issue, the number one issue of concern to the people, require that I support final passage," he said.

The bill was adopted. Voting in favor of it was a momentous decision for a man who had spent his entire career fighting harder and longer than perhaps any other American politician against efforts to restrict gun ownership. Dingell almost immediately came to regret it. He faced howls of outrage from the same gun rights crowd that had once regarded him as a hero and now castigated him as a sellout. Threats poured in, and not just the political kind.

"He had to have police protection for several months," his wife, Debbie Dingell, told me. "We had people scream and yell at us. It was the first time I had seen that real hate."

Beyond the fallout from the assault weapons ban, Democrats in general soon had a rude wake-up call: Republicans swept the November midterms, capturing control of the House for the first time since 1952. It seemed the crime bill wasn't enough to counter larger political forces coursing through a discontented electorate. Voter anger over the North American Free Trade Agreement, a House banking scandal, and President Clinton's ill-fated health-care reform plans were all cited as factors.

But there was little doubt that blowback over gun control had cost Democratic seats in Southern states and rural areas. Some vulnerable Democrats, desperate to avoid the chopping block of public sentiment, scrambled to adjust. Two dozen of them—including five who had voted for the assault weapons ban—signed an obsequious letter to newly installed Republican Speaker Newt Gingrich pledging to support any effort to repeal it. "We believe that a central theme established by the most recent congressional elections is that the American people strongly resent government intrusions into their personal freedoms," the letter said.

Dingell also favored repealing the ban. His staff put together a memo outlining pros and cons if he were to do so, pointing out that "a solid explanation will have to be made to the majority of our voters who favor gun control." The memo concluded that he was in a no-win situation: "People he made happy last year will feel abandoned. His good will with these people may be lost. Gun friends will never restore him to their former level of admiration, despite this action. He may take a lot of flack for 'too little, too late.'"

The repeal never came to pass. Republicans, particularly in the Senate, viewed it as a trap set by Democrats, since Clinton would simply veto any attempt to overturn it and bash the GOP for not supporting the police.

As for Dingell, he never forgave himself for going along with the assault weapons ban. Looking back years later, he was adamant that it "cost us the election" in 1994 and damaged the Democratic brand. He saw danger signs ahead for the future of the party.

"The Democrats are finally beginning to understand," he said, "that most of the red states that you see on the map became red states in good part because of the Democratic Party's position on gun control."

RAMBO ACQUISITION

IT TOOK FIVE hundred years, but the world's oldest firearms manufacturer, which had gotten its start making harquebuses at a medieval European forge, entered the new millennium as just another gun seller accused of enabling violence on the streets of America.

It was an ignominious turn for Beretta SpA.

The family-owned enterprise proudly traced its lineage to Bartolomeo Beretta, who founded it in northern Italy in 1526. Gunsmithing skills were passed down through the generations of Berettas, and the family proved as adept at business expansion as they were at creating high-quality weapons. The company worked for the US military following World War II, repairing and modifying service rifles, and pursued contracts with other governments around the globe.

In the 1970s, Beretta opened a US manufacturing facility, and by 1985 it had bested competitors by winning a Pentagon contract to supply handguns. The 9mm Beretta M9 semiautomatic pistol replaced the old .45-caliber Colt M1911, which had been standard for decades in the US armed forces. To capture the contract, Beretta deliberately offered the guns practically at cost, with the longer-term goal of leveraging the high-profile military relationship to move into law-enforcement and commercial markets.

It proved a good strategy. In the early 1990s, the same guns that Beretta was selling to the military for about $225 apiece were priced at around $400 for police agencies and $625 for civilians. Beretta was pulling in about $30 million from combined sales to the American military and law enforcement. But the much more lucrative civilian market, worth about $60 million at that time, was where the company had set its sights.

"My guess is that ten times more women are buying handguns now than five years ago," Robert Bonaventure, head of Beretta USA, said in 1993. "Boyfriends and husbands are giving them to their girlfriends and wives as gifts."

There is a grand irony to this.

In Beretta's home country of Italy, the commercial market for firearms is much tougher. To buy a gun, you must apply for a license and demonstrate a legitimate reason for having it. The percentage of Italians who own guns is small compared to the percentage of Americans, and not surprisingly, the homicide rate with firearms is twenty times higher in America than in Italy.

As the popularity of Beretta firearms took off in the United States, they started being linked to gun-related crimes, and the company eventually joined other gunmakers as targets of lawsuits by cities and shooting victims. The suits were part of a barrage of litigation against firearm manufacturers in the late 1990s and early 2000s fueled by high-profile killings such as the Washington, DC, sniper attacks, in which seven people were murdered by an army veteran and teenage accomplice using a Bushmaster AR-15–style rifle.

The rifle had been legally purchased despite the federal ban on assault weapons. To be prohibited under the 1994 law, a semiautomatic had to have a detachable magazine and two other combat-style features, such as a folding stock or pistol grip. That left room for mischief by gun companies that were determined to keep selling them.

Unlike Beretta, an international behemoth, Bushmaster was a small Maine-based company, run by an old-school gun guy named Richard Dyke, who had bought a bankrupt firearms business in the 1970s and renamed it. Dyke sold AR-15s primarily to law enforcement and the military, but also was among the first to unabashedly market them to civilians—even after the 1994 ban went into effect. Bushmaster simply fiddled with its rifle design to remove a few prohibited tactical features—essentially cosmetic changes—and voilà! "The rest of the rifle is unchanged," it proclaimed on its website.

Following the DC sniper shootings, Bushmaster defended its

civilian sales of AR-15s by insisting they were not military-type weapons because they were semiautomatic and were only meant to be "used in competitive shooting, target shooting, and small varmint hunting." Nevertheless, the company paid $2.5 million to settle a lawsuit brought by victims of the shootings, while grumbling it did nothing wrong and "would not agree to change the way we do business."

The lawsuits in the late 1990s and early 2000s against Bushmaster, Beretta, and others were largely the work of the Brady Campaign to Prevent Gun Violence, named after James Brady, the White House press secretary who was shot in the 1981 assassination attempt on President Reagan, and Brady's wife, Sarah. The suits were based on a theory of product liability, seeking to hold companies accountable for the damage caused by the things they produced. It wasn't a novel concept—see the tobacco industry—but it was the first time it had been attempted in such a sweeping scale against the gun trade. Similar to the cigarette companies, whose executives refused to acknowledge that smoking can kill you, the firearms makers balked at the seemingly obvious notion that guns are dangerous.

"I think we believe that the guns don't pose any risk at all," Robert Morrison, president of Taurus International, said in a deposition in 2001. "It's the people that are using them that pose the risk."

Taurus International, the US subsidiary of a Brazilian gun manufacturer, is known for its affordable semiautomatic pistols. Another handgun maker, the Austria-based Glock, also found itself on the litigation hot seat and responded with indignation. Paul Jannuzzo, the chief operating officer of Glock's American subsidiary, scoffed at the idea that children shouldn't be allowed in store departments where guns are sold.

"Why? There's nothing intrinsically evil about these things," he said in his deposition. "They don't impart bad vibes or keep you up all night long if they're separated from the ammunition and they're in a counter or locked up or on a chain or a cord. I can't imagine why anybody would even propose such a thing."

The gun industry execs wanted to make sure no one ever read the statements they made under oath, so their depositions were sealed as part of a court-approved settlement. However, I was able to get my hands on them anyway through a confidential source in 2013.

What they showed was that the firearms executives expressed no qualms about their sales practices and pushed back against the suggestion that they had any responsibility to ensure that their guns did not fall into the wrong hands. What if one of their dealers was the subject of numerous trace requests by law enforcement investigating gun crimes?

"That's not for us to enforce the law," said Charles Guevremont, president of Browning, an old-line American gunmaker known for its high-powered hunting rifles and military weapons.

Would they want to know if a retailer that sold their guns was involved in trafficking on the black market? "I don't even know what a gun trafficker is," Morrison replied.

When it was Beretta's turn in the witness chair, the company put forward Ugo Gussalli Beretta. Representing the fourteenth generation to run the family business, he had followed the traditional path, beginning as an apprentice. It was Ugo who had cinched the 1985 contract to supply the US military with handguns and set Beretta on its successful expansion into law enforcement and civilian markets.

Lawyers for the Brady Campaign were used to dealing with hostile American executives and expected as much from the Beretta family scion, whose name was synonymous with one of the most well-known brands in the world. What emerged in his deposition, however, was something else entirely. By comparison to his peers, Ugo seemed downright civil.

Most telling was his response to a line of questioning about whether Beretta bore any responsibility for reckless sales practices by dealers who sold its guns. All the firearms executives had been asked this, and they had uniformly denied it, saying, for example, that there would be no reason to question why somebody wanted to purchase a small arsenal of guns all at once.

When Ugo Beretta was asked that same question, he said he thought it was Beretta USA's policy that its dealers make sure the person had "a legitimate need" to buy so many firearms. Of course, there was no such requirement in America. Ugo was asked why he assumed that there was. He pondered it for a moment.

"Common sense," he replied.

Alas, when it came to guns in the United States, common sense was on the run by the early 2000s. But before it fully left the building, there had been a brief glimmer of hope for advocates of more reasonable policies.

The litigation campaign against firearms manufacturers was barely off the ground when it scored a significant win: Smith & Wesson, an old-line gunmaker famous for its revolvers, reached a settlement in March 2000 with municipalities and the Clinton administration. It appeared to be a game changer.

The provisions called for, among other things, design changes to minimize accidental shootings and prevent the use of high-capacity magazines; restrictions on multiple handgun purchases by a single buyer; a crackdown on dealers who were frequently the source of guns used in crimes; and an oversight commission to enforce the terms of the agreement.

The government intended for it to become a template for the firearms industry. As an incentive to get more companies to sign on, it was announced that federal agencies could give Smith & Wesson preferential treatment when entering into purchase contracts. The Clinton White House trumpeted the deal as a victory for "common sense."

It declared, "Today's agreement represents the first time a major gun manufacturer has committed to fundamentally change the way guns are designed, distributed and marketed. This deal shows what is possible when we work together in good faith."

Truth be told, Smith & Wesson's motivations were atypical. At the time, it was owned by Tomkins PLC, a British firm that had bought the venerable American brand in 1987 for $112 million. By 2000, Tomkins was looking to sell the gunmaker, and the more than two dozen lawsuits pending against it were an impediment to that. As for signing the settlement agreement, a company spokesman said at the time, "It was a business decision."

As such, it quickly proved a disaster.

Reaction from the gun lobby was immediate and vicious. The NRA railed against the agreement, saying the British-owned Smith & Wesson acted in "craven self-interest" and had become "the first to run up the white flag of surrender." Gun laws are much stricter in Great Britain, where less than 1 percent of the population has the mandatory firearms license, compared to the United States, where about a third of Americans report owning a gun.

"Of course," the NRA sneered in a statement, "there is no Second Amendment in Britain, where subjects are barred from owning handguns and many long guns."

The bravado masked a deep concern that Smith & Wesson's decision could lead others to follow suit. Inside NRA headquarters, executives prepared a report to the board decrying "the capitulation of Smith & Wesson to blackmail disguised as litigation" and outlining the scope of the threat:

"The agreement by Smith & Wesson to a laundry list of anti-gun demands affected everyone involved in the manufacture, sale, purchase and regulation of their products.

"Perhaps worse yet, S&W agreed to be bound by the terms of future, stricter agreements negotiated by other firms—an open-ended surrender modeled on a provision rejected by tobacco companies in their own settlement talks."

A counterattack quickly came together. It was summed up in a letter by an executive at Kimber America, another gunmaker, who urged the industry to "boycott Smith now and forever. Run them out of the country.

"You guys need to make sure that no one else is going to join the surrender," he wrote.

That is exactly what they did. Thousands of retailers stopped selling Smith & Wesson guns. Sales tanked. The company's stock price fell to pennies a share. Seven months later, it announced layoffs and the CEO, Ed Shultz, departed. Finally, in May 2001, Tomkins sold Smith & Wesson for $15 million and the assumption of its debt—a fraction of what it had paid fourteen years earlier.

Under new management, the gunmaker soon shed the terms of its historic settlement and worked to restore its good standing among gun buyers and the industry. Shultz, meanwhile, was unrepentant. In an interview with *The New York Times* not long after he left the company, he said he had made the decision to settle "based on the tradition of the company and my own beliefs of what's right."

While acknowledging the practical business considerations, he also pointed to his nagging feeling that the culture of the gun industry needed to change. For instance, when it came to child-safety locks on firearms, Shultz found that "I couldn't answer the question 'Was I doing everything I knew how to do to prevent accidents?'

"Would I put locks on our guns if it might save one child? The answer was yes."

The NRA, certainly, had a very different view of how gun companies should respond to the litigation threat. But the organization itself had been slow to recognize the danger—much to the consternation of Bob Barr.

A libertarian lawyer from Georgia who had been among those swept into Congress during the Republican Revolution of 1994, Barr served on the House Judiciary Committee and helped prosecute the impeachment of President Clinton. He was also known as Mr. Second Amendment for his staunch advocacy of gun rights. And he had another notable entry on his résumé: He was a member of the NRA's board of directors.

In that dual role, he championed firearms bills and policies in Congress that the NRA favored, much like John Dingell had. He was among the first to raise alarm bells about the lawsuits being brought against the gun industry. Not long after he joined the NRA board in 1997, he drafted a bill that would shield firearms companies from liability for the criminal misuse of their guns. But years later, it still hadn't gone anywhere because he couldn't seem to get the industry's attention.

"To date," he complained in one of a series of private memos to the NRA's chief executive, Wayne LaPierre, "I have received absolutely zero interest, much less support, from the firearms industry."

Barr's memos, written on the eve of the new millennium, amounted to a clarion call for action. Like Dingell a generation before him, Barr saw threats everywhere from his perch on Capitol Hill, and not just from liability lawsuits. Gun grabbers, he warned, were trying to use legislation related to such things as juvenile justice and bankruptcy reform as Trojan horses to slip in restrictions on firearms. "This is frightening," he wrote, adding:

"Given the direction in which things are going overall, I am no longer confident we will win this debate. However, while we are facing many obstacles, I also believe there are considerable opportunities here; but only if we seize them, work them, present a united front, and begin to do so now."

The immediate problem, as Barr saw it, was the liability litigation. To be sure, gun companies were very concerned about the lawsuits. But their response had been like a game of Whac-A-Mole, defending against each one as it came. They treated them more like a costly and distracting nuisance, rather than the existential threat that Barr correctly recognized.

Barr's bill, benignly titled the Firearms Heritage Protection Act, would kill all pending liability lawsuits against gun companies and prohibit new ones from being filed. Such litigation, the bill said, punished the industry for "lawfully competing in America's free enterprise system, and constitutes an unreasonable burden on interstate and foreign commerce."

In an added twist, the legislation invoked the Fourteenth Amendment—the Reconstruction-era attempt to extend constitutional rights to freed slaves—saying it should also protect gun dealers from being sued.

Barr may have been first out of the gate, but he wasn't alone in pushing the liability shield. In the Senate, Larry Craig, a Republican from Idaho, and Democrat Zell Miller of Georgia—both of whom were also NRA directors—backed a similar bill in 2004. Together, these NRA men were using their privileged position as elected representatives to advance legislation that the NRA and its allies supported. It seemed like a conflict of interest, yet the only body capable of preventing it was Congress, which saw fit to do nothing.

I wanted to ask them about that, but Miller was dead and Craig—who did not seek reelection in 2008 after being accused of lewd conduct in an airport restroom and pleading guilty to disorderly conduct—never responded to my messages. Dingell also was no longer with us, but his longtime aide Michael Parker came to his defense when I contacted him:

"Mr. Dingell passionately believed in the right of the people to keep and bear arms, and the fact that he used his office to protect it, and them, is not a conflict of interest in any pejorative sense."

Barr was also willing to talk. He explained that he had joined the NRA's board because he was asked to, not because he had sought the position, but that "didn't change how I viewed firearms issues." The organization, he said, "never approached me to do anything that I didn't want to do or that I would not have done anyway.

"I'm doing it as a member of Congress who also happens to be an NRA board member."

As fate would have it, Barr lost his congressional seat because of Democrat-controlled redistricting ahead of the 2002 elections, and it fell to others to pursue his grail of liability protection for the gun industry. A number of NRA allies in the House were happy to do so, notably Clifford Stearns, a Republican from Florida, who introduced what was now being called the Protection of Lawful Commerce in Arms Act. The blunt title showed how the objective of ending lawsuits had come to be more openly embraced in the years since it hid behind Barr's gauzy-sounding Firearms Heritage bill.

Stearns had been a reliable point man for the gun lobby going back to the 1990s, when he introduced legislation seeking to require concealed-carry permits to be recognized across state lines. His files—which I found in the archives of George Washington University—show how the symbiotic process worked.

For example, after Stearns introduced his "right-to-carry" bill in 1996, an NRA staff attorney asked an outside lawyer with longstanding ties to the NRA, Stephen Halbrook, to analyze it. Halbrook responded with a seven-page dissection of the draft bill addressing "problem areas" and suggesting alternatives.

The staff attorney then sent a memo to the NRA president summarizing Halbrook's observations and saying Congressman Stearns "has indicated that he is open to any suggestions that we have for altering the bill and re-introducing it." The attorney then faxed the final verdict over to Stearns's office for action, with instructions to his aide to keep the whole thing "on a 'close hold' basis" so their exchange would not leak out.

Such was the backdrop to Stearns's introducing the rebranded liability protection bill years later. Together with Craig's companion legislation in the Senate, the gun industry shield moved forward, aided by a last-minute gimmick to attract the support of moderates: the addition of a mandate that child-safety locks be included with the purchase of handguns. There was less to this seemingly reasonable step than met the eye. NRA talking points I found in Stearns's files show that, behind the scenes, gun lobbyists reassured conservatives that the provision "does not require any gun owner to actually use the device."

With momentum building in Congress, it was only a question of when, not if, the firearms industry would no longer have to fear victims of their products going to court to hold them accountable. Gunmakers saw blue skies ahead.

There was just one thing left standing in their way.

As the federal assault weapon ban neared its ten-year expiration date in 2004, gunmakers, who already had enough on their hands fending off liability lawsuits, wanted to ensure it was not renewed. They needn't have worried.

There had long been a sharing of common interests between the NRA and the firearms industry. But the existential threat of litigation, combined with the assault weapons ban, had brought the two closer together. NRA Pres. Charlton Heston said as much when he appeared before the gun industry's annual trade show in Atlanta in January 1999 and declared to a cheering crowd that "your fight has become our fight."

"Our enemies will think they can beat you in court because they can't beat us in Congress," he said. "But they don't have the checkbooks and votes of eight million members and thirty million gun owners."

It didn't matter that polls showed almost three-quarters of Americans—and even one-third of NRA members—favored extending the assault weapons ban. Republicans were fully in thrall to the firearms lobby, and Democrats, having touched the hot stove of gun politics, did not want to get burned again. After losing control of Congress in 1994 and the presidency six years later, Democratic Party leaders believed that gun control had cost them as many as twenty congressional seats and enough votes for Al Gore to lose in 2000. Now, the clock was winding down on the ban just as the country faced another bitterly contested national election.

Few profiles in courage were to be found. Democrats staged a couple of events to draw attention to the ban's expiration, but they were muted, and members of Congress, especially those in close races, stayed mostly on the sidelines. When *The New York Times* caught up with Sen. Patty Murray, a Washington State Democrat who voted for the bill in 1994 and was in a tight reelection contest, she sounded less than enthusiastic.

"There are so many issues, education and health care and jobs and the economy in my state right now," she said. "People are really focused on that."

Republicans, meanwhile, were firmly in the iron grip of the NRA. The organization ruthlessly enforced its system of rating candidates based on how they voted on gun issues, and no right-minded GOP candidate could risk straying from the script on the assault weapons ban. Even though Pres. George W. Bush publicly remarked that he would sign an extension if it crossed his desk, he knew that would never happen.

"He knows, because we don't have the votes to pass the assault weapons ban," House Majority Leader Tom DeLay said shortly before it ended. "It will expire Monday, and that's that."

The nation's ten-year experiment with banning assault weapons quietly spiraled down the drain and has never returned. Research into its effectiveness finds mixed results, but it is generally believed to have reduced mass shootings involving military-style rifles.

A 2024 study by researchers at Northwestern and Columbia universities looked at trends over time and estimated the ban prevented up to five mass shootings and could have stopped dozens more had it been renewed. Physicians at New York University concluded in a 2019 study that after the 1994 ban went into effect "the number of deaths from mass shootings fell, and the increase in the annual number of incidents slowed down."

"The data shows an almost immediate—and steep—rise in mass shooting deaths in the years after the assault weapons ban expired in 2004," said Dr. Michael Klein, one of the study's authors. "Breaking the data into absolute numbers, between 2004 and 2017—the last year of our analysis—the average number of yearly deaths attributed to mass shootings was 25, compared with 5.3 during the ten-year tenure of the ban and 7.2 in the years leading up to the prohibition on assault weapons."

Many other reports, with varying degrees of academic rigor, yield similar findings. The NRA prefers to point to outliers that assert the ban did not reduce *overall* gun violence or whose findings on mass-shooting deaths are muddled. For instance, one of its fact sheets cites a 2018 Rand Corporation overview of gun violence research that the NRA claims "found no evidence that 'large capacity magazine' bans and 'assault weapon' bans affect mass shootings." But that is not what the Rand report said.

The Rand authors looked at two studies of state-level bans on assault weapons—an oddly cramped approach—one of which concluded the bans "significantly reduce mass shooting deaths," while the other "found uncertain effects." Based on this, along with questions about the way the studies were conducted, the Rand report declared the evidence to be "inconclusive."

This is where Ugo Beretta's invocation of common sense seems warranted. By the 1990s, semiautomatic assault rifles were increasingly used in mass shootings and, importantly, large-capacity magazines made them more lethal. It is not rocket science to deduce that banning the sale of more of these meant fewer of them available for misuse. We will never know exactly how many lives were saved because a deranged person was unable to acquire an AR-15. But neither is there a precise measurement of lives saved by banning the civilian use of hand grenades—yet we do it anyway.

Furthermore, "law-abiding" gun owners, who we were told would unfairly suffer by not being able to purchase an assault weapon under the ban, somehow survived the decade. So did the firearms industry.

The death of the assault weapons ban was followed months later by final passage of the Protection of Lawful Commerce in Arms Act in October 2005. Fourteen Democrats in the Senate and fifty-nine in the House joined an overwhelming majority of Republicans in approving the bill, which granted extraordinary privileges to an industry whose marketing and sales practices arguably contributed to the slaughter of Americans daily.

Almost overnight, the twin victories turbocharged the financial picture for gun companies. It was only a matter of time before Wall Street came sniffing around.

Just before closing time on Friday, February 17, 2006, the white-shoe New York law firm of Milbank, Tweed, Hadley & McCloy LLP filed papers with the Delaware secretary of state creating a new company called Rambo Acquisition LLC. Per tradition, no information was revealed about its purpose or who owned it.

Delaware is basically America's equivalent of an offshore tax haven, a veritable Cayman Islands of corporate shenanigans that allows the rich and powerful to hide behind opaque shell companies and benefit from favorable state business laws. It's what a tiny state does to create an economic niche for itself.

Millions of companies have been allowed to incorporate in Delaware despite having no tangible connection to the state, and it is often impossible to ever figure out who is behind them or what they're up to. That could've remained true for Rambo Acquisition, if not for a second document that appeared in Delaware public filings less than a month after its formation.

The new filing announced that the short-lived Rambo was changing its name to Bushmaster Firearms International LLC. And it was signed by George Kollitides—an executive at Cerberus Capital Management, one of the world's largest private equity firms.

Cerberus, whose name derives from the mythical three-headed beast that guards the gates of hell, was run by Stephen Feinberg, an ex-trader with a net worth in 2025 estimated at $5 billion (that same year he would be deputy defense secretary in the second Trump administration). Prior to 2006, Cerberus was known mostly for hiring former VP Dan Quayle to chair one of its divisions and had collected a portfolio of investments in retail, transportation, and finance. Firearms were not on its radar.

Wall Street had largely eschewed dabbling in gun companies because of the high risks, both financial and reputational. Few firearms makers were publicly traded, and most of the rest were privately held by families or longtime owners. But with the expiration of the assault weapons ban and enactment of legal protections against liability, the field was suddenly wide-open.

Feinberg saw the opportunity and leaped at it. But before putting his money down, he did some homework. He visited a firearms-training facility in North Carolina run by Blackwater, the private security contractor, and spent a weekend taking instruction in target shooting. An experienced hunter who was in the Reserve Officers' Training Corps in college, Feinberg was a good shot.

Cerberus's Rambo Acquisition was used to purchase Bushmaster for $76 million several months later. The choice of Bushmaster was telling, because as Cerberus noted in one of its annual reports, the gunmaker was "one of the first to introduce modern sporting rifles to the consumer market." The term *modern sporting rifle* was the industry's preferred euphemism for AR-15–style guns, and it was a reliable indicator of what Feinberg had in mind.

A year after its Bushmaster purchase, Cerberus bought Remington for $370 million. Remington, founded in 1816, was at the time the number one American producer of rifles and shotguns for the domestic market and gave Cerberus instant credibility as a serious player in the firearms industry. Remington conveyed respectability and was known as a maker of traditional bolt-action hunting rifles, as well as semiautomatic weapons for the military and law enforcement—but not civilians. Notably, up until then, Remington's long-range marketing plans said that the company "does not participate in marketing military style firearms for sale to the general public." That would change almost immediately once Cerberus entered the picture.

In September 2007—now under the control of Cerberus—Remington's director of marketing exchanged emails with the company's outside advertising firm, Brothers & Co., about the need to "legitimize the AR-15 system as a hunting product." He lamented that "there are so many negative associations with the guns" and suggested some "words to avoid," including *assault*, *combat*, *automatic*, and *weapon*. The company cooked up a new model called an R-15 VTR (varmint tactical rifle), which came in full camo, a feature seen as amping up "the cool factor." Internal emails noted that it was the "most photographed" gun at a demonstration of new Remington weapons for firearms/outdoors trade journalists in June 2008.

Meanwhile, Cerberus continued snapping up firearms companies—DPMS, Marlin, Dakota Arms, Barnes Bullets, and more—and gathered all of them under a new corporate umbrella called the Freedom Group. By 2009, it had acquired both the number one (Bushmaster) and number two (DPMS / Panther Arms) largest makers of assault weapons. Having rolled up most of the major producers of AR-15–style rifles, Cerberus then executed the next step typical of private equity plays: It filed papers to take Freedom Group public and cash in.

In a stock registration statement for Freedom Group that Cerberus submitted to the Securities and Exchange Commission, it boasted of having become the largest producer of modern sporting rifles, a market it said was growing at an annual rate of 36 percent and "faster than the general firearms industry." Indeed, industry data shows that annual domestic production and imports of AR-15–style rifles more than doubled from 2007 to 2009 and would continue to explode, rising from four hundred thousand the year Cerberus entered the market to 2.8 million by 2020.

Cerberus had accurately predicted the trend. Its securities filings bluntly laid out the rationale for investing and made clear that its continued emphasis on assault weapons and associated components was central to its economic growth. Regarding the upward trend in AR-15 sales, Cerberus concluded, "We view this current increase in demand as having significant long-term benefits."

It took a few years, but by 2010, Remington's commitment to incorporating military-style rifles into its traditional sportsman's lineup was solidified. Key to this evolution was the involvement of Bushmaster, which was merged with Remington within the Freedom Group. A Remington executive told an NRA publication in October 2010 that they "relied on Bushmaster quite a bit to get this AR project started."

The benefits of this relationship flowed both ways. Remington essentially took over the marketing of Bushmaster AR-15s and used Brothers & Co. to do it. Whereas in the past Brothers came up with fairly conventional plans to market hunting rifles, starting in 2009 they launched an over-the-top campaign to promote the Bushmaster ACR (adaptive combat rifle), creating what became a notorious ad showing the new gun with the line "Consider your man card reissued." Subtle as a brick, the ad continued with the line at the bottom "If it's good enough for the military, it's good enough for you."

This was in keeping with the strategy, described in a 2010 internal memo, to use the "same overall tone/attitude" to promote a new Remington assault rifle to both law enforcement and civilian customers. It was a big departure from the conservative, traditional advertising that both Remington and Bushmaster had used before being absorbed by Cerberus; whereas in the past the companies had made distinctions between the police, military, and civilian markets, now they were essentially viewed as one and the same.

And something else was new as well. Remington was trying its hand at product placement in violent video games. In January 2010, the vice president of marketing emailed a colleague, recounting how a contractor working on his house had raved about the Bushmaster rifle used in *Call of Duty: Modern Warfare 2*: "He went on to tell me that the ACR in the gaming world was gaining quite a following amongst gamers due to the fact that it is being endorsed by some of the more respected gurus in the community."

Sales and marketing were not the only areas where the Freedom Group was putting its money. In the bitterly fought arena of gun politics, lobbying was an increasingly important line item in any firearms company budget—and the NRA was more than happy to take the industry's cash.

Just as Wall Street had quickly moved to exploit the newly attractive firearms industry in 2005, the NRA around the same time created a "corporate partners" program called Ring of Freedom to collect big donations from gun companies. Donors at the $1 million level included the Freedom Group, Beretta, and Smith & Wesson, and by 2013 the program had brought in as much as $60 million.

The industry was also lavishing money on targets more directly connected to Capitol Hill. The National Shooting Sports Foundation, the firearms industry's trade group, was one of the largest donors to a charity whose ostensible purpose was to provide nonpartisan "advice, support and information" to Congress about issues affecting outdoor recreation. In reality, the NSSF and its allies used it as a vehicle to sponsor junkets for lawmakers and push for gun-friendly policies.

The NSSF had evolved dramatically since it was formed in 1961 to represent gun manufacturers and dealers in rather prosaic matters, such as safety standards and organizing an annual trade show. By the 2010s, it had become increasingly aggressive in promoting gun rights and defending the sales of assault weapons and high-capacity magazines. Among other things, the NSSF led the way in promoting the term *modern sporting rifle* to sublimate the military pedigree of the AR-15.

But whereas the NRA had long ago situated its headquarters close to the epicenter of political power in Washington, DC, the NSSF's home base still reflected its more low-profile origins. It occupied a tasteful colonial-style building on Mile Hill Road in the quiet suburb of Newtown, Connecticut—about a ten-minute drive across town from where a gun enthusiast named Nancy Lanza lived.

In March 2010, Lanza went to a gun shop to purchase a Bushmaster AR-15–style rifle, the kind that Remington had worked to integrate into violent video games. She then returned to her home on Yogananda Street, where her son, Adam, spent much of his days in the basement playing *Call of Duty*. Adam would use the modern sporting rifle his mother had bought to kill twenty-six children and adults at Sandy Hook Elementary School.

To carry out his murderous rampage more efficiently, he duct-taped together thirty-round magazines in staggered pairs to quickly eject an empty one and slap in the next. Where did he get the idea to do that? Josh Koskoff is pretty sure he knows.

Koskoff, a lawyer representing parents of the Sandy Hook victims, was familiar with *Call of Duty* because one of his sons played it. When he eventually saw crime-scene photos of the taped-up magazines found at Sandy Hook, "the hair on my arms stood up." The Bushmaster rifle in the video game used a staggered pairing identical to what Adam Lanza used.

"Remington may not have known him," said Koskoff, "but they'd been courting him for years."

COMMON SENSE

I WAS STANDING IN the kitchen working on my third cup of black coffee when I noticed a commotion on the small TV that sat in a corner of the cluttered countertop. The sound was muted, but a worried-looking news anchor was saying something. Behind her were flashing police lights and what looked like a brick school building.

I turned up the volume. Then I messaged my wife, saying there had been a school shooting in Newtown. She replied immediately to ask whether we should take our kids out of school. The Connecticut town we lived in was not far from Sandy Hook Elementary, where my wife had recently applied for a job as the school librarian. The stepdaughter of a journalist friend of ours was a substitute teacher there, and our son's Boy Scout troop was part of the same small district that served Sandy Hook.

Now, according to the television report, someone had shot up the school. There were casualties. Other schools were going into lockdown. My wife and I quickly decided to go pick up our son and daughter.

On the way there, my phone buzzed with a new message. It was my editor at *The New York Times* telling me to call ASAP. Two minutes later, I got another message, this one from an old college friend asking if my kids were all right. He lived in Parkland, Florida. We could not have known that someday I would be sending him the same anxious message.

You could run out of superlatives describing the tragic significance of Sandy Hook in the story of guns and violence in America.

The December 14, 2012, mass shooting was the worst at a K-12 school in the country's history. The twenty dead children were all first graders, six and seven years old. The other victims were the school principal, a psychologist, and four teachers—including my friend's stepdaughter.

Newtown is relatively wealthy, with a median family income of about $150,000 in 2024 and where the average home costs more than $600,000. Historically, the percentage of gun deaths in Connecticut is quite low, though the blue state is hardly pacifist, given it is the birthplace of Colt and other gun companies and the defense industry is one of its largest employers.

A sense of "it couldn't happen here" contributed to the shock and horror. But more than that, there was a feeling of trend lines going in the wrong direction and that America had reached a tipping point.

By the 2010s, the frequency of mass shootings had steadily been rising. Studies were starting to appear linking the internet and social media to mental health problems in young people. Gun sales were skyrocketing, driven in part by cynical messaging from the industry and its political allies that President Obama was coming for your firearms.

On its own, the scale and circumstances of the Sandy Hook tragedy were bad enough. But I knew I wasn't alone in feeling that the real crisis, laid bare by the sacrifice of so many innocents, was existential. How the country chose to respond would be a defining moment.

In the aftermath of Sandy Hook, pressure built on political leaders to finally do something, anything, to address the scourge of mass shootings that was tearing at the fabric of society. President Obama wanted to make an announcement quickly. VP Joe Biden, assigned to come up with recommendations, personally spoke to the traumatized Sandy Hook parents. He also met with gun control groups, health experts, police, and the National Rifle Association.

In January 2013, he sat down with members of a Democratic House task force working on its own set of proposals. It was not a public meeting, and the White House, wary of political trip wires as it sought a path through the impossible terrain of gun rights, didn't plan to talk about it afterward.

But I've since obtained twenty pages of handwritten notes taken by someone at the closed-door meeting. They reveal a fatalism and skittishness infecting politicians' private discourse around guns that was often at odds with their strong public statements. The cold reality was that, despite public outrage, the gun lobby effectively had a lock on the Republican-controlled House, and while Democrats had the Senate, they did not have a supermajority needed to overcome procedural hurdles.

As a result, while they outwardly proclaimed their determination to crack down on easy access to military-style weapons, privately the Democrats on the task force were resigned to failure before they even got started. Biden began the meeting by explaining the basic objective: "how to keep weapons out of the hands of bad people." But there were political and legal realities to contend with, including the Supreme Court's expansive interpretation of the Second Amendment, the rights of the mentally ill, and the legitimate interests of law-abiding gun owners.

Biden said President Obama intended, among other things, to propose reinstating the assault weapons ban that had expired a decade ago. The vice president, however, had concerns about that idea. He feared expending too much capital on it could detract from other more promising actions.

"We don't want all the energy to go into an assault weapon ban," Biden said. "We do not want it to take all the oxygen in the room so that you can't talk about anything else."

Jackie Speier, a Democratic congresswoman from California, agreed. Speier knew from personal experience the havoc caused by guns in the wrong hands. As a young staffer for Congressman Leo Ryan in 1978, she had been part of a delegation that went to Guyana to investigate allegations of human rights abuses by the cultish followers of Jim Jones. Her group was ambushed as they were leaving, and five people, including Ryan, were killed. Speier was shot multiple times and almost died before help arrived.

She had a long track record of fighting for gun control and helped enact an assault weapons ban in California. Immediately after Sandy Hook, Speier wrote a newspaper column demanding the same thing on a national level and she later cosponsored a bill to do it: "I ask my colleagues to join with me, to pledge with me that we will not rest until assault weapons are banned."

But aware of the political landscape, she was now bluntly telling her colleagues she didn't think it was doable: "I do not think an assault weapons ban can pass. The chances are slim to none."

Another Democratic congresswoman in the room, Carolyn McCarthy of New York, had had her own tragic encounter with gun violence. In 1993, her husband was one of six people killed and her son was injured in a mass shooting on the Long Island Rail Road. McCarthy also called for banning assault weapons and after Sandy Hook said publicly, "I'm not going to be shy anymore."

However, like Speier, she privately worried it was not feasible and suggested that maybe focusing on large-capacity magazines was a better idea. "We want something which works," she said. "We don't want something that looks pretty but won't work."

Biden agreed that it might be more realistic to restrict magazines "instead of dealing with assault weapons," adding that there were additional ideas, including broadening the categories of dangerous people ineligible for gun ownership; doing more to require safe storage of guns in the home; incentivizing so-called smart-gun technology; and expanding treatment options for the mentally ill.

One thing not on the table was the NRA's proposal to arm schoolteachers.

"That's the dumbest thing we can think about doing," Biden said.

Going around the room, other House members offered their own suggestions. Mike Thompson of California, the task force chair, talked about strengthening background checks. Bobby Scott of Virginia favored improvements in mental health treatment and youth programs.

Then there was John Dingell, the long-serving Democrat from Michigan and former NRA board member. Dingell, eighty-six, jokingly referred to himself as the "skunk at the picnic" and reminded everyone that back in the 1970s he had been responsible for helping create the NRA's lobbying operation.

"The reason it's so good," he quipped.

Dingell explained how his support for the Clinton assault weapons ban in 1994 had "cost me dearly" and that any new gun controls should not only respect the rights of sportsmen and hunters, but also reflect political realities. Firearms "are part of our culture," he said, and Democrats ignore that at their peril.

"You need to show no desire to take Second Amendment rights away," Dingell warned.

The vice president, who had known Dingell for decades and liked to highlight his own Second Amendment credentials by saying he owned a shotgun, was not unsympathetic. In his comments to the group, Biden also spoke of the need to not trample on the rights of law-abiding gun owners.

Continuing around the room, Ed Perlmutter, a Colorado Democrat, was particularly well-versed in the technology and pathology of mass shootings. His congressional district included Aurora, where the previous July a deranged man wielding an AR-15–style rifle equipped with a hundred-round magazine killed thirteen people and wounded fifty-eight others at a movie theater. And in 1999, Perlmutter was a state senator representing the area around Columbine High School when the massacre occurred there.

Going after high-capacity magazines and the ability to purchase ammunition online were priorities, Perlmutter said, adding that he would also support banning assault weapons. But he cautioned that the politics of doing the right thing were often unforgiving. Remember the blowback, he said, that followed passage of Obamacare and the Clinton assault weapons ban.

"We need to be prepared," he said. "We've got to get ready for the consequences."

Summing up, Biden sought to distill what he was hearing from the lawmakers: a desire for action but leavened with a heavy dose of cold reality.

"We need to posture ourselves for common sense," he said.

The investigations unit at *The New York Times* is different from the rest of the newspaper. Our stories can take a long time to produce because we're engaged in the difficulty of delving beyond the daily headlines to uncover hidden truths that readers deserve to know.

Since most journalists live to see their names in print, the deliberative pace of investigative reporting can be a source of angst. It's sort of like being a designated hitter in baseball—you don't get much playing time, so you better hit a home run.

Reporters covering the Sandy Hook shooting in the days afterward did invaluable work under difficult circumstances. Their stories, often done quickly to meet deadlines, helped people understand how the horrific attack unfolded. They had profiled the victims, talked to loved ones, and provided the public with ways to lend support to the shattered Sandy Hook community.

I had assisted with that early coverage because I lived nearby and had experience reporting on gun violence. In the immediate aftermath—along with attending the funeral of my friend's stepdaughter, the substitute teacher, who died trying to shield her students—I talked to law enforcement sources and sought divorce records for the shooter's parents, seeking any clues to his background and behavior.

Amid all the frenetic news gathering, my editor, Matt Purdy, posed a simple question. Matt was always a thoughtful and calm presence in what could otherwise be a crazy environment, and the question he posed reflected his best instincts: "Do you see something we should be doing that we're not?"

As a matter of fact, yes, I did.

I explained to Matt that this was actually the second time I had been personally touched by a mass shooting. And I saw parallels between the two tragedies.

The first one had occurred years earlier, in 1998. As a reporter then for the *Hartford Courant*, I had returned to the newsroom one day to find a strange man sitting in my chair, Matthew Beck. A thirty-five-year-old accountant at the Connecticut State Lottery, he wanted to alert the media to what he claimed was corruption and incompetence at his workplace. He was being interviewed by one of my colleagues and had pulled my chair over to an adjacent cubicle.

I tapped Beck on the shoulder and he jumped up. He seemed tightly wound. Without really looking me in the eye, Beck rolled the chair back to me, while my colleague, Lyn Bixby, found him another one. Afterward, Lyn commented that Beck was odd and added, half jokingly, Lyn was glad Beck didn't have a gun on him.

Beck later called the newsroom and left a message saying he wanted to meet again. Lyn was out of town and didn't hear it until the next morning. By then, Beck had killed the top four officials of the state lottery before shooting himself. He had previously attempted suicide and was committed to a psychiatric hospital, which should have made him ineligible to possess firearms. But in the house where he lived with his parents, Beck had a half dozen guns, including two assault weapons. Afterward, Beck's father, Donald, wept while second-guessing his decision to let his son keep guns in the home: "I will regret that to my dying day."

Nancy Lanza was another parent of a troubled young man who hadn't foreseen the danger of having guns around. She kept multiple firearms in her home, including an AR-15, semiautomatic pistols, high-capacity magazines, and hundreds of rounds of ammunition. She did so even as her deeply disturbed twenty-year-old son, Adam, spent his days in the basement immersed in violent video games and grew increasingly isolated. Nancy had taken him to gun ranges and taught him how to shoot. Adam killed her first, with her own gun, before driving to Sandy Hook Elementary.

There were obvious differences between Matthew Beck and Adam Lanza. But there were also intriguing commonalities: two mentally ill young men with access to firearms because they still lived at home with a well-meaning parent. Where did Nancy Lanza, in particular, get the idea that introducing guns to her son was an acceptable way to connect with him? And what made these troubled young men so attracted to high-powered weaponry?

In the weeks after Sandy Hook, as political leaders in Washington held emergency meetings, I proposed that the *Times* commit to a year-long investigation of gun violence. A colleague in my department, Michael Luo, joined me in coming up with a list of story ideas examining the culture, commerce, and politics of firearms in America. In a memo outlining our plans, I mentioned that I had already started digging into one possible story, an exposé of how the gun industry was spending millions to get firearms into the hands of kids and young men, in part by convincing parents that it was a great way to teach them responsibility.

"The effort, with echoes of the strategy employed by tobacco companies to foster a new generation of smokers, is backed by extensive social research and carried out by an array of nonprofit groups financed by the gun industry," I wrote in the memo.

Among the tactics gun companies were using: marketing a discounted AR-15–style rifle for "junior shooters" and promoting brand-name semiautomatic weapons in a target-shooting video game.

Three days after the vice president's meeting with the congressional task force, the White House released President Obama's fifteen-page plan to combat gun violence.

"The President strongly believes that the Second Amendment guarantees an individual right to bear arms," the White House said. "But to better protect our children and our communities from tragic mass shootings like those in Newtown, Aurora, Oak Creek, and Tucson, there are four common-sense steps we can take right now."

Entitled "Now Is the Time," the plan laid out goals for banning assault weapons and high-capacity magazines, strengthening background checks, making schools safer, and improving mental health treatment. "Common sense" was a recurring theme. It would be implemented through roughly two dozen executive orders, along with a dozen proposals to be introduced in Congress.

But the executive orders were mostly incremental steps around the margins. The president could only do so much without seeking legislative approval, and it showed in Obama's list, which included low-impact items such as writing a letter to states "highlighting the importance" of using the national background-check system and issuing "a memo encouraging every US Attorney's Office to renew domestic violence outreach efforts."

Congress was where the heavy lifting would need to happen. Polls showed that a majority of Americans favored much of what Obama was asking for, including banning assault weapons and high-capacity magazines. Nearly 90 percent supported expanding background checks for gun purchases to cover online sales.

At the *Times*, Michael and I were continuing to pursue the stories we had proposed at the start of the year. We did what investigative reporters do, asking questions, obtaining documents and data, talking to people. We pored over medical examiner reports of children killed by guns and found that official government statistics grossly undercounted accidental shooting deaths every year, suggesting there were basic safety steps that could be taken to reduce the toll.

We scraped data from a website where guns were bought and sold and identified felons who were illegally obtaining them because no background check was required for those private online purchases. We collected court records showing how dangerously mentally ill people, drug addicts, and domestic abusers often had no trouble getting a gun and committing violence, despite laws barring them from possessing firearms.

We obtained confidential testimony of firearms-industry executives from lawsuits revealing that, even under oath, they refused to acknowledge the havoc their products caused or to take responsibility for their own reckless sales practices. And we shined a spotlight on the gun industry's lobbying tactics, disclosing how it spends millions of dollars a year cozying up to members of Congress, wining and dining them and inviting them to junkets and shooting contests.

The stories struck a nerve. Politicians waved them around as proof that change was needed. They were cited in law reviews and court filings. Thousands of readers left comments, some of them relating their own experiences with gun culture. A family doctor in Pennsylvania expressed amazement at the blasé attitude of his patients when it came to gun safety: "People have smoke detectors and lock up their drain cleaner but leave loaded firearms in the hall drawer." A woman in Washington State recounted being shot at by an adolescent girl while trying to return a lost dog to the child's home: "This young lady, only 13, had access to guns and ammo when she was left home alone with her siblings."

Many readers focused on the power of the NRA. Those who lived outside the United States couldn't believe that one group could hold such sway over gun policy.

"The gun culture in America is a form of collective psychosis," one wrote. "How long will we allow this insanity to continue?"

Indeed, if anyone had a playbook for how to deal with exactly the sort of crisis gripping the country, it was the NRA. But for them, the nature of the crisis was not that Americans were being shot to death at alarming rates. Rather, it was what the nation's elected leaders intended to do about it. And the organization had long experience in addressing that problem.

Gun companies were happy to let someone else take point. The National Shooting Sports Foundation, located a stone's throw from Sandy Hook, mostly kept silent while the NRA geared up. This was perhaps unsurprising, since the millions of dollars the firearms industry had shoveled into NRA coffers in preceding years meant the symbiotic relationship between the two was stronger than ever.

The NRA had successfully blocked every meaningful action on Capitol Hill to address gun violence over the past two decades, while also advancing pro-gun interests in new ways. No member of Congress was more helpful than Dingell. Huddling a few days before the task force meeting in January 2013, Dingell and NRA executives had discussed how to contain efforts to impose new gun restrictions.

The NRA men said they would be willing to support school safety measures and stronger punishment for crimes involving guns, but not much else. Dingell's notes of the meeting summed up the plan: "Need to buy time to put together package can vote for, and get support, also for sensitivities to die down."

The wind was at the NRA's back and it showed in the confidence expressed by the group's leaders. Wayne LaPierre, the longtime CEO, held a press conference after the Sandy Hook massacre to condemn a roster of villains: the creators of violent movies and video games, street gangs, ineffectual politicians, the media—everything but guns.

In fact, LaPierre famously explained, the real solution to the problem of school shootings was more firearms in the right hands. "The only thing that stops a bad guy with a gun," he said, "is a good guy with a gun."

The NRA's lobbying unit went into high gear, circulating sets of talking points for friendly members of Congress to undermine gun control bills. One claimed an assault weapons ban would be ineffective, citing a 1997 study that found that rifles were only used in about 2 percent of all murders. It was a brazenly misleading factoid. In the 2010s, assault weapons were used in a third of mass shootings, a trend that had steadily been rising.

Other talking points attacking a proposal for universal background checks were similarly cynical. They claimed such checks would "criminalize all private firearms transfers, even between family members or friends who have known each other all of their lives."

The bipartisan compromise bill being considered in Congress specifically *did not* do that. Introduced by two senators with A ratings from the NRA, Democrat Joe Manchin of West Virginia and Republican Pat Toomey of Pennsylvania, the legislation was designed to address the gun lobby's concerns while also being effective.

"I don't consider criminal background checks to be gun control," said Toomey. "It's just common sense."

But none of that mattered. The NRA had long ago determined that ideological rigidity on Second Amendment issues sold better with its base, and being seen taking a stand against gun safety measures—even ones deliberately fashioned to be as inoffensive as possible—took priority. The NRA mobilized its 4 million members, mounting a pressure campaign to force vulnerable lawmakers in line. Sandy Hook parents would later say that senators who privately claimed to support them ended up voting against the bipartisan gun legislation out of fear of losing their seats.

On April 17, 2013—the same day we published a story showing how the lack of a background-check requirement allowed felons to buy guns online—the Senate failed to pass the background-check bill, falling short of the sixty votes needed to overcome procedural hurdles. As for the assault weapons ban, that proposal never stood a chance. It went down to defeat the same day, by a vote of forty to sixty.

In the end, the "common sense" proposals for curbing gun violence went nowhere, having run headlong into the implacable power of the gun lobby. But there had also been a failure by the Obama administration and congressional leadership to marshal the sort of energy, creativity, and will that drove, say, the Affordable Care Act.

Years of playing political footsie with gun rights, for fear of losing swing states during elections, had left the president weakened from the start. Obama never exhibited the kind of focused force that Bill Clinton had when the latter personally got on the phone and managed to browbeat Dingell, of all people, to vote for an assault weapons ban, or the angry brute strength of Lyndon Johnson, who rammed through the Gun Control Act in 1968.

Outside the White House after the defeat on Capitol Hill, an emotional President Obama appeared with Vice President Biden and families of the Sandy Hook victims to rail at the NRA and Republicans who were mostly responsible for Congress's inaction. It was clear the parents, having been let down by their elected leaders, would need to carry the ball going forward.

Mark Barden, whose seven-year-old son, Daniel, was killed at Sandy Hook, stepped to the microphone. Looking sad but determined, he read from a prepared statement, saying the families of the victims had "always known this would be a long road, and we don't have the luxury of turning back.

"Our hearts are broken. Our spirit is not."

In the days after the Sandy Hook shooting, I had been watching television news coverage of it when a recognizable face appeared on the screen. It was Msgr. Robert Weiss, or, as I knew him, Father Bob, the Catholic priest who had presided over my wedding.

He was actually the second priest enlisted in that effort.

When my soon-to-be wife and I were planning our ceremony back in 1990, we had a little trouble with the first priest. Like any profession, the clergy has its share of disappointments, and that particular fellow was a dour stiff who seemed too hung up on rules and regulations—getting married in the Church shouldn't be like serving time at the DMV.

Aggravated, we turned to another priest, this one at a church in the Connecticut town where we had recently rented an apartment. We were hesitant at first because we had no real connection to him or his parish, but Father Bob couldn't have been more positive and welcoming. Without a second thought, he agreed to preside over our ceremony, and he did so with warmth and humor. At the altar, he presented us with a small box of crayons and went through the colors, explaining how they represented the ups and downs of marriage.

For a few years afterward, before we moved away, Father Bob remained a presence in our lives. When our infant daughter was in pediatric intensive care and we feared the worst, he came to the hospital to be with us. Thankfully, she recovered. Father Bob's decision to drop everything and answer our call was an act of kindness for which my wife and I were forever grateful.

Now, here he was on my TV talking about Sandy Hook. He had since become the parish priest at Saint Rose of Lima Church in Newtown, where the school was located, and spent days tending to grief-stricken families and accompanying police officers to some of the parents' homes to confirm the horrific news that their child was gone. I took a measure of comfort knowing that, in its moment of need, at least Sandy Hook was in good hands.

In the years since December 2012, the shattered community has struggled to return to some sense of normalcy. The date of the shooting is referred to locally as 12/14. A memorial was built and there are annual vigils. Sandy Hook school was torn down and replaced; the new one has bullet-resistant windows.

One community member that chose not to stick around was the National Shooting Sports Foundation—the group eventually picked up and moved to another Connecticut town a half hour away.

Father Bob did stick around. As the tenth anniversary of the massacre approached in 2022, he was turning seventy-five, and under Church tradition he was supposed to retire. But he didn't feel right about it. Many of those who had led the town through the aftermath of the tragedy had since stepped back, and Father Bob wanted to keep a sense of continuity as the community continued to heal.

He wrote to Church leaders and received permission to stay on a few more years.

"The first selectman's gone, the school superintendent's gone, the police chief is gone, half of the ministers have left," he said. "There are very few of us who were really involved in the heart of this thing."

When Father Bob talked about Sandy Hook, he tried to focus on the positive. It's the character trait that I had appreciated in my own dealings with him many years before. He recalled how, after a round of painful house calls on the night after the massacre, he returned to Saint Rose of Lima at 2:00 a.m. and encountered something both unexpected and hopeful.

"And I walked into church, and there were two pews"—he choked up and paused before continuing—"two pews of college kids who had all gone to Saint Rose school, kneeling there saying the rosary. And I thought, *They got it*."

It affirmed for Father Bob the importance of being present, rising to the occasion, and making yourself available: "Jesus was never sitting in the temple. He was out with the people, listening to their needs.

"Sandy Hook showed that you don't always have to be saying something," he said, adding: "But you do have to be there for the people."

Alas, being there for the people seemed to elude the nation's leaders after Sandy Hook. It would be everyday citizens and leaders outside Washington who made progress on gun violence prevention where the official political class had not.

In response to Sandy Hook, former Congresswoman Gabby Giffords—who had narrowly survived being shot by a deranged man in 2011—together with her husband, Mark Kelly, formed Giffords: Courage to Fight Gun Violence, to lobby for firearms safety and support reform-minded candidates. That was followed a year later by the creation of Everytown for Gun Safety, funded largely by former New York Mayor Michael Bloomberg as an effort to match the lobbying capacity of the NRA.

Both Giffords and Everytown developed litigation arms focused on using the courts to pursue changes where legislative efforts failed, something that gun rights groups had been doing for decades.

A mass shooting at Marjory Stoneman Douglas High School in Parkland, Florida, in February 2018 (thankfully my old college friend's kids were not hurt) ignited a movement of young people demanding stronger laws and changes in attitudes toward guns. A group called March for Our Lives held protests that rivaled the student demonstrations of the Vietnam War era and launched a new generation of activism. Witnessing the courage of these kids moved retired Supreme Court Justice John Paul Stevens to start a public discussion of repealing the Second Amendment and replacing it with something appropriate to the modern era.

"Rarely in my lifetime have I seen the type of civic engagement schoolchildren and their supporters demonstrated in Washington and other major cities throughout the country," Stevens wrote in an op-ed for *The New York Times*, adding, "These demonstrations demand our respect."

In 2022, the parents of Sandy Hook, acting on their own, finally achieved a measure of justice when a lawsuit they initiated led to a landmark settlement. Remington, the manufacturer of the assault weapon used in the massacre, agreed to pay $73 million and release internal company documents revealing how guns were allegedly marketed to at-risk young males through provocative ads and placements in violent video games—echoes of the story I had written a decade earlier entitled "Selling a New Generation on Guns."

Although partly the result of favorable state laws in Connecticut, the legal victory reflected a potential new strategy to hold gun companies accountable for irresponsible sales practices. It has since been replicated elsewhere. In July 2025, a New York State appeals court allowed a lawsuit to proceed against the manufacturer of a firearm accessory that plaintiffs say made it easier for a white supremacist to shoot Black shoppers at a Buffalo grocery store.

And while Washington remains paralyzed by partisan division, state legislatures have offered more fertile ground. In 2025 alone, nearly three dozen states passed more than eighty gun safety measures, including gun-friendly Alabama and North Dakota, which took action to make it harder for domestic abusers to obtain guns. At the same time, of course, many states also moved to loosen restrictions on firearms or to make it harder to sue gun companies, so progress for gun safety advocates remains halting and incremental.

Still, any progress is a testament to the sort of vigor and imagination at a grassroots level that was absent in the nation's capital in 2013, when the White House and Congress debated the same old nonstarters and then watched them fail.

CHILDISH THINGS

I'VE ENCOUNTERED A lot of death in my line of work.

On the city police beat at my first daily newspaper job, I more than once showed up at a crime scene before the cops did, having heard the call on the radio scanner I carried. One time I parked my car by the curb where the body of a young Black man, shot in the head, was lying in the grass. I stood there alone, notebook in hand, looking at him. It was just the two of us. He seemed peaceful, as if he were taking a nap on that bright sunny day, except for the small round hole in his temple.

Another time I found myself on an interstate observing what little was left of two truckers who had been run over by an eighteen-wheeler while standing outside their own rig checking on a faulty tire. The tractor trailer had been going so fast that the men were knocked out of their work boots, which were scattered across the highway. Two large pinkish stains on the pavement marked their last moments.

There were many more—the parents whose adoptive son killed them with a sledgehammer and burned their bodies in the backyard; the mob victim whose rotted remains were pulled from a harbor. But somehow, mass shootings are the worst. There are a couple of reasons for that. One has to do with the survivors.

When Matthew Beck killed the top officials at the Connecticut Lottery in March 1998, he did so in front of their friends and coworkers, who could do nothing but scream and cry. I interviewed one woman who had hidden in some trees outside the building and watched as Beck chased the lottery president across a parking lot, felled him with a pistol shot, and then stood over him as he begged for his life. Beck, out of breath, leveled his gun at the man's head. From the trees, the woman and others shouted pleas for Beck not to do it. But he did. And then he killed himself.

As the woman recounted this for me, she started hyperventilating and sobbed uncontrollably, making animal-like sounds I will never forget.

We don't know the full psychological consequences of mass shootings, thanks largely to the NRA, whose allies in Congress succeeded in quashing federally funded research into such things. Still, some studies have been done. One found that 95 percent of survivors report post-traumatic stress afterward, and 80 percent still experience it almost a year later. Other research suggests that the aftereffects on mental health are far worse than those of most natural disasters. There is also the corrosive impact on the community at large, where family members, first responders, and others must process these tragedies.

That brings me to the other reason that mass shootings are the most insidious on the roster of horribles I've covered as a journalist: their virality.

Unlike crimes of passion, ignorance, or greed, mass shootings in the modern era are often connected. Like fungi, their cankered tendrils reach out and entwine one another through manifestos, live streams, chat rooms, and other virtual guano that provide fertilizer for evil cogitations. They are, to apply another metaphor, a contagion.

It's hard to point to a patient zero. But, increasingly, there is a profile of the typical carrier of this deadly virus.

One year after the Connecticut lottery shootings, on April 20, 1999, two students walked into Columbine High School in Colorado and shot to death twelve classmates and a teacher. As details trickled in and the names of the shooters became known, I went online and did some searching.

The internet was still a relatively new thing. In an America Online chat room I found what appeared to be a posting by one of the teens, Eric Harris, saying "today is my last day on earth" and "be prepared." Other toxic digital droppings had been left behind as well.

Harris, eighteen, and Dylan Klebold, seventeen, had seemed to find a perverse sense of community in this new online space, bonding with faceless others in a little cell they called the Trenchcoat Mafia and sharing helpful tidbits such as "Pipe bombs are some of the easiest and deadliest ways to kill a group of people." They created websites, uploaded violent video game files, and generally embraced the fledgling frontier of the web to incubate their dark fantasies.

This felt new and deeply unsettling.

As the phenomenon of the mass shooter metastasized over the past half century, the perpetrators were mostly men who tended to skew younger—but not *that* young. Charles Whitman was twenty-five when he shot people from the University of Texas tower in 1966. Matthew Beck was thirty-five when he killed his coworkers at the state lottery in 1998. In the 1970s and 1980s, the worst public mass shootings were committed by men in their early forties.

But there had never been a case of teenagers, steeped in the new medium of the internet, methodically planning and executing a mass murder and then committing suicide. As the nation searched for answers, the relative youth of the shooters stood out as an obvious, and perhaps vital, factor.

Anyone who has ever known, raised, or been an adolescent boy understands that, as much as you might love those boys, you wouldn't want to bet the farm on their capacity for self-control or common sense. Many will charge into battle and win wars—and also drive their car into a tree or recklessly jump off a cliff.

The reasons are mostly biological.

"There's a lot of research about how their brains are not fully developed in terms of regulation," said Jonathan Metzl, a psychiatry professor at Vanderbilt University.

Studies have shown that the prefrontal cortex—the portion of the brain responsible for processing executive functions—doesn't completely form until about age twenty-five in males, a few years later than in females. This means that for many young men, whose already turbulent passage through adolescence is further addled by testosterone, the ability to regulate impulses lags behind. And, like any segment of the population, some of them also have mental health problems. Adding guns into this unstable mix can be like tossing a match into a pool of gasoline.

It helps explain why more than half of all homicides in the United States are committed by young men under the age of thirty, and mass shooters, about 95 percent of whom are male, increasingly are in their early twenties or even younger. While teenagers carried out six mass shootings in the twenty-five years before 2000, they have committed twice as many in the twenty-five years since then.

Jaylen Fryberg was fifteen when he used his father's Beretta pistol to murder four students, including a girl who had rejected his advances, at his Marysville, Washington, high school in 2014. Beau Wilson was eighteen when, armed with an AR-15 and two handguns, he randomly shot and killed three people on the street in Farmington, New Mexico, in 2023.

"We see two clusters when it comes to mass shooters," said Jillian Peterson, a criminology professor at Hamline University. "People in their forties who commit workplace-type shootings, and a very big cluster of young people—eighteen, nineteen, twenty, twenty-one—who seem to get caught up in the social contagion of killing."

A lot has been made of the possibly exacerbating role of the web, video games, and movies in influencing antisocial behavior among the cohort of adolescents who commit mass shootings. A research protocol has yet to be developed that can, once and for all, determine a causal link between any of those things, and doing so may prove impossible.

But some studies show that electronic media, and the internet in general, have allowed dangerously unstable youths to feed off one another, drawing inspiration, justification, or technical know-how for their actions. The Institute for Strategic Dialogue, in a report published in 2024, described how its researchers, posing as children, created social media accounts and quickly found that a "content ecosystem glorifying mass casualty shooters exists and is readily accessible to minors across platforms." They found 127 videos "glorifying a range of mass casualty attackers" on TikTok alone and tracked how the material migrated to darker corners of the web where more intimate connections between troubled users can occur out of sight:

"Young mass shooting fans, or those with an initial interest in mass shootings, find each other on more open and mainstream platforms such as TikTok. There they exchange information about how to communicate on more opaque platforms such as Discord and Telegram."

Payton Gendron, eighteen, found such platforms useful when he was making preparations to shoot Black people at a supermarket in Buffalo, New York, in 2022. Gendron spent untold hours on Discord, a chat site favored by gamers, where he obsessively detailed his plans and justification for his racist attack. He said he drew inspiration from a mass shooting a few years earlier at a mosque in Christchurch, New Zealand, in which the killer wrote a manifesto and live streamed his attack on Facebook. Gendron did precisely the same thing—live streaming his killing of ten people on the social media platform Twitch and uploading his own 180-page manifesto, much of it plagiarized from extremist message boards on yet another online platform, 4chan.

In the years leading up to the Sandy Hook massacre, Adam Lanza had also spent much of his free time on his computer, researching mass shootings—particularly Columbine, about which he collected an enormous amount of online material. The Columbine shooting has become a lodestar for many budding mass shooters. Investigators discovered Lanza frequently visited a blog devoted to Columbine and other shootings and "exchanged e-mails with others who were interested in the topic," according to the state's final report on Sandy Hook. The report detailed a partial list of what was found on Lanza's computer, including a video "game titled 'School Shooting' where the player controls a character who enters a school and shoots at students."

Many fair-minded and sincere advocacy groups, scholars, and researchers point to the internet and electronic media overall as accomplices to gun violence. Then there is the gun lobby.

After Sandy Hook, NRA chief executive Wayne LaPierre appeared before a throng of reporters to rail against video games, Hollywood, and the music industry, among others, for polluting adolescent brains with violent content.

"A child growing up in America witnesses sixteen thousand

murders and two hundred thousand acts of violence by the time he or she reaches the ripe old age of eighteen," LaPierre said. "And throughout it all, too many in our national media, their corporate owners, and their stockholders act as silent enablers, if not complicit coconspirators."

Not mentioned, of course, was guns or the NRA's own role in getting them into the hands of America's youth to legally purchase at the "ripe old age of eighteen." That took a concerted effort that began long before anyone had ever heard of *Call of Duty*, Columbine, or the World Wide Web.

I always had a basic understanding that the gun industry, like a lot of business interests, took steps to cultivate young people as the next generation to buy their products. It didn't surprise me to learn, for instance, that firearms dealers often donated guns and ammunition to youth groups, such as the YMCA camp where I learned to shoot as a kid.

But it wasn't until I obtained a previously unseen trove of internal NRA records from the early 1980s that I discovered just how calculated, far-reaching, and early the effort was. What the records showed was that commercial incentives were only a part of it.

"More important from a political point of view, and for the future of firearms ownership in the United States," one of the documents explained, was the goal of "'socializing' youngsters to think of guns as sporting and useful."

The files included a transcript of a meeting in January 1980 of the NRA executive committee, along with mimeographed handouts, describing an ambitious plan for "expanded large-scale junior shooting programs" to develop a stronger pro-gun sentiment in American society. Together, the files offered a rare fly-on-the-wall look at a pivotal moment in the gun lobby's long-term effort to bend public attitudes in a direction favorable to its agenda.

Leading the meeting was the group's director of general operations, an Olympic sports shooter named Gary Anderson. He presented the NRA directors with a hand-drawn chart showing the relative proportion of Americans for and against guns, noting a "massive uncommitted population" that could be persuaded.

The NRA had to be laser focused on that uncommitted demographic, Anderson said, for reasons that were both ideological and practical. Fostering a greater acceptance of gun rights was core to the organization's mission and would also benefit it financially.

"We need majority public support," he told the group.

Anderson believed he had a plan to achieve that: The NRA had to relentlessly focus on America's children.

This was not an entirely new proposition. So-called junior shooter clubs had been part of the organization since its earliest days. Among groups that the NRA supported were the Boy Scouts, 4-H, and the JROTC, or Junior Reserve Officers' Training Corps, a military program that operates in schools. The idea was that if you train young people in the safe use of guns through competitive target shooting, at least some of them will stick with it into adulthood and become the next generation of firearm owners and NRA members.

"The objective of our junior programs is to expand this pro-gun portion of the population as much as we can," Anderson reminded the directors. "The reason we have junior programs in the NRA goes back to our need to respond to the problems we have identified."

But that tradition was in decline. By 1980, internal numbers showed that membership in the NRA's junior shooter programs had fallen to sixty-five thousand from about eighty thousand in 1975, as hundreds of local gun clubs folded. Around the country, almost half of indoor shooting ranges at colleges and high schools had been shuttered because of concerns about lead hazards, poor ventilation, and changing attitudes among educators, some of whom viewed them as cultural anachronisms.

Indeed, even that smaller number of junior shooters was being supported by an anachronism—courtesy of the federal government. A 1916 law, passed in the throes of World War I, had created the Office of the Director of Civilian Marksmanship, which opened military shooting ranges to the public. It supplemented an even earlier program, authorized by Pres. Theodore Roosevelt, allowing the sale of surplus guns and ammo to certain rifle clubs, such as the NRA.

More than a half century later, this Defense Department initiative was keeping youth gun groups awash in materiel—12 million rounds of ammunition distributed to more than three hundred Boy Scout summer camps in 1979 alone. Yet it still wasn't stanching the steady erosion of interest in firearms among kids and their parents.

Retired V. Adm. Lloyd Mustin, who had just finished a term as NRA president, listened to Anderson's presentation and voiced frustration with the predicament. He pointed out that the group's leadership had long been told, "If we don't bring in the juniors, the name of the game is death and we'd better get going.

"But there is not an awful lot of positive achievement on the record, as reflected by some of these declines in recent years."

Anderson agreed. Recognizing that the NRA had limited resources—"I didn't intend this to be a pitch for more money"—he described a strategy to achieve their goals "and get somebody else to spend the money." Part of it was to use public schools as an on-ramp for gun use.

A board member named Dr. Nathan Arenson liked that idea. A radiologist from Pensacola, Florida, Arenson said it would work best if you could find "a practical method of getting a shooting program introduced into the school system" without causing undue alarm.

"That is, to tie shooting in with something that might be a little more palatable and acceptable," he said. "For instance, in Pensacola we have tied the shooting program into a biology course."

The biology class included a study of wildlife conservation, which was "a natural step" to discussion of hunting and a hunter-safety course. "And then from hunter safety, it went to firearms, firearms and ballistics, and firearms recognition."

That was precisely Anderson's plan. He explained that the NRA's relatively new lobbying arm—only five years old at that time—had begun conferring with state education departments around the country about getting shooting programs integrated into school physical education curriculums. It was seen as a stealthily convenient way of introducing guns to kids.

"We believe very much that if you can get shooting into the schools in this way, if it is in as a physical education activity, it is accepted in a very positive context and nobody argues about it," Anderson said.

"We just feel that this is a good way to slip it in. Nobody questions it."

The amount of resources thrown at the NRA's campaign to capture America's youth was stunning. Although its leaders had talked wistfully in those early days of relying on public money by using school physical education as a sort of Trojan horse, they soon realized the NRA would need to open its wallet for the plan to work.

Whereas in 1975 the group had spent a total of $882,000 on children's activities, by the 1990s and 2000s it was pouring tens of millions of dollars into youth activities across the country. And while they were successful in getting firearms training introduced into schools, it was not just through gym curriculums, but also by building on programs, such as JROTC, that were already in the classroom.

The NRA's school grants proved effective. Instructors at many schools that received the money promoted the NRA to students and their parents, encouraging them to join the organization and, at times, explicitly mixing politics with the message. A school district in Texas, for instance, wrote in its grant application that the NRA's support for JROTC would foster "positive attitudes toward Second Amendment rights for these future voters and their families."

Not everyone is thrilled with this. Rick Jahnkow, a nationally known nonviolence activist who lobbied for decades against introducing guns to children, said schools that get involved with JROTC programs, in particular, ignore the "dangerous implications of giving such a mixed message about guns to young people.

"Think about it. A child can be disciplined for bringing a squirt gun to class, but school officials and the Pentagon get a pass when they train students to use rifles with shooting ranges inside our schools."

The JROTC was started by the US Defense Department a century ago as a high school version of the ROTC that is embedded in colleges and universities. While not explicitly a recruitment tool—the Pentagon is not permitted to do that with children—the junior corps focuses on instilling discipline, responsibility, and respect for authority, which are essential components of the armed services. There are about thirty-five hundred JROTC units in schools around the country, partially subsidized by the federal government and frequently staffed by retired veterans.

A major part of the JROTC experience is firearms training. In many schools, learning how to shoot air rifles and compete in marksmanship contests is the primary draw for students. Which is where the NRA enters the picture.

While the Pentagon funds some portion of JROTC activities, schools have to come up with the rest of the money themselves, and they frequently turn to the NRA for help paying for the guns component.

In 2016, Marjory Stoneman Douglas High School in Parkland, Florida, received a $10,827 NRA grant for its JROTC competitive-shooting program, part of more than $2 million the NRA distributed to hundreds of schools that year. It was a popular activity at Stoneman Douglas and attracted some stellar students, including Peter Wang, the son of immigrant parents, who loved seeing him in his dress uniform.

Peter, fifteen, was wearing his JROTC polo shirt on Valentine's Day in February 2018 when the sound of loud bangs reverberated through Building 12 on the Stoneman Douglas campus shortly after 2:00 p.m. On the third floor where Peter was, panicked students began streaming out of classrooms into the hallway. As students rushed toward a stairwell, Peter held the door open to allow them to escape. That's where he was standing when he was fatally shot twelve times with an AR-15.

The nineteen-year-old former Stoneman Douglas student holding the rifle, Nikolas Cruz, was wearing his own JROTC polo shirt.

Cruz should never have been allowed to have a firearm—let alone participate in a school activity involving guns. Deeply troubled, he had a long history of making threats and bouncing around between psychiatrists and special education programs. Different authorities over the years had repeatedly determined that he should be involuntarily committed for mental health evaluation, which would have barred him from purchasing a firearm when he turned eighteen.

As early as 2013, when Cruz was fourteen, doctors recommended he be placed in a residential treatment facility. The next year, a clinician's memo described him as "moody, impulsive, angry, attention seeking, annoys others on purpose and threatens to hurt others." By 2016, Cruz was cutting himself, claimed to have drunk gasoline because he didn't want to live, was punching holes in walls, and talked about getting a gun.

"My friends constantly reported that he was threatening them," said Megan Bonner, a student at Stoneman Douglas at the time Cruz was there.

But despite the mounting evidence of trouble, Cruz was never committed to a psychiatric hospital. Meanwhile, he had been permitted to take part in JROTC rifle training at Stoneman Douglas, where he earned a sharpshooter badge. He was among the cadets who received several awards for participating in JROTC and got ribbons for "consistently presenting an outstanding appearance" and demonstrating "outstanding conduct throughout the school."

While in JROTC, Cruz was also enrolled in Cross Creek School, an alternative program for students with emotional and behavioral problems. A psychiatrist there had recommended that Cruz not be allowed to take part in JROTC. But the JROTC instructor at Stoneman Douglas claimed he had been unaware of that. The instructor, John Navarra, said he knew Cruz had emotional issues and social impairments, but that he never personally witnessed any problems with the boy.

"He was quiet and well-behaved," Navarra said, "and oftentimes that is worth a lot in a classroom."

Cruz was eventually barred from participating in JROTC rifle training and kicked out of Stoneman Douglas for escalating behavioral problems. He continued to act out in ways that led to the police visiting his home and even a complaint being filed with the FBI warning about threats he had made. On social media, he brazenly posted that he wanted to be "a professional school shooter."

None of this disqualified him from purchasing seven guns after he turned eighteen, including the AR-15 he would eventually use to commit his massacre. It took Cruz less than six minutes, firing 139 bullets, to kill seventeen people before dropping his gun and escaping by blending in with other students. He was caught about an hour later walking in a neighborhood a couple of miles away.

JROTC members were among the Parkland students credited with acting bravely that day. Some helped barricade classrooms to try to prevent the shooter from entering. In addition to Peter Wang, two other JROTC students, Alaina Petty, fourteen, and Martin Duque, fourteen, were also killed. All three were later awarded heroism medals by the US Army, and Peter was posthumously granted admission to West Point's class of 2025.

It would be wrong to say that Nikolas Cruz did what he did because he was in JROTC. There is no evidence that the program could turn someone into a school shooter. Its basic objective, after all, is to instill positive character traits.

But its underlying assumption that using guns is an acceptable way to achieve that objective is a different matter.

Time and again, parents have succumbed to the notion that introducing firearms to a troubled child will somehow help them cope with behavioral problems or teach them how to be responsible—with devastating consequences.

The parents of Ethan Crumbley bought a pistol that his mother referred to as his Christmas present, and they made target shooting a family pastime, despite Ethan's escalating behavioral problems, which included suicidal thoughts and violent drawings. When he was fifteen years old, in 2021, Ethan used the handgun to kill four students and injure seven more at Oxford High School in Michigan.

Colin Gray gave his son, Colt, an assault weapon for Christmas, even though the latter had been exhibiting antisocial behavior and was questioned by police about making threats. The father told a sheriff's deputy who came to the house that Colin was using firearms as a way "to get him interested in the outdoors." When Colt was fourteen, in 2024, he used his Christmas gift to murder four people at Apalachee High School in Georgia.

Where would parents get the idea that deadly weapons are a sensible way to relate to their kids? It's a theme that the gun industry has been pushing for decades.

The NRA's scheming back in the early 1980s was only the start of what would become a concerted industrywide effort. Much like the tobacco companies, gunmakers spent millions trying to wheedle their way into the lives of kids, financing youth camps, after-school groups, and other activities that promote the use of guns.

A 2012 study commissioned by the National Shooting Sports Foundation described the objective. It recommended deploying children from gun-friendly families to recruit other young people inexperienced with firearms. The report, which focused on children ages eight to seventeen, said these "peer ambassadors" could be used to introduce wary friends to guns slowly through less intimidating activities, such as paintball or archery.

"The point should be to get newcomers started shooting something," the report said, "with the natural next step being a move toward actual firearms."

The industry helped finance *Junior Shooters* magazine, which ran ads offering a discount coupon for an assault weapon and encouraged young readers to tell their parents about it: "Who knows? Maybe you'll find a Bushmaster AR-15 under your tree some frosty Christmas morning!"

Oftentimes the pitch from local educators to get kids involved with guns was more explicitly tied to the idea that it would be helpful to those who required special attention. School officials in Kentucky who applied for an NRA grant to support a JROTC program said they saw it as an "opportunity to engage a set of at-risk students to shooting sports."

Some educators have expressed concerns. Deborah Teal, a high school teacher in Orange County, California, said that despite some positive aspects of JROTC, she worried about the preoccupation with guns. "The militarization of the kids, especially vulnerable kids, is what bothered me," she said.

More broadly, the idea that children—and in particular, teenagers, whose brains are still developing—are equipped to make proper decisions about handling firearms is problematic, said Dr. Jess Shatkin, a psychiatrist at the Child Study Center at New York University's medical center.

"There are lots of ways to teach responsibility to a kid," Dr. Shatkin said. "You don't need a gun to do it."

A child may not yet have the critical thinking skills necessary to avoid dangerous mistakes, but adults are generally expected to. Yet, time and again the combination of grown-ups and guns has proven to be just as allergic to sensible decision-making, due in part to the complexities of how people evaluate risk. And often it is children who are hurt because of adults' bad choices.

The risk-perception gap is the space between the likelihood of negative consequences from engaging in a certain behavior and how we perceive that likelihood. Because human judgment is shaped not solely by statistics but also emotions, learned experience, basic necessity, and lack of information, we are famous for making seemingly irrational assessments of risk in our daily lives.

As a result, calculating the odds of something bad happening often yields unexpected outcomes when deciding, say, whether to drive in a snowstorm, how to safely slice a bagel—or when to give a machine gun to a little girl.

In the summer of 2014, Alex MacLachlan, an Ivy League–educated investment banker from New Jersey, and his wife, Alison, were vacationing in Las Vegas with their three children when they decided to visit a place called Bullets and Burgers just across the state line in Arizona. After a monster-truck ride, they went to the shooting range, where Alex tried his hand at firing an Uzi submachine gun.

Fully automatic machine guns are one of the few firearms that remain virtually unobtainable in the civilian market, but a loophole in the law allows for the transfer of ones legally owned before 1986 with federal registration. They are popular attractions at ranges, and in Arizona even children can fire them under adult supervision.

After Alex had his shot, he let his nine-year-old daughter take a turn. The instructor, Charles Vacca, put the Uzi in her hands, got her positioned correctly, and let her fire a single shot in semiautomatic mode. Then he flipped the switch to fully automatic, meaning her next squeeze of the trigger would release a burst of repeated gunfire and the strong recoil associated with it.

The girl, dressed in pink shorts and with a braided ponytail, fired the weapon and immediately lost control of it. The machine gun lurched to the left and kept firing, striking Vacca in the head. As he fell to the ground, the girl dropped the weapon and ran to her family. Vacca was airlifted to a hospital, where he was pronounced dead.

One might think that such a needless tragedy, in which a man is killed and a child scarred for life, would inspire thoughtful reconsideration of putting lethal weaponry in the hands of kids—the absurdity of treating machine guns as playthings. Instead, gun rights proponents got their backs up or sought to explain it away.

A physician with Doctors for Responsible Gun Ownership, a pro-gun-rights project of the Second Amendment Foundation, wrote a column downplaying the tragedy's significance, saying there had been only one similar incident in recent years. Dr. Robert Young said, "We might wonder why the instructor did not steady the weapon by gripping it as the child held it."

"While we can learn from our hindsight critique of adult mistakes in these two cases," he said, "let's recognize that a great many children (and adults) have emerged unscathed from their experience of safely, successfully shooting automatic weapons in these venues."

A bill was introduced in the Arizona State legislature to prohibit children under sixteen from using machine guns—"I'm disgusted that we even need such a law," said its Democratic sponsor—but it didn't get far. Law enforcement closed its investigation of the incident with no charges, concluding it was an "industrial accident." Gun enthusiasts quickly moved on.

On an online travel-review site for Bullets and Burgers, amid glowing comments about how fun it is to shoot big firearms, a lone visitor posted a discordant message:

"What in the name of Jesus is wrong with us, Americans? Automatic weapons as toys?"

It's safe to say that in America, when it comes to firearms, the risk-perception gap can be as wide as the Grand Canyon. There are several reasons.

Guns are deeply ingrained in the country's history, so any calculation of whether or how to interact with them starts from a place of generalized acceptance. There is also what I would call an artifice of safety loosely wrapped around gun commerce that can give the consumer a false sense that they are "doing it right." Someone may take a gun-safety class, entrust their kid to a trained instructor at a shooting range, or obey the laws around carrying a weapon and feel as if they're being responsible.

But the numbers alone belie any notion that such measures make a decisive difference. In all but one of the last ten years, the number of accidental shootings has exceeded the number of times a gun was fired in self-defense, according to data collected by the Gun Violence Archive, a nonpartisan project that tracks shootings in the United States. In 2024, more than twenty-seven thousand people killed themselves with guns. Firearms remain a leading cause of death generally and are used in about 80 percent of all homicides.

The permissiveness around gun ownership in many parts of the country can contribute to the misguided sense of personal security, leading to unintended consequences. Some border on farce. In St. Louis in May 2022 a man openly carrying his AR-15 inside a grocery store for self-defense—it's legal to do that in Missouri—was robbed of the weapon on his way out. The thief held a pistol to the back of the victim's head and took the rifle. The victim then retrieved a second gun from his vehicle and shot the robber. During the mayhem, a *third* armed man surfaced (a "good guy with a gun" perhaps?) and also shot the robber. Two innocent women were hit with stray bullets.

Unintended consequences with firearms are all the more painful when kids are involved. Because adults cannot be counted on to always act responsibly, there are statutes and regulations to provide a safety net for most things. We childproof swimming pools, laundry detergent, and car seats, but there is no federal law requiring that a gun be secured in a home with children.

Numerous attempts over the years to require the use of gun locks and storage devices or to incentivize the development of smart-gun technology, where a gun can only be fired by its biometrically paired owner, have been stymied. The one law that came close, the impressively named Child Safety Lock Act of 2005, only mandates that a lock be included when a pistol is sold, not that anyone actually use it.

Similarly, we also protect consumers from defective products. We enforce standards for extension cords, chainsaws, and lawn mowers, but not for guns, which might accidentally discharge or misfire. Congress made sure they were exempt from regulation by the Consumer Product Safety Commission.

Against this backdrop, the combination of kids and guns inevitably produces tragic results. And it's even worse than imagined. When I looked into the circumstances of accidental shootings involving children, I was shocked to discover that the official numbers undercounted the actual frequency of these tragedies by about 50 percent. That's because of quirks in the way local coroners report deaths.

One would think that when a toddler picks up a loaded handgun from a dresser drawer and shoots his nine-month-old brother, as happened in a Texas household in 1999, it would obviously be ruled accidental. But I got the Bexar County medical examiner's report and found that the death was declared a homicide—because it occurred "at the hands of another." Intent wasn't even considered.

That case, and hundreds of others, don't show up in the federal statistics for accidental shootings, which are, of course, compiled for the purpose of helping Americans weigh the risks.

The heedless integration of firearms into American life is not solely explainable by historical undercurrents, such as the grand schemes of the NRA and the gun industry to inculcate pro-gun attitudes in young people. Larger cultural and social forces have also become increasingly important.

As I began exploring them more deeply, it quickly became apparent that modern-day gun culture has entered a phase akin to the late-stage Roman Empire, when success and power devolved into selfish extravagance. No longer was it enough to argue that sports shooting, hunting, and self-defense justified an expansive interpretation of the Second Amendment—simply having fun with guns was now a God-given right.

On a 550-acre desert expanse in the unincorporated township of Pahrump, Nevada, you can pay for Rolling Thunder, an "adrenaline-fueled experience" of high-speed tactical shooting from an off-road vehicle, offered by Staccato Vegas, an offshoot of the Staccato gun company. A marketing brochure shows a blond woman wearing mirrored shades blasting away with a semiautomatic rifle painted like an American flag.

For a $1,000 annual Patriot membership plan, you get 50 percent off on "run-n-gun" courses, free firearms cleaning, and unlimited monthly guest passes. If you're willing to pay $3,000 to upgrade to the Freedom plan, you get additional perks such as concierge services, on-demand food and beverage, preloaded magazines for your pistol or rifle when you arrive, and exclusive access to the Staccato 368 Lounge (368 supposedly was a code used for the word *liberty* by Revolutionary War patriots).

If all of this sounds rather silly, Staccato wants you to know that it is their solemn obligation as red-blooded Americans. At Staccato, you see, "We believe in protecting freedom and celebrating liberty:

"It's a part of who we are as Americans, allowing us the freedom to be individuals and for each of us to pursue our own unique happiness."

To join this assembly of patriots, you must buy at least one Staccato pistol.

Sport-shooting clubs have been around for at least a century. In olden days, they mostly entailed well-to-do men gathering at some secluded retreat to drink, smoke, play cards, and occasionally shoot bolt-action rifles at targets or maybe go out for a hunt. They were genteel affairs.

In recent decades, entrepreneurs have taken this concept and jacked it on steroids. Numerous oases of controlled violence dot barren landscapes in Nevada, Arizona, and Texas, with indoor facilities as well in Los Angeles, Chicago, and Philadelphia. In Las Vegas, the Range 702 offers bachelorette parties, where ladies can shoot machine guns and get a free shot glass, followed by drinks and a "limo to Larry Flynt's Hustler Club."

Luxury is a defining theme. An NRA blog post from 2017 explained the emergence of a new name to describe the phenomenon: *guntry club*. Acknowledging that "gun culture could inspire thoughts of dark and cold ranges, dusty or muddy outdoor environments or even loud, brash and unforgiving crowds," guntry clubs sought to combine the shooting experience with luxury accoutrements of traditional country clubs.

Some of these places are fashioned as family theme parks, combining sightseeing, swimming, and horseback riding with shooting machine guns and grenade launchers. "Drive a tank! Crush cars!" blares an ad for Bullets and Burgers, the apocalyptic playground in Arizona where the shooting instructor was accidentally killed by a nine-year-old girl with an Uzi. If you're willing to part with $2,300, the Super Platinum Shooting Package gets you access to eight machine guns of your choice, a flamethrower, and a gigantic .50-caliber tripod-mounted sniper rifle "used in several Hollywood hits including *Jumanji* and *Rambo II*."

The relative wealth and professional status of the tragedy-struck MacLachlan family came as somewhat of a surprise to me. I suppose that betrays my own biased assumptions about the type of person who would want to go to a place such as Bullets and Burgers. Part of my preconception was based on my experience in the 1990s visiting gun ranges such as the one in Kentucky where you could pay to blow up gas-filled barrels—"Machine gun and flame thrower rentals available Friday, Saturday and Sunday!" It was the epitome of "loud, brash and unforgiving."

Since then, it seemed, the audience had expanded to include a demographic I had not thought would be as interested in it. When I learned about the MacLachlan incident it immediately brought to mind an eerily similar case I knew of involving a physician from Connecticut. In that tragic incident, the doctor's eight-year-old boy was accidentally shot in the head when he lost control of an Uzi submachine gun he was given at a range in Massachusetts (unlike the Arizona case, this one led to criminal indictments and changes in the law).

Well-educated, well-off parents with the freedom to choose any number of healthy, memorable adventures for their children gravitated to ones centered around instruments of lethal violence as entertainment. Some of this was undoubtedly influenced by the gun lobby's decades-long effort to position firearms as an acceptable way to teach responsibility to kids by making shooting a family-friendly pastime.

But there were deeper societal currents working as well. Legally purchasing and maintaining a decent firearm has never been cheap. One consequence of restricting imports of inexpensive guns such as so-called Saturday night specials—which in the 1960s and early '70s could be bought for as little as $10—is that it allowed American-made guns to be sold at even higher prices. Gun control advocates such as Sen. Thomas Dodd were often accused of pushing import bans, in part, to protect homegrown manufacturers, such as Colt, Winchester, and Sturm, Ruger in Dodd's state of Connecticut.

Import restrictions under the 1968 Gun Control Act required firearms to be for "sporting purposes" and go through licensed dealers. The foreign-made guns that continued to be imported, such as the Beretta, tended to be higher quality and thus more costly. And as the AR-15 took off as a cultural icon, the money required to partake in the fun increased exponentially. Gun industry marketing adjusted to target higher earners, who could more easily afford the advanced weaponry they were selling.

By 2014, households earning more than $90,000 were nearly twice as likely to have guns in the home than those earning less than $50,000. A 2019 study found that "slightly less than half of US guns were owned by persons whose household income was $100,000 a year or more."

At the same time, the typical education level of the people buying these weapons was also on the rise. In 1994, 29 percent of gun owners had some college education. By 2017, that figure had risen to 34 percent, and by 2022 it was 40 percent. Of course, educational attainment for Americans in general has been trending upward, but the concentration of gun ownership among wealthier households outpaced the extra income that accompanies higher levels of schooling.

There is no better window into this phenomenon than the history of the Staccato Vegas gun range in Pahrump, Nevada. The place actually began under a different name and ownership. It started as the vision of Ignatius Piazza, a chiropractor from California, who founded a firearms training program he called Front Sight. But it wasn't just about shooting.

From the beginning, Piazza imagined more than dusty target ranges nestled in the desert canyons. He obtained a development agreement with the county to build a "vacation club and resort" that would include thousands of time-share condos, single-family homes, a hotel, and a recreational park, among other amenities—a veritable town dedicated to gun lovers.

To join Front Sight required paying membership fees that could reportedly exceed $200,000 at the topmost "lifetime" tiers, which included a luxury home site. I had a hard time believing anyone would actually pay that much, but fortunately there was a way to find out: Front Sight filed for bankruptcy protection in 2022, and buried in the thousands of court records I found a list of close to three thousand members and the amounts they were said to have paid. The membership costs ranged from $500 to $350,000.

There was the real estate sales and investment consultant from California who paid $165,000; an oncologist and vineyard owner, also from California, was in for $148,000; a corporate lawyer in Illinois paid $106,000; for a physician in Arizona it was $50,000; a tech consultant in New Jersey, $48,000. And on and on.

The chief operating officer of Front Sight once described the clientele this way:

"We've got people that are college students to Forbes 400 guys. The economic spectrum is quite broad, but what we find is there's very few, like forty or fifty, who actually want a residence. What they want is an upscale place to stay for the week or two that they're out here."

What motivates them? Bruce, a "gold status" member and CEO of a tech company in Orange County, California, explained why he brought his fourteen-year-old son and members of his family's church group to the range: "The feeling of security that I come home with, that I'm able to protect my family with all the craziness going on in this world."

Michelle, a tax accountant from Liberty, Missouri, spent weeks at Front Sight with relatives and "girls from my office" learning to shoot and "be ready to defend our family." Grant, a software-company executive from Bloomington, Minnesota, came with friends because "it's really important to be able to defend myself and defend my family if I ever got into that situation."

As much as self-defense may be the practical, mature rationale participants offer when asked, many also gravitate to these guntry clubs for entertainment. The industry has been remarkably successful at selling the eat-your-spinach objective of skills training in a sugary wrapper of fun, comfort, or excitement.

And for that, the lure of cool "forbidden" stuff comes in handy.

Desert Wolf Tours in Arizona offers packages for bachelor and bachelorette parties and corporate retreats that combine off-road ATV driving with shooting machine guns, which they are licensed to operate. One of them, priced at $314 per person, is the Machine Guns and Suppressors Adventure, which is cosponsored by a company that makes silencers or, in the industry's preferred parlance, suppressors:

"Shoot REAL, Federally-Restricted Machine Guns and Suppressors! These are the REAL DEAL!"

The use of guns for entertainment and over-the-top recreation may be all in good fun (the wisdom of it notwithstanding), but a darker element to the modern idolization of firearms and violence can be found in our political discourse. Here, the societal effects are especially profound because, for better or worse, our elected leaders both reflect and set the tone for what's considered "normal."

For schoolchildren, a visit to their class by a politician once conveyed a sense of seriousness and civic duty. Students today could be forgiven for confusing it with professional wrestling.

To be sure, American politics has a long history of bare-knuckle excesses. The 1828 presidential campaign featured accusations, circulated in dueling handbills, that Andrew Jackson was a cannibal and John Quincy Adams a pimp. In modern times, negative attacks on opponents have tended to emphasize fear as much as slander and innuendo. Democrats can lay claim to one of the most notorious examples—the "Daisy ad" of 1964, showing a little girl plucking flower petals followed by a nuclear blast, the unsubtle message being that a vote for Republican Barry Goldwater meant the end of the world.

At the same time, as the NRA made support for gun rights a potent political signifier, it became increasingly common for candidates from both parties to flaunt their love of firearms. Traditionally, they struck relatively tame poses—hunting ducks or shooting at targets—just enough to reassure voters for whom guns were important. But in the 2010s, political messaging around guns took a sharp turn. Conservative opposition to President Obama and the rise of the Tea Party movement propelled a class of antiestablishment Republicans to the fore, along with increasingly agitated campaign ads of a different caliber—literally.

In Arizona, there was Pamela Gorman bragging about her NRA rating in 2010 by firing a machine gun, an AR-15, and a semiautomatic pistol. Another Arizona candidate, Jesse Kelly, promoted a campaign event that year where supporters could "shoot a fully automatic M16" with him. Around the same time, Christina Jeffrey in South Carolina ran an ad in which she brandished an AK-47 while asserting that gun rights were necessary "to ensure that our limited government stays limited."

Will Brooke, who unsuccessfully sought the Republican nomination for Congress in Alabama in 2014, ran an ad in which he used a small arsenal of semiautomatic weapons to blow holes in a printed copy of the "Obamacare" law. He was mimicking a milder ad from four years earlier showing West Virginia Sen. Joe Manchin, a Democrat, shooting a bolt-action rifle at a different bill.

In the 2016 Missouri governor's race, Eric Greitens, a Republican and former Navy SEAL, took gun imagery to new heights in two ads, one showing him firing a mounted machine gun while pledging to "fight Obama's Democrat machine and their corrupt attacks." In the other, he shot an assault-style rifle at an unseen target until it blew up. And in 2018, there was the not-so-subtle ad for Republican Kay Ivey, the governor of Alabama, showing two men loading pistols at a range while saying they are "sick of those DC politicians" and that Ms. Ivey "protected our monuments."

What was different about these is that the political messaging featured a firearm but, unlike in the past, the focus was neither pro-gun nor pro–gun control. Rather, the gun itself was a prop used as a sort of ominous exclamation point for some other argument.

The careless flaunting of firearms by these twenty-first-century pols stood in stark contrast to earlier generations of elected leaders, who may have supported gun rights but didn't shove it in people's faces. The discourse had become so militant that even John Dingell, the archetype of the pro-gun politician, was having doubts.

In a memoir published shortly before he died in 2019, Dingell recounted watching his wife, who had succeeded him in Congress, give a speech pleading for reason and a spirit of compromise to address gun violence. Thinking about it the next day, he said he found himself regretting that "the gun debate had gotten too polarized."

"As Debbie had said with such passion the night before, 'Can't we have a *discussion*?'" Dingell wrote. "And I thought about the role I know I played in contributing to that polarization."

Compromise, however, does not sell as well with certain constituencies as performative antics, which have only gotten more extreme in the years since Dingell's ruminations. Republican Congressmen Thomas Massie of Kentucky and Andy Ogles of Tennessee sent out Christmas cards in 2021 showing their families posing with assault rifles. A Republican Senate candidate in Georgia, Josh Clark, held weekly giveaways of AR-15s in 2022 to ensure voters are equipped to "fight tyranny and evil" and filmed himself with his kids shooting one of the rifles. And in 2024 in Missouri, Republican attorney general candidate Will Scharf fired a grenade launcher at a stack of documents from Trump-related court cases.

Watching these ads, I found myself thinking of another politician from a bygone era, Robert F. Kennedy, and his remarks about gun ownership after his brother, the president, was assassinated:

"We have a responsibility to the victims of crime and violence. It is a responsibility to think not only of our own convenience but of the tragedy of sudden death. It is a responsibility to put away childish things, to make the possession and use of firearms a matter undertaken only by serious people who will use them with the restraint and maturity that their dangerous nature deserves and demands."

WAR OF ATTRITION

THE NRA'S MAIN shooting range can be found in the bowels of the beast, directly below the group's headquarters in the Washington, DC, suburbs. To get to it, you loop around past the NRA café to a parking garage and down a ramp into a gloomy concrete bunker.

I had gone there in the fall of 2024 at the invitation of the American Suppressor Association, the lobbying group for the industry that makes and markets silencers. It used to be called the American Silencer Association, but decided a rebrand using the term *suppressor* would help disassociate the devices from their negative connotation as tools of assassins.

Frankly, I was a little surprised they got me in. The NRA has never returned my calls over the years, having apparently written me off as a "libtard" journalist who's not with the program when it comes to guns. When I arrived, a team was waiting that included two NRA execs, including a wary-looking public-affairs rep keeping an eye on me, and two guys from the suppressor association.

Their purpose that day was to educate me on the benefits and harmlessness of silencers.

There are few clearer windows into the state of American gun culture than the campaign to gin up public demand for an obscure firearm accessory known mostly as a favorite of spies and Hollywood hit men. Doing that would require changing laws and regulations, some of them in place for more than a century. They were enacted by state legislatures and Congress during the 1900s in response to what was commonly viewed as an unnecessary risk posed by silencers, which were being used in stealthy murders, Prohibition-era gang violence, and illegal hunts.

Now, an industry-driven effort was afoot to mainstream and ultimately deregulate silencers by repurposing them as health-care devices for preventing hearing damage to hunters and sports shooters.

When I first learned about this campaign, I was fascinated by how it fit in with the overall movement to broaden gun rights. On the one hand, it was just the latest example of the gun lobby pushing the boundaries of what is acceptable. From ghost guns and bump stocks to public carrying of weapons, the goal is virtually unlimited freedoms—and profits—under the protective umbrella of the Second Amendment.

However, it became apparent that the push to unfetter silencers could also be viewed as a sort of capstone to the modern gun lobby's decades-long project to transform Americans' relationship to firearms by advancing a particular view of freedom. Having vanquished attempts to ban assault weapons, secured protection against liability, achieved a radical reinterpretation of the Second Amendment, and captured popular culture, what was left to conquer?

To that end, it was worth exploring how exactly the campaign worked and, importantly, what it revealed about the gun lobby's endgame. Because while the silencers saga was uniquely significant, it was also part and parcel of the larger ongoing effort by the gun rights movement to cement its wins in the war of attrition against limits on firearms.

My journey would not only take me to the basement of the NRA, but also put me on the trail of phantom advocacy groups fueled by millions in dark money and bring me to the doorstep of an elusive academic whose controversial pro–gun rights research was cited by the Supreme Court. It began, however, in the archives of Hiram Percy Maxim.

Maxim was the son of Hiram Stevens Maxim, the inventor of the machine gun, and he inherited his father's knack for creative engineering.

The younger Maxim graduated from the Massachusetts Institute of Technology in 1886 and became fascinated with combustion engines, which propelled the new "horseless carriages." But after several years of attempting to build his own engine, he grew less sanguine about them, writing later that they "shook and trembled and rattled and clattered, spat oil, fire, smoke, and smell.

"It was revolting," he declared.

Maxim turned his attention instead to taming another by-product of the industrial revolution that he found particularly annoying: loud noise. Using various configurations of baffles encased in metal tubes, he came up with the first exhaust mufflers for car engines. The concept was later applied to other types of motors and machinery for boats and factories.

But his interest in sound-dampening was not limited to industrial uses. Maxim had grown up in a family steeped in firearms. In addition to his father, his uncle, Hudson Maxim, also was heavily involved in that field, having invented new forms of smokeless gunpowder and high explosives. The younger Maxim enjoyed target shooting at his home, but did not want the earsplitting cracks of gunfire to bother neighbors, so he applied his muffler design to the problem.

The result: the first silencer for guns. Maxim, who received a patent for the device in 1909, set about marketing it not only for a quieter sports-shooting experience, but also for militaries to confuse the enemy on the battlefield. Before long, however, criminals also discovered the benefits of stealth conferred by Maxim's silencer.

One by one, states started banning silencers after they turned up in shootings, murders, and illegal hunts, and by the Prohibition era they were regularly associated with gang violence nationwide. Amid the public uproar, Maxim finally stopped making firearm silencers in 1930.

But the basic technology was now out in the wild, and the federal government finally moved to crack down on it. When Congress drafted the National Firearms Act of 1934, its restrictions covered not only machine guns and short-barreled shotguns, but also silencers. No one seriously questioned the wisdom of this.

Historically, it was widely recognized that the only real civilian use for silencers was to more sneakily kill someone. In the modern era, they can make it harder to recognize the sound of an active shooter in a school, shopping mall, or other public space. As a federal appeals court said in a 1970 gun case, "The government does not suggest that there are legitimate uses for silencers, and none come to mind; uses which do come to mind are assassination and armed robbery. . . . The relation between silencers and violent crime is so obvious."

The restrictions proved effective. When Payton Gendron was planning his mass shooting in Buffalo in 2022, he thought it would be helpful to have a silencer for his AR-15–style rifle. In addition to mitigating sound and muzzle flash, a silencer would reduce recoil, making it easier to quickly continue aiming and shooting. However, because of laws in place, Gendron could not readily obtain one.

"Unfortunately," he wrote in his manifesto, "suppressors are hard to get in the U.S. legally, and I don't have the machining equipment to make one."

The current project to mainstream silencers, which began in the 2010s and really hit its stride during the first Trump administration, has been driven by the industry from the start. The CEO of Sturm, Ruger told Wall Street analysts in 2017, "Our big focus right now is going to be on suppressors" because they "are an emerging market that really have taken the whole shooting industry by storm."

Key to that would be pushing the idea that silencers are necessary to protect against hearing loss. Of course, sports shooters and practice ranges commonly use ear protection already, and Americans have been hunting with unsilenced firearms for centuries. But now the industry was insisting that such activities were an urgent public health issue and was pushing legislation in Congress to remove silencers from the National Firearms Act.

Under the federal law, silencer purchases had to be registered and required submitting fingerprints and a photograph, undergoing a background check, and paying a $200 tax—which in 1934 was equivalent to almost $5,000 today. Initially, that steep fee effectively kept silencers out of circulation, but it was never adjusted for inflation and was, in 2025, repealed as part of President Trump's budget bill. More problematic for the firearms industry are state laws restricting silencers—eight states, including New York, where Payton Gendron was located, don't allow them at all.

But the gun lobby has been chipping away at those restrictions, filing legal challenges with the ultimate goal of elevating one up to a sympathetic Supreme Court. Despite the legal hurdles, gun companies have achieved remarkable success in destigmatizing and marketing silencers—roughly 5 million were registered in 2024, up from 285,000 in 2011.

Despite the nerdy earnestness of industry lobbyists citing audiology studies, you won't find many silencer ads focusing on ear protection. Instead, the imagery and branding is all about coolness and masculinity, with big-biceps guys in black T-shirts brandishing tactical-looking guns with silencer brands named Spectre, Scythe, or Wolfman.

That vibe, however, was absent when I met the men from the silencer industry at the NRA shooting range. The suppressor association president was Knox Williams, a well-spoken young man who graduated magna cum laude from the University of Georgia with a degree in history.

"We think the law-abiding citizen should have the ability to purchase a suppressor and exercise their Second Amendment rights, whether it's hunting, recreational shooting, using it for self-defense," Williams told me. "We think people should be given the tools, and given the choice to pick the tools, that they use to help protect one of their five senses when they're shooting."

All of us donned safety glasses and ear protection, and Williams began by firing some guns with, and without, a silencer to demonstrate the difference in sound. He then let me do the same thing using an AR-15–style rifle.

I'm always struck by the seductive qualities of the AR-15 once it's in your hands. It's almost like the malevolent ring in the Tolkien novels that infuses you with a desire to wield its dark power. You can see why it has so completely captured the imaginations of gun enthusiasts. Aiming the rifle at the target downrange, I had a fleeting thought of what it would be like to point it at a frightened unarmed civilian, and the spell was broken.

The bottom line of this little adventure was that while a silencer—a baffled cylinder that redirects expanding gases from a fired round—can reduce noise below the 140-decibel limit for what is considered safe, it doesn't eliminate it completely. A suppressed gunshot can still be loud.

And this is the sweet spot the silencer industry wants. It wishes to promote the hearing-protection benefits, while at the same time asserting that the sound is still loud enough to mitigate public-safety concerns about making gunshots harder to recognize. One problem, though, is that although a suppressed gunshot may be noisy, it can sound different—less like a booming crack and more like a thin *thwap*.

During a mass shooting in 2019 at a municipal complex in Virginia Beach, in which a city employee, DeWayne Craddock, used a silencer when he shot and killed twelve people, witnesses said they mistook the sound for nearby construction workers operating a nail gun. Christi Dewar, who was in the building at the time, said if it had sounded like "a regular gunshot we would've definitely known a lot sooner, even if we would've had thirty or sixty seconds more."

The altered sound is such that the company that sells ShotSpotter gunfire-detection services to police departments does not guarantee in its contracts that it can pick up shots fired with a silencer.

To be sure, instances of silencers linked to crimes remain low, though they have been gradually increasing. Gun rights groups claim this shows criminal use of silencers is not a problem, while gun safety advocates say it is simply proof that regulation works.

In May 2024, a Pennsylvania man was sentenced to ten years in prison for selling "hit kits" comprising untraceable ghost guns, silencers, and special ammunition that is quieter than regular rounds. Elsewhere in the world, a silencer was used in the assassination of a businessman on a street in Istanbul in August 2024. That same month, a shop owner in a city in Colombia was targeted by someone using a silencer. Poachers in South Africa were sentenced to jail a few months later for using a silencer to quietly kill protected rhinos.

To get a better sense of the risks, I talked to a couple of experts not associated with the gun industry. Thomas Chittum, a former ATF official, said that although, historically, suppressed gunfire still made an identifiable noise, technological advancements were changing that. Subsonic ammunition that travels slower than the speed of sound and thus does not create a sonic boom when it exits the muzzle of a gun can render a shot almost completely quiet.

"Silenced is a misnomer," Chittum said, "but with development of subsonic ammo and a high-quality silencer, they're getting pretty close."

That's a big red flag for Robert Spitzer, a political scientist and gun scholar at the State University of New York, who has testified against deregulating silencers. He told me that being able to easily recognize the sound of gunfire is "critical, whether it's criminal use of a gun or a mass shooting or you're out hiking in the woods and somebody is hunting.

"If the gun industry was really interested in protecting hearing, they would provide for free or at a reduced cost a set of hearing protectors when guns are sold, the same way they do with gun locks. This is all driven by commercialism."

It's worth dwelling on the strategy used in this deregulatory effort, for it is a textbook example of how the gun lobby seeks to change laws and influence public perceptions with the slippery use of information that is sometimes misleading, exaggerated, or false.

Industry lobbyists began by working with Republicans in Congress to introduce pro-silencer bills with names like SHUSH, for Silencers Help Us Save Hearing. To promote the legislation, the National Shooting Sports Foundation, the firearm industry's trade group, produced a fact sheet that asserts American restrictions on silencers are out of step because the use of them has "long been mandated in many countries." In other statements, the foundation claimed some European nations "require the use of a suppressor for recreational shooting and hunting."

However, I couldn't find any such laws in Europe or elsewhere around the world. When I asked the foundation to point to examples of it, it could not do so.

"At this time, I cannot direct you to definitive law that specifically requires the use of a suppressor," said a spokesperson for the foundation.

Similar claims surfaced elsewhere. The American College of Emergency Physicians posted an article extolling the benefits of silencers that said, erroneously, they are mandatory "in many European countries" and that gun owners in France "are fined and penalized for firing guns without a suppressor." French gun laws are stricter than those in the United States, and while silencers are legal, there is no requirement to use them. Asked to provide sources for his information, the article's author, a doctor at the University of Illinois, told me he could not recall where those details came from.

An industry-backed lawsuit in Illinois that sought to overturn a state ban on silencers cited a line from a study by Stephen Halbrook, the firearms scholar and lawyer who has worked closely with the NRA. The study said silencers are allowed in many countries under varying degrees of restrictions, and that in Germany they "may be required" for professional hunters and others. But German laws governing firearms do not require the use of silencers. In an email to me, Halbrook noted that he wrote "may be"—not "are"—and added that "where wildlife must be culled near populated areas, local authorities likely require noise reduction measures via use of suppressors."

The Illinois lawsuit also said that the Centers for Disease Control has "recommended the use of suppressors for hearing protection," a claim that gun companies have also made in marketing materials. Those assertions stem from studies of workplace hazards for shooting instructors at two federal-government training facilities, including one where extremely loud military weapons were used.

But a spokesperson for the CDC told me in 2024 that the National Institute for Occupational Safety and Health, the subagency that conducted the studies, "has no policy statement specific to the use of suppressors on firearms." She said neither study—which noted the sound-reduction benefit of silencers but also urged the use of traditional ear protection—made recommendations related to the civilian use of silencers for hunting or recreation.

When I asked Williams, the president of the suppressor association, about this, he suggested the government was splitting hairs. The "dangers associated with exposure to impulse noises as loud as gunfire do not discriminate between military, law enforcement, or civilian applications," he said. "At the end of the day, we are talking about the same human ears."

In September 2025, the suppressor association, along with the NRA and a newer gun rights group called the Firearms Policy Coalition, announced another federal lawsuit, this one seeking to declare the National Firearms Act of 1934 unconstitutional as it applies to silencers and short-barreled rifles. The argument was that because Congress earlier in 2025 had zeroed out the NFA tax on those items, there was no longer constitutional support for other elements of the law, including registration requirements.

In making its case, the lawsuit quoted some of the usual experts, such as Halbrook and David Kopel, and compared the registration requirements for buying a silencer to the disarming of the Jews by the Nazis and the tyranny of King George III. It also cited the Supreme Court's 2022 ruling in *Bruen*.

The *Bruen* case has proven incredibly helpful to the gun lobby as it goes around the country challenging restrictions on assault weapons, large-capacity magazines, and more. As I looked into the legal front of the gun rights movement, I was amazed at how this particular ruling quickly rose to the top of its arsenal—*Bruen* was cited ten times in the newest silencer lawsuit, three more than the *Heller* ruling.

I decided to try to find out more about how that consequential decision was made. It was widely viewed in legal circles as opening a Pandora's box of unintended effects, and indeed the Supreme Court has tried to do cleanup in several follow-up cases that cited the logic of *Bruen* to try to invalidate laws barring alleged domestic abusers or drug users from having guns. What did the court base its *Bruen* decision on in the first place, and what role did the gun lobby play in securing that big win for itself?

Part of the answer to those questions can be found in a nondescript building on Painted Mirage Road, just north of the Las Vegas Strip, where $189 could get you a corporate address and the option to rent office space by the hour. In virtual Suite 320 is where one finds the Center for Human Liberty, whose high-minded purpose is to "defend and advance individual liberty and freedom."

In exchange for pursuing its selfless goals, the Center for Human Liberty was relieved from having to pay taxes.

"We're pleased to tell you we determined you're exempt from federal income tax under Internal Revenue Code Section 501(c)(3)," the IRS informed the center in a letter. "Donors can deduct contributions they make to you."

The center's first significant contribution, in 2021, was for $100,000 and came from something called the FPC Action Foundation—an offshoot of the Firearms Policy Coalition. The foundation shares the same virtual office suite and leadership as the center, and its tax-exempt mission sounds similar: "to create a world of maximal liberty and freedom."

The Center for Human Liberty has no staff or website. There's nobody to call or email if one was curious about what exactly the center has done in pursuit of its charitable mission. But there is one place where you can find some trace of its activities: the US Supreme Court.

On July 20, 2021, the center—which had been created only a couple of months earlier—joined a professor, William English, in filing an amicus brief in the *Bruen* case. The center's brief showcased a new piece of research by Dr. English: the 2021 National Firearms Survey. English, a political scientist at Georgetown University with no public track record of doing gun studies, had just days before come out with the results of his survey of more than sixteen thousand gun owners—the largest of its kind ever conducted. He posted his findings on the Social Science Research Network website, where just about anyone can upload academic papers that have not been published or peer-reviewed.

The findings purported to show that guns, including AR-15–style rifles and high-capacity magazines, were commonly used for self-defense, bolstering arguments that Americans should enjoy an expansive Second Amendment right to own them. As for why the Center for Human Liberty had joined the professor in promoting his research, it explained in the amicus brief that it "shares English's interest in ensuring that the court is presented with the most objective and accurate social science evidence and analysis available."

The brief ended up carrying weight during the Supreme Court's proceedings. The lead attorney for the pro-gun plaintiffs in the case, a former US solicitor general, cited it during oral arguments, referring the justices to its "very rigorous statistical analysis." And Justice Samuel Alito invoked it in his concurring opinion, when the court's conservative majority issued their ruling siding with the plaintiffs.

The center would surface again in other cases challenging restrictions on firearms. In 2023, it filed an amicus in a Hawaii court, this time partnering with someone described as a former professor and writer, whose record of scholarship seemed limited to a handful of unpublished history papers. That same year, the center filed its own brief, by itself, in another Supreme Court case, siding with a violent drug dealer who challenged a federal law denying guns to people under domestic-violence protective orders. To justify its interest in the matter, it explained it was simply advancing its mission to "promote the protection of liberty."

Despite its murky origins, that respectable lawyers write and cite the Center for Human Liberty's legal briefs lends it credibility, and even its name would seem to convey an air of gravitas. It has managed to get itself heard and taken seriously in judicial proceedings across the country, including the highest court in the land.

All in a day's work for the gun lobby's latest sock puppet.

Supreme Court dockets were not always Potemkin villages where special interests hide behind seemingly independent amicus filers like so many phony storefronts. Ironically, the practice traces its origins to progressive efforts to improve working conditions for vulnerable women a century ago.

The history of amicus, or "friend of the court," briefs dates to the early 1900s, when future Supreme Court Justice Louis Brandeis, then a progressive lawyer, broke with tradition and submitted a filing filled with references not to legal precedents but actual data points about harsh labor practices in factories.

His was not an amicus brief. Rather, it was a plaintiff's argument, but it differed from usual practices in that it entered into the record nonlegal information about real-world conditions. What would become known as the Brandeis Brief would change the way the high court deliberated over cases and opened the door to what eventually became an assembly line of amicus filers bearing baskets of supposed facts.

Though in principle the notion of the justices having to consider empirical input from outside the narrow legal confines of a case sounds appealing, in practice it has sometimes proven to be a dangerous embarrassment. The high court has no mechanism for vetting the content or authorship of amicus briefs. This makes it easy to game the system with multiple submissions to create a false appearance of broad-based support and enter into the record biased, or unreliable, information.

When it came time for gun rights advocates to line up behind the NRA-backed plaintiffs in the Supreme Court's *Bruen* case in 2021, the usual roll call of scholars was there.

Stephen Halbrook filed an amicus brief on behalf of the National African American Gun Association. David Hardy and Joyce Malcolm each appeared with separate briefs, filed jointly with the Firearms Policy Coalition, an aggressive litigation group that has replaced the NRA as the most prolific filer of pro-gun lawsuits in the country.

Compared to the NRA, the coalition is a relative newcomer. It was formed in 2012 by several West Coast groups to try to bring younger people into gun rights advocacy. With the social media mantra "Superior firepower through superior memes (and lawsuits)," it hawks hoodies and coffee mugs with in-your-face messaging such as "Abolish the ATF." Its leader, Brandon Combs, a California gun rights activist, has a knack for drawing attention. He once told a newspaper that replicating New Zealand's assault weapons ban in the United States would lead to "armed resistance, if not outright armed conflict."

For all its edginess, the coalition is also tightly entwined with an influential network of established lawyers and scholars that has been central to the gun lobby's success. In addition to its work in *Bruen* with Malcolm and Hardy, the group is frequently represented in other gun cases by Erik Jaffe, a former law clerk to Justice Clarence Thomas, who wrote the majority opinion in *Bruen*.

The coalition, through its related entity, the FPC Action Foundation, was behind the creation of the Center for Human Liberty, the phantom outfit that operates out of a virtual office space in Las Vegas. If this daisy chain of organizations is hard to follow, that's at least partly by design.

In my reporting on *Bruen*, I discovered that the Firearms Policy Coalition was connected to *at least six* briefs filed with the high court by various organizations, including the Madison Society Foundation and California Gun Rights Foundation. Still other groups that seemed to have come out of nowhere for the *Bruen* case had such names as Asian Pacific American Gun Owners Association and League for Law Enforcement, Sportsmen and Defense, each formed days or weeks before filing amicus briefs.

A number of briefs cited the work of Dr. English, the Georgetown professor whose work was promoted by the Center for Human Liberty. Though I was first made aware of him through *Bruen*, I became intrigued when I noticed how the influence of English's work had since stretched far beyond that case. He and his gun study were being cited in scores of other lawsuits, as well as in judges' rulings overturning restrictions on assault weapons and high-capacity magazines.

His work was also facing criticism from some researchers, who asserted that the way English conducted his survey could skew the results in a pro-gun direction. Far from his claim that Americans defend themselves with guns 1.67 million times a year, other studies, while ranging widely, have put the figure as low as seventy thousand. One longtime firearms researcher, Dr. Matthew Miller at Northeastern University, dismissed English's findings as "absurd."

How did English come up with such a high number?

For one thing, his definition of self-defense with a firearm was so broad it included someone simply telling another person they had one, without actually using it. English also counted respondents whose purported self-defense incident could have happened years or even decades ago, potentially inflating the numbers. And in the paper he wrote describing the results, he omitted setups to some of the survey questions that potentially influenced the responses.

Joseph Blocher, codirector of the Center for Firearms Law at

Duke University, said he was "struck by the enormous attention and influence" English's study had achieved, given the questions swirling around it.

"It just sort of came out of nowhere, posted online without going through formal peer review, and by a guy most of us had never heard of," he said.

I was curious to learn how English suddenly burst onto the scene with his firearms survey, when he seemed to have no history with the subject. On his website, he describes his research focus as human behavior, including ethics and "how to lie with data science." Adding to the mystery was, despite having a lengthy record of publishing his work in well-regarded journals, English did not do that with his firearms survey. Instead, he simply uploaded it to the web.

He had rarely spoken publicly about his motivations for the survey, but when he did, he described it as part of an ongoing book project. In one news article, he made it sound almost like happenstance: "It kind of dawned on me that there's a real opportunity here just as a scholar to contribute to this literature."

The aw-shucks air of serendipity heightened the value of English's work to gun rights groups because, unlike the more established gallery of academics and lawyers whose connections to the NRA were well-known, English appeared to have no such ties. His interest, as his *Bruen* brief asserted, was simply "ensuring that the court is presented with the most objective and accurate social science evidence and analysis available."

But was that really all there was to it? In early 2024 I started digging and eventually found that English did have prior connections to the gun lobby. He served as an expert witness for pro-gun plaintiffs in several lawsuits, including one backed by the NRA in which he produced a poll of gun owners that served as a precursor to his national survey. And he received tens of thousands of dollars from a mysterious pro-gun nonprofit, whose contact info was a nonworking email address and a UPS Store mailbox. The grant to English from the nonprofit, called the Constitutional Defense Fund, was among millions of dollars in payments the group made to the Firearms Policy Coalition and Second Amendment law firms in the lead-up to the *Bruen* ruling.

I tried to talk to English about all this. I emailed, called, left messages. I visited his office at Georgetown. I went to his house and rang the bell. No response.

Apparently I was not the only one having difficulty getting him to talk. Among the lawsuits that invoked his research was one brought by the Firearms Policy Coalition to try to overturn Washington State's ban on assault weapons. The state sought to question English about his survey methods, but he pulled the same disappearing act with the government lawyers.

They emailed him, called, and sent a certified letter. When a process server with a subpoena went to English's house, no one would accept it, even though someone inside "looked at the door, then turned away," according to court records. Interestingly, after the state sought a judge's order to compel English to testify, the pro-gun plaintiffs suddenly decided to drop all references to his work from their case, saving him from having to answer questions.

Even after I partnered with a colleague, Jodi Kantor, to write an article for *The New York Times* about English's work, he still didn't respond to our reporting directly. Instead, he ran to a friendly outlet, *The Wall Street Journal*, which published an op-ed under his name with the provocative headline "Antigun Activists Ambushed Me."

In it, the professor defended his methodology, saying he used a reputable polling firm and that his results were in line with other surveys. He also griped about getting subpoenaed and complained about my trying to talk to him (he suggested a "journalist" trespassed at his house, a rather breathless way to characterize someone ringing your doorbell and then leaving when nobody answered). His article also contained several artful dodges, such as this line challenging the assertion that he failed to disclose the funding for his national firearms survey: "The *Times* article insinuated that I hid my funding, compensation and expert-witness work. But my funding has been fully disclosed, in accordance with academic practice, in every journal article accepted for publication."

Well, yes, but his survey was never published in a peer-reviewed journal, so its funding was never disclosed. And given the opportunity to finally do so, in the op-ed, he still did not disclose it. Instead, he went on to attack those who had scrutinized him and his research. He accused journalists, "progressive law clerks," and government lawyers of conspiring to "cancel academics who state inconvenient facts.

"Those of us who want to foster an evidence-based public-policy discourse should reject these tactics, and courts should take note of them."

Several months after my story was published, a court did take note. English's survey had been cited by gun rights groups seeking to overturn Illinois's assault weapons ban, and a federal judge offered his opinion of it:

"The Court agrees with the Government that the methodological errors and inherent biases raise concerns about the reliability of Professor English's survey relating to his determination that various challenged semiautomatic firearms and large-capacity magazines are in common use. Therefore, this Court elects NOT to rely on the English Survey in resolving any questions of fact in this case."

In June 2025, a new development in the Illinois case flew largely under the radar. It was yet another amicus brief, this one filed by the United States of America—backing the plaintiffs seeking to overturn the state ban on assault weapons. Atty. Gen. Pamela Bondi, the brief explained, had directed the Department of Justice "to use its full might to protect the Second Amendment rights of law-abiding citizens."

The brief was followed in the months afterward by the initiation of full-blown lawsuits by the Justice Department to overturn state gun laws in California, Washington, DC, and elsewhere. It marked a sea change in the government's role in the ongoing legal battle over firearms regulation, positioning the United States itself at the forefront of knocking down limits on AR-15s, high-capacity magazines, carrying of weapons, and more.

It was, in many ways, the apotheosis of a half century of efforts to reframe the country's relationship with firearms. "For too long, the Second Amendment, which establishes the fundamental individual right of Americans to keep and bear arms, has been treated as a second-class right," Bondi said in announcing the policy change. "No more."

Her comments came exactly sixty years after one of her predecessors, Atty. Gen. Nicholas Katzenbach, testified before Congress on the same issue. In impassioned tones, he warned that those opposed to reasonable gun restrictions—"in a country which has lost four presidents to assassins' bullets"—were disingenuously twisting the history and purpose of the Second Amendment for selfish ends. It was past time, Katzenbach said, that the nation act to "challenge interests which have thrived on the present state of unregulated chaos." And then he closed with a simple question that, all these years later, still bedevils Americans:

"Which is more significant: The right to not be slightly inconvenienced in the purchase of a firearm? Or the right not to be terrorized, robbed, wounded, or killed?"

CONCLUSION

WHAT IS TO BE DONE?

HISTORY SUGGESTS THAT any consideration of where the country goes from here would need to begin with the basic premise that two important freedoms must coexist in equilibrium: bearing arms and living in peace. Many Americans would argue that the excesses of the former have made the latter impossible.

Living in peace means kissing a child goodbye in the morning without fear they will be shot, and not turning schools into fortresses or asking teachers to pack a gun. It means not enduring active-shooter drills at the office or nervously eyeing some bozo who's grocery shopping with an AR-15 slung over his shoulder.

It means exercising your First Amendment right to peacefully demonstrate without being intimidated by armed counterprotesters. It means going to a movie, concert, or church service and not taking mental note of the escape routes in case of a mass shooter. It means running your small retail shop without worrying that the jingle of the front door opening may be the last thing you hear.

Alas, aside from its stated purpose of insuring domestic tranquility and the "blessings of liberty," the Constitution does not specifically enumerate a right to live in peace. The closest it comes may be the Fourth Amendment's safeguarding of "the right of the people to be secure in their persons, houses, papers, and effects, against unreasonable searches and seizures." A theoretical argument could be made that unfettered gun rights run amok is a form of unreasonable seizure of liberty, but it is unlikely to survive outside debate class.

The potential steps to reform run from the incremental to the existential. Boxed in by Supreme Court rulings, gun safety advocates work around the edges, seeking age minimums for assault rifles, limits on open carry, and bans of untraceable ghost guns. Even these measured steps are met with lawsuits, Republican pushback, and cries of "Tyranny!"

One legal avenue for victims of gun violence that has found renewed success is suing firearms manufacturers for reckless marketing and advertising, as in the successful settlement with Remington by families of those killed at Sandy Hook. It is a path similar to that previously taken against Big Tobacco. Cigarettes, of course, are not namechecked in the Bill of Rights. Nevertheless, there are many parallels between the two regulatory challenges.

The tobacco industry for decades seemed like an unconquerable force, having built a powerful and aggressive lobbying machine that owned congressional majorities, intimidated critics and the media, and cranked out pseudoscience to obfuscate the harm caused by its products. Only through litigation, aided by a few brave whistleblowers, was the brazen nature of the industry's lies and deception laid bare. Critical mass was achieved and tobacco companies were finally forced to compensate victims, laws were passed, and a sea change in cultural attitudes, once unthinkable, took hold.

Again, there are crucial differences. One is hard-pressed to find any redeeming qualities in smoking, while guns obviously have a utility and purpose that cigarettes do not. Guns also are not only referenced in the Constitution, but their manufacturers were granted specific immunities by Congress via the 2005 Protection of Lawful Commerce in Arms Act. However, that unprecedented liability shield is not impenetrable.

"The law has been held to deny victims their day in court in some otherwise-viable cases and makes it more difficult to hold gun companies accountable for their contribution to gun violence," said Jonathan Lowy, a longtime legal advocate for gun safety. "But courts have confirmed that 'more difficult' does not mean impossible."

The Connecticut Supreme Court laid the groundwork in a nuanced ruling that allowed the Sandy Hook plaintiffs to go ahead with their lawsuit. Acknowledging the barriers put in place by Congress, the court rejected the idea that "merely by selling semi-automatic rifles" do gun companies become responsible for their misuse. But the court identified "one narrow legal theory" sufficient for the plaintiffs to proceed.

Many states, including Connecticut, have consumer protection laws against reckless, dangerous, or deceptive sales practices. The only question was whether PLCAA, the 2005 federal shield law, effectively nullified them. The Connecticut justices pointed out that the federal law contains an exception for when a gun company knowingly violates an underlying statute "applicable to the sale or marketing" of a firearm—precisely what was being alleged in the Sandy Hook case. The court then yanked back the state's ability to maintain law and order in this context: "The regulation of advertising that threatens the public's health, safety, and morals has long been considered a core exercise of the states' police powers."

The federal shield law also does not protect retail gun sellers against certain claims of negligence. A Milwaukee jury found a gun shop guilty of ignoring evidence that a customer was illegally purchasing a pistol for an underage friend, who later used it to shoot two police officers. As a lawyer for the officers said, the verdict was "a wake-up call for licensed gun dealers who now knew that PLCAA was not an impregnable wall."

Despite these legal tremors rippling through the gun industry, the unique nature of America's relationship with firearms suggests that for those who are fed up with the status quo, suing their way to a solution, ultimately, is not realistic.

Politics and the law often follow social movements. The radical experiment of Prohibition arose after a century of concerns about the deleterious effects of alcohol on public order, home life, and the workplace. A constitutional amendment banning booze, unimaginable today, was so popular it was ratified by all but two states (a lesser number voted for repeal fourteen years later). Similar shifts in public sentiment propelled civil rights laws, legalization of gay marriage, and deregulation of marijuana. Even with tobacco, the legal strategy against it emerged as smoking was already becoming stigmatized by a younger, more health-conscious generation that recoiled from it.

Most of these issues had something in common: a well-organized, broad-based movement seeking to win public acceptance and convert it into lasting change. But that has generally eluded those trying to affect gun culture.

A dynamic at play here is best explained through analogy. I once investigated the dangers posed by highway construction. Accidents at roadside work zones kill almost a thousand people and injure tens of thousands more each year. Pointing to the risks for construction workers, Congress allocates billions for police enforcement and public-awareness campaigns targeting reckless motorists.

Yet, when I dug into the data, I found it's not careless drivers who are the problem—it's the road-building industry itself. Motorists, not construction workers, account for about 85 percent of the fatalities, many of them caused by poorly designed or mismanaged work zones. Most of the remaining 15 percent are workers killed by construction vehicles or some other occupational mishap; only a handful of workers are actually struck by passing cars. This tiny segment receives almost all of the attention because the road-building industry is eager to avoid scrutiny of its own negligence.

More to the point, what I also discovered was that this misdirection is allowed to persist because of an absence of any cohesive interest group speaking up on behalf of the victims. Work zone crashes happen randomly across the country, on back roads and interstates, killing people from all walks of life. Each one might generate a local news story or a lawsuit, but collectively there is no unifying force for change. Nobody is protesting outside statehouses, fundraising for politicians, spending millions on ads, or fostering influencers on social media in favor of dead motorists.

It's hard not to see parallels to the victims of gun violence. Barring something catastrophic, such as a particularly horrific school massacre, the daily trickle of bloodshed flows largely unnoticed, never cresting with the sustained energy needed to address it. A single plane crash that kills two hundred people will trigger a massive government, industry, and media response; two hundred people killed in scattered shootings across fifty states does not.

Put simply, the gun lobby succeeded on a macro level in buying time, as John Dingell put it after Sandy Hook, "for sensitivities to die down"—roughly forty thousand deaths a year is now just background noise.

At the same time, many proponents of stronger gun laws do themselves no favors by not acknowledging that firearms have a legitimate place in American life. By not embracing the reality that the vast majority of gun owners are law-abiding and well-intentioned, they risk abandoning a portion of the population to partisans who eagerly stoke fears of crime, gun confiscation, and cultural division.

The Democratic Party tends to struggle with this balancing act the most. Democrats have often allowed themselves to be caricatured as soft on public safety, which surveys show is the single biggest motivator, by far, for people buying a firearm. Democrats have also been criticized for self-defeating approaches to the unforgiving politics of guns.

When Beto O'Rourke, the Texas Democrat, was seeking his party's nomination for president in 2019, he famously proclaimed, "Hell yes, we're going to take your AR-15." That may have sold well with primary voters, but the comment also became instant fodder for Republicans and the NRA, who regularly trot it out to portray Democrats as gun grabbers. O'Rourke abandoned his presidential bid two months later, lost a campaign for governor in 2022, and hasn't held elective office since.

The takeaway from such experiences is not that proposing to ban assault weapons is necessarily a bad idea, but that the politics of how to do it have to be contended with. The battle over gun rights is fought with the conditions as they exist, not as one side or the other wishes they were.

Among Democrats, Joe Manchin probably came closest to navigating this terrain. The former senator defied political gravity for years by winning elections in ruby-red West Virginia and earned rebukes from gun control advocates with his 2010 campaign ad showing him firing a hunting rifle at a piece of legislation he opposed.

But once in Congress, he cosponsored a bill to strengthen background checks and was a key figure in passing the 2022 Bipartisan Safer Communities Act, the first major gun safety legislation in a quarter century. When he retired from the Senate in 2024, Everytown for Gun Safety praised him as a "guiding light" for how to get results on firearms issues.

Republicans who are inclined to support efforts to reduce gun violence face their own challenges. Sen. John Cornyn of Texas, no fan of gun control in general, nevertheless worked to find common ground with Democrats on the Bipartisan Safer Communities Act in 2022. As originally envisioned, the bill was to include a national "red flag" law empowering police to temporarily seize guns from people deemed a danger to themselves or others. Many gun rights proponents objected. Cornyn got flak back home in Texas and was heckled at a state GOP convention by Republicans shouting, "No red flag."

But fortified by private polling showing widespread support for it, and not facing reelection until 2026, Cornyn continued with negotiations over the bill. The resulting compromise provided $750 million for states to implement their own red flag laws, along with other crisis interventions, allowing the Republicans to frame it as respectful of states' rights. It also strengthened background checks for young gun buyers and restrictions on domestic abusers seeking firearms.

To be sure, it is hard for politicians to gain footing on any issue without a strong, organized cultural base from which to draw support.

A majority of Americans in most major polls favor banning assault weapons and high-capacity magazines, strengthening background checks, raising age minimums, restricting how firearms are marketed, and more. But while there clearly is fuel to start a wildfire, those longing for more sensible gun policies have yet to find a match.

In this vacuum, the gun lobby, cohered by the reliable motivators of political power and commercial profits, steamrolls onward. Its road to success started with a false dichotomy: that restrictions must only impact criminals and not law-abiding citizens. This sounds reasonable, until you realize that we would need to know, in advance, who all the criminals are and somehow fashion laws to keep guns out of their hands without limiting the rights of anyone else (many of the worst mass shooters were "law-abiding citizens" up until the fateful moment they were not).

Because such clairvoyance is not possible, the result was to allow gun rights advocates to proclaim that virtually *any* attempt to impose limits on guns is illegitimate. It is similar to the argument made by drug companies behind the opioid crisis, who insisted that their dangerous products were intended only for law-abiding patients and not the criminals who abuse them. Such rhetorical artifice is useful for undermining regulatory efforts while seeming to stand up for the rights of average Americans.

Having made steady headway with this framing, pro-gun interests worked to preserve their gains with the help of allies in the conservative legal movement that took root at the dawn of the Reagan era. Eyeing the long game, ideologues planted seeds that gradually altered the jurisprudence of firearms, much in the same way overturning a half century of legal precedent on abortion was methodically planned and carried out despite a strong majority of Americans favoring the status quo.

There is nothing stopping those who want to stem gun violence from pursuing their own long-term legal strategy similar to what proved so successful for the gun lobby.

It could take a generation or more, but ultimately the surest way to effect lasting change, as Dingell and the NRA knew, is to foster a legal climate friendly to your needs. While amending the Constitution may be a quixotic pursuit, adapting Americans' understanding of the Second Amendment to the demands of modernity is not. As Michael Waldman, a Second Amendment scholar who runs the Brennan Center for Justice at the NYU School of Law, has pointed out, winning popular support for sensible gun laws "is not an alternative to a legal strategy." The two must go hand in hand.

"How the Supreme Court sees the Constitution is ultimately up to us," he said. "A full scan of American history shows that the public, fully engaged, has made constitutional law every bit as much as jurists and lawyers."

And to be sure, there have been glimpses of what is possible when the unanswered desire for reform meets charismatic or politically adept figures able to deliver it. In the 1930s it was Franklin D. Roosevelt, disgusted by gangland shootings, aided by women's groups just as angry about domestic violence. In the 1960s it was the Kennedy brothers who found the words and moral authority to elevate the debate on guns. In the 2010s it was Parkland High School students who galvanized public attention with their passion and purpose.

These moments are fleeting. Consequential as they were, they still didn't get down to the roots of the current problem, and eventually their energy dissipated. What is at the roots?

I've often thought that so much of what passes for American gun culture today is wrapped up in a caricature of exaggerated masculinity, and if you could somehow strip away the cartoonish "coolness" of it, the effect would be to reveal the emperor has no clothes. Guns are being marketed, essentially, as an erectile-dysfunction drug that promises to put you back on top where you belong (recall Remington's "Consider your man card reissued" ad for assault weapons).

The insecurity revealed by such messaging might be laughable if it weren't so dangerous and sad. When the gun industry indulges in such tactics and pays to get its products into violent video games and movies or into the hands of hypermasculine influencers on YouTube, it's because that's where the demand is.

Much has been made of the crisis of young men and boys. By an alarming array of measures, American males have been slipping beneath the waves. They are far more likely than women to die by suicide or drug overdose, and their educational and professional attainments lag behind women's. Behavioral problems are increasing and loneliness is endemic. More young men don't date. The percentage of them who say they had at least a half dozen close friends dropped by half over the past thirty years, and 20 percent of single men report having no close friends at all.

Some people make the mistake of rolling their eyes at this—women, after all, have obviously long endured their own debilitating societal hurdles—but the potential consequences are everybody's problem.

"One could speculate that there's something that ties male loneliness to violence," said Dr. Nathaniel Glasser, a physician-researcher at the University of Chicago Medicine. "That in situations where boys and men feel loneliness, they—not always, but occasionally, arguably too frequently—turn to violent mechanisms to reconcile or cope or otherwise deal with their loneliness."

In this context, the exacerbating effects of the internet go beyond the usual concerns about its influence on young people's mental health—it's also made obtaining a firearm as easy as ordering a pizza. In 2022, just days after turning eighteen, Salvador Ramos, a troubled loner who expressed anger toward girls, went online and legally bought an AR-15–style rifle before killing nineteen students and two teachers at Robb Elementary School in Uvalde, Texas.

His $2,024.28 digital receipt from Daniel Defense included a link to a customer survey so the company "can better serve you in the future."

Until the country comes to grips with its boys-and-young-men emergency, continued easy access to firearms is not sustainable, particularly when an entire industry is eager to profit off the darker recesses of male psychology while turning a blind eye to the risks.

In 1992, three centuries after the Pequot War decimated much of the Indian population in southeastern Connecticut, a massive edifice rose above the treetops at the forested reservation I had visited as a young schoolboy.

Gone are the trailers and makeshift exhibits of Native American culture I remembered. In their place looms Foxwoods Resort Casino, one of the largest gaming establishments in North America, built by descendants of those who survived the massacre in 1637. The sprawling complex includes a state-of-the-art museum showcasing the history of the Pequots. Among the displays is a collection of musket balls fired during the siege of the Pequot fort by Capt. John Mason and his men. Some of them are misshapen from impact.

The reservation where the casino is located, like all federally recognized tribal areas, is governed by its own laws. Ever since the Pequots gained official recognition in 1983, they've had a rule: No outsiders can carry guns onto their land.

ACKNOWLEDGMENTS

AUTHORS OFTEN SAY, upon release of a new book, that it's one they had been thinking about writing for years. In my case, it's been decades.

Ricochet would not have come about without the support and encouragement of many people, starting with my agent, Andrew Stuart, always a thoughtful and positive force spurring me to action. Libby McGuire at Simon & Schuster, who took an interest in my reporting for *The New York Times*, and Julia Cheiffetz, who thought enough of my book proposal to take it on, were instrumental in getting the ball rolling. As much as I believed that I knew what I wanted to say in writing *Ricochet*, it was Alessandra Bastagli, my editor and the publisher of One Signal, whose expert and patient hand gave it voice. Her guidance was invaluable.

As I mentioned, the cumulative experiences that led me to want to write this book trace back a long time. I want to acknowledge my former colleague and reporting partner at the *Times*, Michael Luo, with whom I spent a year after the tragedy at Sandy Hook investigating the culture, commerce, and politics of guns in the United States. Our editors, Matt Purdy and Paul Fishleder, shared our commitment to trying to help readers make sense of it all. Later, it was Rebecca Corbett, the investigations editor at the *Times*, who encouraged and honed my deep dive into the untold history of the National Rifle Association that helped jump-start my idea for *Ricochet*.

When deadline pressures and distractions made writing difficult, my old friends Bob Cunniff and Sheila Brennan generously offered a quiet place to seclude myself and get work done. Most of all, I want to thank my wife, Maggie, for her unflagging encouragement, good humor, and support, without which this endeavor would not have been possible.

NOTES

INTRODUCTION

4 *carnage wrought:* Jennifer Mascia and Chip Brownlee, "Newest CDC Data Confirms Gun Deaths Fell in 2024, but Were Still Higher Than Before the Pandemic," *Trace,* July 19, 2025.

A COWARDLY CONTRIVANCE

11 *Accompanying Capt. John Mason:* John Mason, *A Brief History of the Pequot War* (Boston: S. Kneeland & T. Green, 1736).

12 *The fort was actually a palisade:* "1637—the Pequot War," Society of Colonial Wars in the State of Connecticut, colonialwarsct.org.

12 *farming colony along the Connecticut River:* "Massachusetts Bay 12: The Pequot War, Pt. 2," *American History Podcast,* January 18, 2018.

12 *"This insolent Nation":* John Underhill, *Newes from America* (London: Peter Cole, 1638).

12 *Bay Colony, starting in the 1630s:* Capt. Robert K. Wright Jr., *Massachusetts Militia Roots: A Bibliographic Study* (Washington, DC: Departments of the Army and the Air Force Historical Services, July 19, 1986).

13 *Connecticut law required:* Spencer P. Mead, "The First American Soldiers," *Connecticut Magazine* (Hartford), 1906.

13 *As the English watched:* Philip Vincent, *A True Relation of the Late Battell Fought in New England Between the English and the Savages* (London: Nathanael Butter, 1637).

13 *release of the two girls:* "The Battlefields of the Pequot War," National Park Service, pequot war.org.

13 *"Owanux!":* Mason, *Brief History of Pequot War.*

14 *"the providence of God":* Underhill, *Newes from America.*

14 *While the initial round of gunfire:* Vincent, *True Relation of Late Battell.*

14 *Englishmen were struck in the face:* Dr. Kevin McBride et al., "Battlefields of the Pequot War, 1636–1638," Mashantucket Pequot Museum & Research Center, pequotmuseum.org.

15 *"Great and doleful":* Underhill, *Newes from America.*

15 *"Sometimes, the Scripture":* Ibid.

16 *five thousand muskets:* Aitziber Muga, "Following in the Footsteps of the Marquis de Lafayette," *Noticias de Gipuzkoa,* April 30, 2017.

17 *As knowledge of black powder:* Tom Wintringham, *The Story of Weapons and Tactics* (Boston: Houghton Mifflin, 1943).

17 *"very complicated things":* Ibid.

17 *"How darest thou shoot":* David Ayalon, *Gunpowder and Firearms in the Mamluk Kingdom: A Challenge to Medieval Society* (United Kingdom: Taylor & Francis, 2013).

18 *"It is a shame":* Christopher Hare, Bayard: *The Good Knight Without Fear and Without Reproach* (United Kingdom: J. M. Dent & Sons, 1911).

18 *kinetic energy:* Richard Moore, "The Production of Muskets and Their Effects in the Eighteenth Century," *Forbes & Fifth* (University of Pittsburgh) 6 (Fall 2014).

18 *Bayard had his horse shot out:* Hare, *Bayard.*

19 *There have been plenty of studies:* Nicholas C. Borgogna et al., "The Precarious Masculinity of Firearm Ownership," *Psychology of Men & Masculinities*, February 2022.

20 *Sassacus, a Pequot sachem:* "History of the Pequot Indians," Society of Colonial Wars in the State of Connecticut, colonialwarsct.org.

20 *the end of any hope:* Jill Lepore, *The Name of War: King Philip's War and the Origins of American Identity* (New York: Alfred A. Knopf, 1998).

20 *Their weaponry and training:* Harold E. Selesky, *War and Society and Colonial Connecticut* (New Haven, CT: Yale University Press, 1990).

DIN OF ARMS

21 *"Men rushed madly":* Harold E. Crofts, "Traitor's Daughter," *Connecticut Magazine* (Hartford), 1901.

21 *later in an affidavit:* Charles Hervey Townshend, *The British Invasion of New Haven, Connecticut* (New Haven, CT: Tuttle, Morehouse & Taylor, 1879).

22 *"They instantly fired upon me":* Ibid.

22 *"Because it is the exercise of war!":* Ibid.

22 *"acute and excruciating pain":* Ibid.

23 *"robbed and enslaved":* Sara Sidner and Elizabeth Joseph, "Texts and Video Reveal Details of the Alleged Domestic Terror Plot to Kidnap Governor Whitmer," CNN, October 19, 2020.

23 *Adam Fox, lived in the basement:* Emma Nicolas, "Shop Owner Shocked by Ties to Whitmer Kidnapping Plot," WZZM (Grand Rapids, MI), October 8, 2020.

23 *forty-five rounds per minute:* Matthew Medsger, "AR-15 Briefly Explained," *Boston Herald*, May 27, 2022.

23 *ten times the accuracy:* "Musket vs. AR-15: How Do They Compare?," *Wired*, October 2016.

24 *44 million:* Colin Dickey, "The Curse of the AR-15," *New Republic*, October 2023.

24 *Militia Model:* Franklin Armory, www.franklinarmory.com/shop/firearms/complete-firearms/franklin-armory-militia-model-m4-sbr-m.

24 *"founded with one goal":* Militia Armory, www.militia-armory.com/about.

24 *Republican leaders:* David Kirkpatrick and Mike McIntire, "'Its Own Domestic Army': How the G.O.P. Allied Itself with Militants," *New York Times*, February 8, 2021.

24 *"strict subordination":* State of Michigan Constitution, www.legislature.mi.gov/Publications/MIConstitution.pdf.

25 *"a lethargy seemed to have seized":* Townshend, *British Invasion of New Haven.*

25 *"Address to the Inhabitants of Connecticut":* Ibid.

26 *their ability to make their own:* "A Revolution in Arms: Weapons in the War for Independence," American Revolution Institute, www.americanrevolutioninstitute.org.

26 *training requirements of New England:* Spencer P. Mead, "The First American Soldiers," *Connecticut Magazine* (Hartford), 1906.

26 *Stiles acknowledged that the first:* Diary of Pres. Ezra Stiles, vol. 9, Yale College.

26 *"Perhaps one-third":* Ibid., vol. 14.

27 *"Jim Hillhouse and his men":* Crofts, "Traitor's Daughter."

27 *Capt. James Hillhouse was:* Rev. Leonard Bacon, *Sketch of the Life and Public Services of Hon. James Hillhouse* (New Haven, CT: 1860).

27 *"We have had a little difficulty":* Charles Hervey Townshend, *A Pictorial History of Raynham and Its Vicinity* (New Haven, CT: Tuttle, Morehouse & Taylor, 1900).

28 *"Gen. Tryon was very polite":* Crofts, "Traitor's Daughter."

28 *battle of Camden:* John Buchanan, *The Road to Guilford Courthouse* (New York: John Wiley & Sons, 1997).

29 *Bookish, five feet four:* Alexander C. R. Hammond, *Heroes of Progress, Pt. 44: James Madison* (Washington, DC: Cato Institute, May 15, 2020).

30 *The founding document that emerged:* US Constitution, article I, section 8, clause 16.

30 *purpose of the militia:* Ibid., clause 15.

30 *"one of the greatest mischiefs":* Jonathan Elliot, *The Debates in the Several State Conventions on the Adoption of the Federal Constitution as Recommended by the General Convention at Philadelphia in 1787* (Washington, DC: Taylor & Maury, 1836).

30 *"no such thing":* Alexander Hamilton letter to George Washington, September 2, 1794, National Archives.

30 *"the misjudged exaggerations":* James Madison, *Federalist Papers*, no. 46, January 29, 1788.

30 *"the sober apprehensions":* Ibid.

30 *"To these would be opposed":* Ibid.

31 *"neglected and rendered unfit":* Elliot, *Debates in the Several State Conventions.*

31 *"I cannot conceive":* Ibid.

31 *"what I do not like":* Thomas Jefferson letter to James Madison, December 20, 1787, in *The Papers of Thomas Jefferson* (Princeton, NJ: Princeton University Press, 1950).

32 *woven into the text:* "James Madison Introduces the Bill of Rights," National Constitution Center, www.constitutioncenter.org.

32 *"freedom of the press":* "Virginia Declaration of Rights," June 22, 1776, National Archives.

33 *"all men are equally":* Ibid.

33 *"That a well regulated militia":* Ibid.

33 *"the people have a right":* Pennsylvania Constitution of 1776, in Francis Thorpe, *The Federal and State Constitutions, Colonial Charters, and Other Organic Laws of the States, Territories, and Colonies Now or Heretofore Forming the United States of America* (Washington, DC: Government Printing Office, 1909).

33 *Madison's first crack: Annals of Congress*, House of Representatives, 1st Cong., 1st Sess., June 8, 1789 (Washington, DC: Gales & Seaton, 1834).

34 *"The decision to recast":* Saul Cornell, *A Well-Regulated Militia: The Founding Fathers and the Origins of Gun Control in America* (Oxford: Oxford University Press, 2006).

34 *"Framing the right":* Ibid.

34 *"To place any dependence":* George Washington letter to John Hancock, September 25, 1776, National Archives.

35 *an unmitigated disaster:* Colin G. Calloway, "The Biggest Forgotten American Indian Victory," Project of Smithsonian and Arizona State University, June 9, 2015.

THE AMERICAN MIND

36 *"if not checked in time":* Letter from Charles Pinckney to George Washington, September 20, 1791, National Archives.

36 *Stono Rebellion:* Herbert Aptheker, *American Negro Slave Revolts* (New York: Columbia University Press, 1943).

37 *"surprised a warehouse":* Mark E. Smith, Stono: *Documenting and Interpreting a Southern Slave Revolt* (Columbia: University of South Carolina Press, 2005).

37 *numbering close to one hundred:* Ibid.

37 *"This is to be said":* Ibid.

37 *"it shall not be lawful":* South Carolina Slave Code (1740), Gilder Lehrman Institute of American History, www.gilderlehrman.org/ap-african-american-studies/unit-2/origins-enslavement/south-carolina-slave-code-1740.

37 *"No freeman shall be debarred":* Jefferson first draft of Virginia Declaration of Rights, June 1776, National Archives.

37 Patrick Henry fretted: Jonathan Elliot, *The Debates in the Several State Conventions on the Adoption of the Federal Constitution as Recommended by the General Convention at Philadelphia in 1787* (Washington, DC: Taylor & Maury, 1836).

38 *Nat Turner in Virginia:* Aptheker, *American Negro Slave Revolts.*

38 *other states that didn't already:* Robert J. Cottrol and Raymond T. Diamond, "The Second Amendment: Toward an Afro-Americanist Reconsideration," *Georgetown Law Review*, 1991.

38 *Fugitive Slave Act:* Gene Demby and Natalie Escobar, "From Negro Militias to Black Armament," NPR, December 22, 2020.

38 *two hundred rifles for Brown's raiding party:* John Warren, "The Last Days of John Brown: Pikes, Rifles, and Revolvers," *New York Alamanack*, September 13, 2021, www.newyorkalmanack.com/2021/09/the-last-days-of-john-brown-pikes-rifles-and-revolvers/.

39 *limited access to firearms:* William R. Tonso, "Gun Control: White Man's Law," *Reason*, December 1985.

39 *"shall or give to any Indean":* J. Hammond Turnbull, P*ublic Records of the Colony of Connecticut, Prior to the Union with New Haven Colony, May, 1665* (Hartford, CT: Brown & Parsons, 1850).

40 *The state legislature responded:* Patrick Charles, *Vote Gun* (New York: Columbia University Press, 2023).

40 *reaching for his ID:* Catherine Shoichet, "Philando Castile Shooting: In Their Own Words," CNN, July 2016.

40 *mistook him for a suspect:* Daniel Victor, "Black Man Killed by Police in Alabama Was Shot from Behind, Autopsy Shows," *New York Times*, December 4, 2018.

40 *judge threw out a charge:* Todd Richmond, "Explainer: Why Did Judge Drop Rittenhouse Gun Charge?," Associated Press, November 19, 2021.

40 *the metastasizing of violence:* Kelly Carter Jackson, "The Story of Violence in America," *Daedalus*, Winter 2022.

41 *"sustained by violence":* Theodore Parker, *The Collected Works of Theodore Parker*, vol. 5 (London: Trübner & Co., 1863).

41 *"ruthless vigilantism":* Randolph Roth, *American Homicide* (Cambridge, MA: Harvard University Press, 2009).

41 *"Murderers elsewhere":* Ibid.

41 *flooded the country:* Ibid.

41 *General Order of 1866:* Edward McPherson, *A Handbook of Politics for 1868* (Washington, DC: Philip & Solomons, 1868).

42 *"armed citizenry model":* Patrick J. Charles, *Armed in America: A History of Gun Rights from Colonial Militias to Concealed Carry* (Amherst, NY: Prometheus Books, 2019).

42 *Post–Civil War constitutions:* Saul Cornell, "The Right to Regulate Arms in the Era of the Fourteenth Amendment: The Emergence of Good Cause Permit Schemes in Post–Civil War America," *University of California Davis Law Review*, September 2021.

42 *1869 Texas constitution:* Ibid.

42 *Florida in 1885:* Ibid.

42 *Idaho constitution of 1889:* Ibid.

42 Cruikshank *in 1876: United States v. Cruikshank*, majority opinion, US Supreme Court, 1875.

43 *"This is not a right":* Ibid.

44 Presser v. Illinois: *Presser v. Illinois*, majority opinion, US Supreme Court, 1886.

44 *"prohibit the people":* Ibid.

44 *One was William Ellis Niblack:* Niblack, William Ellis, 1822–1893, *Biographical Directory of the United States Congress*, bioguide.congress.gov.

45 *hardscrabble upbringing: History of Pike and DuBois Counties, Indiana* (Evansville, IN: Goodspeed Bros. & Co., 1885).

45 *"irrepressible conflict":* "Speech of the Hon. William E. Niblack, of Indiana, on the Admission of Kansas, Delivered in the House of Representatives, April 11, 1860," Slavery and Anti-Slavery: A Transnational Archive, www.gale.com/primary-sources/slavery-and-anti-slavery.

45 *"when interpreted as John Brown":* Ibid.

45 *In another speech:* "Speech of the Hon. William E. Niblack, of Indiana, on the Admission of Kansas, Delivered in the House of Representatives, Feb. 9, 1867," Slavery and Anti-Slavery: A Transnational Archive, www.gale.com/primary-sources/slavery-and-anti-slavery.

46 *Runyan, a Democrat: Runyan v. State*, majority opinion, Indiana Supreme Court, 1877.

46 *"If the person assailed":* Ibid.

46 *"to the wall":* Richard Maxwell Brown, "No Duty to Retreat American Self-Defense," *Chronicles: A Magazine of American Culture*, January 1994.

47 *"should not be permitted":* Charles, *Armed in America.*

47 *"A very brief examination": Runyan v. State.*

48 *"Apart from its role":* Richard Maxwell Brown, *Strain of Violence: Historical Studies of American Violence and Vigilantism* (New York: Oxford University Press, 1975).

48 *"One significant feature":* Ibid.

48 *"even to save human life": Runyan v. State.*

48 *"a true man": Beard v. United States*, majority opinion, US Supreme Court, 1895.

48 *all but a handful of states:* "Self-Defense and Stand Your Ground," National Conference of State Legislatures, www.ncsl.org/civil-and-criminal-justice/self-defense-and-stand-your-ground.

48 *in 2013 by George Zimmerman:* Lizette Alvarez and Cara Buckley, "Zimmerman Is Acquitted in Trayvon Martin Killing," *New York Times*, July 13, 2013.

49 *Maurice Byrd, a Black man:* Mensah M. Dean, "Maurice Byrd Shot a White Man and Claimed Self-Defense. His Acquittal of Murder Makes Him an Exception," *Trace*, April 24, 2025.

49 *"The doctrine of 'retreat to the wall'": State v. Gardner*, majority opinion, Minnesota Supreme Court, 1905.

50 *Upson was a sixteen-year-old:* Virginius Dabney, "Sherman's March and Other Campaigns," *New York Times*, March 14, 1943.

50 *"The truth is":* Theodore F. Upson, *With Sherman to the Sea: The Civil War Letters, Diaries and Reminiscences of Theodore F. Upson* (Baton Rouge: Louisiana State University Press, 1943).

51 *He paid $35:* Ibid.

51 *"I think the Johnnys":* Ibid.

51 *"I took off my coat":* Ibid.

A REAL MENACE

53 *Union Station in Kansas City:* "Kansas City, MO—Union Station (KCY)," Great American Stations, www.greatamericanstations.com/stations/kansas-city-mo-kcy/.

53 *At 7:15 a.m.:* "Kansas City Massacre and 'Pretty Boy' Floyd," Famous Cases and Criminals, fbi.gov.

54 *adoption of metallic cartridges:* Frank C. Barnes, *Cartridges of the World* (Iola, WI: Krause Publications, 1965).

54 *Thanks largely to French gunsmiths:* Roger Pauly, *Firearms: The Life Story of a Technology* (Westport, CT: Greenwood Publishing, 2004).

54 *the first machine gun:* Malcom W. Browne, "100 Years of Maxim's 'Killing Machine,'" *New York Times*, November 26, 1985.

55 *tommy gun:* Ibid.

55 *slang for "government men":* "George 'Machine Gun' Kelly," Famous Cases and Criminals, fbi.gov.

55 *The three lawmen:* "Kansas City Massacre."

55 *crystal chandeliers:* "Kansas City, MO."

55 *"Up! Up!":* "Kansas City Massacre."

55 *"Let 'em have it!":* Ibid.

55 *level the playing field:* "Timeline," fbi.gov.

56 *the murder rate:* Mark Thornton, "Alcohol Prohibition Was a Failure," Policy Analysis No. 157, Cato Institute, July 17, 1991, https://www.cato.org/policy-analysis/alcohol-prohibition-was-failure.

56 *number of inmates:* Ibid.

56 *Dodge City and Tombstone:* Matt Jancer, "Gun Control Is as Old as the Old West," *Smithsonian Magazine*, February 25, 2018.

56 *the NRA today:* Robert Farago, "NRA-ILA: The Myth of Effective Wild West Gun Control Exploded," Truth About Guns, March 5, 2018, https://www.thetruthaboutguns.com/nra-ila-myth-effective-wild-west-gun-control-exploded/.

57 *"Be it therefore resolved":* "Reports of the Wyoming Stock Growers Association, Important Resolutions No. 11, 1887," Duke Center for Firearms Law.

57 *"primed with whiskey":* Ross Collins, "Gun Control and the Old West," History News Service, July 1999.

57 *"Cattlemen should unite":* Ibid.

57 *a majority of homicide victims:* Lizabeth Remrey, "Homicide Victimization in the United States, 2023," US Department of Justice, Bureau of Justice Statistics, May 19, 2025.

57 *rates of offenses:* Roger D. McGrath, *Gunfighters, Highwaymen & Vigilantes: Violence on the Frontier* (Berkeley: University of California Press, 1984).

58 *"While men have hope":* Ibid.

58 *"with the shocking result":* "The Sale of Deadly Weapons," *New York Times*, May 29, 1873.

58 *"The proper way":* Ibid.

58 *the Sullivan Act:* Peter Duffy, "100 Years Ago, the Shot That Spurred New York's Gun-Control Law," *New York Times*, January 23, 2011.

58 *assassinate Pres. Franklin D. Roosevelt:* Blaise Picchi, *The Five Weeks of Giuseppe Zangara: The Man Who Would Assassinate FDR* (Chicago: Chicago Review Press, 2003).

59 *"For some time":* Rep. Robert Doughton, June 13, 1934, *Congressional Record* (Washington, DC: Government Printing Office, 1934).

59 *National Firearms Act:* "National Firearms Act," Bureau of Alcohol, Tobacco, Firearms and Explosives, www.atf.gov/rules-and-regulations/laws-alcohol-tobacco-firearms-and-explosives/national-firearms-act.

59 *"I do not believe": National Firearms Act Hearings Before the Committee on Ways & Means, House of Representatives, April 16, 18, and May 14, 16, 1934*, testimony of Karl T. Frederick (Washington, DC, Government Printing Office, 1934).

60 *army Gen. Milton Reckord:* Ibid.

60 *"any weapon designed":* Ibid.

60 *"A gun which fires automatically":* Ibid.

61 *"The definition which I suggest":* Ibid.

61 *Samuel Billingsley Hill:* Ibid.

62 *pronounced the final bill "a joke":* "Club Women Insist on Anti-Pistol Bill," *New York Times*, May 25, 1934.

63 *Following a raucous convention:* Ibid.

63 *"We hold you accountable":* Ibid.

63 *"some ladies' organizations":* Representative Doughton, *Congressional Record.*

63 *it wasn't until 1920:* Carolyn B. Ramsey, "Domestic Violence and State Intervention in the American West and Australia, 1860–1930," *Indiana Law Journal*, Winter 2011.

63 *marital rape was illegal:* Marnie Rothschild Shiels, "Spousal Rape Laws: 20 Years Later," Domestic Violence Report, Civic Research Institute, August/September 2000.

63 *Jack Miller lying:* "O'Malley Gang Trial Witness Slain," *Muskogee (OK) Daily Phoenix*, April 6, 1939.

64 *While working as a bouncer:* "Blow on Jaw Caused Death of Tulsa Man," *Oklahoman*, August 29, 1924.

64 *after stealing about $22,000:* Brian Frye, "The Peculiar Story of *U.S. v. Miller*," *New York University Journal of Law & Liberty*, 2008.

64 *state police in Arkansas:* Ibid.

64 *again Ragon batted it away:* Ibid.

65 *no one represented them:* Ibid.

65 *"the collective body":* Brief for the Government, *U.S. v. Miller*, 1939.

65 *"With obvious purpose": U.S. v. Miller*, majority opinion, US Supreme Court, 1939.

65 *"In the absence of any evidence":* Ibid.

66 *"What does* Miller *tell us?":* Frye, "Peculiar Story."

66 *"personally of the opinion": National Firearms Act Hearings*, testimony of Frederick.

DROP BY DROP UPON THE HEART

69 *Albert Leslie Hertz:* Résumé of Albert Leslie Hertz, Los Angeles Police Department report, July 9, 1968.

69 *the Watts district:* Denise DiPasquale and Edward L. Glaeser, *The LA Riot and the Economics of Urban Unrest* (Cambridge, MA: National Bureau of Economic Research, February 1996).

70 *went to the Pasadena Gun Shop:* LAPD report, July 9, 1968.

70 *the ignominious distinction:* Will Dabbs, "The Anarchist Assassin Who Killed a President: An Iver Johnson Safety Automatic Put to Bad Use," *American Handgunner*, July/August 2024.

70 *Hertz and the salesclerk:* LAPD report, July 9, 1968.

71 *Spain and the Dominican Republic:* Benjamin F. Jones and Benjamin A. Olken, "Hit or Miss? The Effect of Assassinations on Institutions and War," *American Economic Journal: Macroeconomics* 1, no. 2 (July 2009).

71 *Thomas Crooks was twenty:* Meghan Schiller, "What Have Investigators Learned About Trump Rally Shooter Thomas Matthew Crooks?," CBS News, July 18, 2024.

71 *he wore a T-shirt:* Nick Penzenstadler, "Texas Gun Influencer Says He's Shocked to See His Logo on Trump Shooter," *USA Today*, July 15, 2024.

72 *George Wallace being shot:* Ben A. Franklin, "Shooting of Wallace Spurs a New Effort to Tighten Gun Controls," *New York Times*, May 17, 1972.

73 *"Throw it in the dump": Trial of Sirhan Bishara Sirhan*, vol. 13, testimony of Sarah Hertz, February 18–20, 1969.

73 *"He was a collector":* Robert Blair Kaiser, *R.F.K. Must Die! Chasing the Mystery of the Robert Kennedy Assassination* (New York: Overlook Press, 2008).

73 *Thomas J. Dodd, the Connecticut:* Senate Bill 1975: A Bill to Regulate the Interstate Shipment of Firearms, 1963.

74 *"no real obstacle":* Sen. Thomas Dodd, Statement to the Senate Commerce Committee, December 13, 1963.

74 *"a growing prejudice":* Rep. John Dingell, Statement to the Senate Commerce Committee, December 13, 1963.

74 *"Present-day firearms legislation":* Ibid.

74 *heated disagreement arose:* "The Gun Under Fire," *Time*, June 21, 1968.

75 *a pitch for cooperation:* Transcript of meeting, April 1967, John D. Dingell Jr. Papers, Bentley Historical Library, University of Michigan.

75 *irked the NRA men:* Ibid.

75 *"I hope that Senator Kennedy":* Ibid.

77 *interrupted a campaign speech:* "Indianapolis, 1968: Bobby Kennedy, Martin Luther King, and a Historic Call for Peace," video recording of speech, www.rfkhumanrights.org.

77 *"I like Hemingway":* "Gun Under Fire."

78 *Erhard showed the pistol: Trial of Sirhan Bishara Sirhan*, vol. 13, testimony of George Erhard, February 18–20, 1969.

78 *Joe reported to work:* Kaiser, *R.F.K. Must Die!*

78 *Meanwhile, in Alhambra:* Los Angeles Police Department Report, October 4, 1968.

78 *A short time later:* Ibid.

78 *Not long after that:* Ibid.

78 *While they were talking:* Kaiser, *R.F.K. Must Die!*

79 *"All too widely":* "Gun Under Fire."

79 *"It is just tragic":* Ibid.

79 *"the sportsmen of America":* Joel Achenbach, Scott Higham, and Sari Horwitz, "How NRA's True Believers Converted a Marksmanship Group into a Mighty Gun Lobby," *Washington Post*, January 12, 2013.

79 *laws in Nazi Germany:* Letter to John Dingell from Lewis C. Coffin, July 10, 1968, Dingell Jr. Papers.

79 *wrote to the US Postal Service:* Letter to Timothy J. May from John Dingell, June 25, 1968, Dingell Jr. Papers.

79 *tracking public sentiment:* "Gun Legislation Letters" tracking memos, July 16, 18, and 24, Dingell Jr. Papers.

80 *Dingell was the only one:* Vote to Pass H.R. 17735, July 24, 1968, www.govtrack.us.

80 *not "suitable for sporting":* Public Law 90-618, October 22, 1968.

80 *"laws are pathetically weak":* Mary Ellen Leary, "Story of the Gun: How Weapon Was Traced," *Washington (DC) Daily News*, June 13, 1968.

80 *cut the army's support:* "Sen. Edward Kennedy Leads Effort to Derail Competition: 1967 National Matches," NRA Shooting Sports USA, January 16, 2025, www.ssusa.org.

80 *opened an FBI investigation:* "Memo to SAC Washington Field Office from Director of FBI," October 31, 1968.

81 *"scurrilous and unaccurate":* Ben A. Franklin, "Rifle Unit Split over Gun Curbs," *New York Times*, December 7, 1964.

81 *"Two of them are members":* FBI interview with Louis F. Lucas, October 23, 1968.

81 *"several members of Congress":* FBI interview with Frank C. Daniel, October 23, 1968.

81 *The precise origins of Dingell's:* Mike McIntire, "The Secret History of Gun Rights: How Lawmakers Armed the NRA," *New York Times*, July 30, 2023.

82 *at the NRA meeting:* Transcript of meeting, April 1967, Dingell Jr. Papers.

82 *"Let me say":* Letter to Dingell from Ashley Halsey, April 4, 1967, Dingell Jr. Papers.

82 *"It was great":* Letter to Dingell from Frank C. Daniel, May 1, 1967, Dingell Jr. Papers.

THE PRICE WE PAY FOR FREEDOM

84 *the late Zell Miller:* Zell Miller Papers, Special Collections Libraries, University of Georgia.

84 *there was Bob Barr:* Bob Barr Papers, Ingram Library, Special Collections, University of West Georgia.

84 *had nothing to hide:* Todd Spangler, "Dingell Papers Go to University of Michigan," *Detroit Free Press*, May 6, 2015.

84 *"Bentley has officially":* "Former Congressman John Dingell Donates Archive to Bentley," https://web.archive.org/web/20150906020202/https://bentley.umich.edu/news-events/news/former-congressman-john-dingell-donates-archive-to-bentley/.

85 *"are not open for research":* Email to author from Lara Zielin, January 4, 2023.

85 *"anyone wishing to write":* "Former Congressman John Dingell Donates."

85 *"I can confirm":* Email to author from Lara Zielin, January 9, 2023.

85 *one other author:* Patrick Charles, *Vote Gun* (New York: Columbia University Press, 2023).

86 *"It would appear":* Letter to Donald M. Smith from Dingell, September 10, 1968, John D. Dingell Jr. Papers, Bentley Historical Library, University of Michigan.

86 *Nicknamed "the truck":* Mary McGrory, "Run over by 'the Truck,'" *Washington Post,* June 19, 1999.

86 *He derided Senator Dodd's gun control bill:* Twelve-page draft speech, undated, Dingell Jr. Papers.

87 *"The citizenry at large":* Ibid.

87 *"old style civil libertarian":* Letter to J. W. Viecelli from Dingell, December 2, 1975, Dingell Jr. Papers.

87 *back in 1963:* Rep. John Dingell, Statement to the Senate Commerce Committee, December 13, 1963.

87 *"good guy with a gun":* Aliyah Frumin, "NRA Breaks Silence: We Need Guns in Every School in America," NBC News, December 21, 2012.

88 *The history of the NRA:* Mike McIntire, "The Secret History of Gun Rights: How Lawmakers Armed the NRA," *New York Times,* July 30, 2023.

88 *wrote a letter that September:* Letter to Franklin C. Daniel from Dingell, September 10, 1968, Dingell Jr. Papers.

88 *"should be bottomed":* Ibid.

89 *1939* Miller *ruling: U.S. v. Miller,* majority opinion, US Supreme Court, 1939.

89 *"no basic conflict":* Letter to Viecelli from Dingell.

89 *he placed a call:* Letter to Charles W. Harris from Dingell, March 28, 1973, Dingell Jr. Papers.

89 *helping draft a proposal:* Letter to Robert Lindahl from C. R. Gutermuth, November 26, 1974, Dingell Jr. Papers.

89 *one-page typed outline:* A Resolution to Establish a Firearms Rights Institute, March 1973, Dingell Jr. Papers.

90 *"affiliated with AFL-CIO":* Ibid.

90 *"Notify NRA":* Dear Colleague memo entitled "Sign the Discharge Petition on High Capacity Ban Legislation," July 21, 1999, Dingell Jr. Papers.

90 *"His insights and guidance":* Letter to Howard Dean from L. M. Mustin, October 24, 1978, Dingell Jr. Papers.

90 *"strategy and tactics":* Ibid.

90 *slipped in an amendment:* Benjamin L. Cavataro, "Regulating Guns as Products," *George Washington Law Review,* February 2024.

90 *he boasted to constituents:* Press release entitled "Congressman Dingell Pushed Stronger Bill to Prohibit 'Saturday Night Special' Handguns," February 5, 1974, Dingell Jr. Papers.

90 *explained privately:* Letter to Sherman M. Arnold Jr. from C. R. Gutermuth, December 6, 1974, Dingell Jr. Papers.

91 *"damn little about":* Letter to Dingell from C. R. Gutermuth, April 17, 1975, Dingell Jr. Papers.

91 *"all out action program":* Letter to Lindahl from Gutermuth.

91 *Over pancakes:* Letter to Dingell from Robert Lindahl, January 15, 1975, Dingell Jr. Papers.

91 *"old goats":* Ibid.

91 *"He is disturbed":* Letter to Harold W. Glassen from Robert Lindahl, November 15, 1974, Dingell Jr. Papers.

92 *voted to adopt his plan:* Minutes of NRA Executive Committee Meeting, January 11–12, 1975, Milton A. Reckord Papers, Historical Collections, University of Maryland Libraries.

92 *thirty-three-page blueprint:* Plan for the Organization, Operation and Support of the NRA Institute of Legislative Action, July 23, 1975, Dingell Jr. Papers.

92 *"Maintain files for each":* Ibid.

93 *a leadership structure:* Letter to Merrill W. Wright from Harlon B. Carter, January 26, 1975, Dingell Jr. Papers.

94 *Carter was a familiar:* Elena Saavedra Buckley, "Sons of Guns," *Epic*, November 17, 2021.

94 *youngest chief of the agency:* Ibid.

94 *Operation Wetback:* Ibid.

94 *Carter was investigated:* John Crewdson, "Hard-Line Opponent of Gun Control Wins New Term at Helm of Rifle Association," *New York Times*, May 4, 1981.

95 *"I have a feeling":* Joseph P. Tartaro, *Revolt at Cincinnati* (Buffalo, NY: Hawkeye Press, 1981).

95 *"purification of dedication":* Ibid.

95 *"NRA should not concede":* Undated memo, with "Given to Gen. Rich" written at the top, Dingell Jr. Papers.

96 *Dingell huddled with a close aide:* Memo to Dingell from Michael Parker, April 9, 1975, Dingell Jr. Papers.

96 *"what stationery":* Draft of April 11, 1975, letter to NRA Board of Directors from Dingell, Dingell Jr. Papers.

96 *"bombarded with garbage":* Memo to Dingell from Parker.

96 *"poisoning the well":* Ibid.

96 *His April 11, 1975, letter:* Letter to NRA Board of Directors from Dingell, April 11, 1975, Dingell Jr. Papers.

97 *Six months later: Hearings Before the Subcommittee on Crime, Committee of the Judiciary, House of Representatives*, October 1, 1975 (Washington, DC: US Government Printing Office, 1976).

97 *roughly 170 bills:* Ibid.

97 *"the punks and the criminals":* Ibid.

97 *hewed to the same:* Ibid.

98 *Twelve-year-old Salvatore Pena:* "Carter Murder Trial Gets Under Way," *Laredo (TX) Times*, April 14, 1931.

98 *"What were you doing":* "Carter Trial Testimony Ends," *Laredo (TX) Times*, April 15, 1931.

98 *"We asked him why":* Ibid.

99 *"Son, you hurt that boy!":* Ibid.

99 *"There is no evidence":* Crewdson, "Hard-Line Opponent."

99 *The jury convicted Carter:* Ibid.

99 *appellate court reversed:* "Retrial for Harlan Carter," *Laredo (TX) Times*, December 23, 1931.

99 *Salvatore had been caught:* Ibid.

100 *Harlon-with-an-o:* Crewdson, "Hard-Line Opponent."

100 *"I cherish the freedom": Hearings Before the Subcommittee on Crime.*

SCORNED AND DENIGRATED

103 *a strange young man:* Tom Humphrey, "The Last Time a President Visited the Grand Ole Opry . . . ," United Press International, September 12, 1984.

103 *A few days later:* Charles Mohr, "Gun Traced in 16 Minutes to Dallas Pawn Shop," *New York Times*, April 1, 1981.

103 *seeing a psychiatrist:* Lincoln Caplan, *The Insanity Defense and the Trial of John W. Hinckley, Jr.* (Boston: D. R. Godine, 1984).

103 *"Guns are fun!":* Ibid.

103 *Devastator bullets:* Philip Taubman, "Explosive Bullet Struck Reagan, FBI Discovers," *New York Times*, April 3, 1981.

103 *In Hinckley's wallet:* "Famous Trials," University of Missouri–Kansas City School of Law, https://famous-trials.com/johnhinckley.

103 *committed to a psychiatric hospital:* Dan Collins, "Mark David Chapman Says He Sought Mental Help," United Press International, August 6, 1981.

104 *more than 30 million:* "Gun Ownership in America: 1973 to 2021," Violence Policy Center, November 2022.

104 *ten thousand deaths a year:* Alexia Cooper and Erica L. Smith, "Homicide Trends in the United States, 1980–2008," US Department of Justice, Office of Justice Programs, Bureau of Justice Statistics, November 2011.

104 *three-quarters of Americans:* Tom W. Smith, "The 75% Solution: An Analysis of the Structure of Attitudes on Gun Control, 1959–1977," *Journal of Criminal Law and Criminology*, Fall 1980.

105 *formed by Laura Fermi:* Andrew C. McKevitt, *Gun Country* (Chapel Hill: University of North Carolina Press, 2023).

105 *"security and safety":* "Club Women Insist on Anti-Pistol Bill," *New York Times*, May 25, 1934.

105 *"Let us see who will win":* McKevitt, *Gun Country*.

105 *rape and murder:* Ibid.

105 *Groups such as Handgun Control Inc.:* Robert Spitzer, "US Tragedies from Guns Have Often—but Not Always—Spurred Political Responses," *Conversation*, June 8, 2022.

106 *brainchild of Alan Gottlieb:* Jim Halpin and Paul de Armond, "Merchant of Fear," *Eastsideweek*, October 26, 1994.

106 *H. L. Richardson, who once belonged:* John Berthelsen, "Calif. Gun Owners Advocate Is Making Liberals Uneasy," *Washington Post*, November 11, 1980.

106 *"carve this government":* Ibid.

106 *episode of* Firing Line*: Firing Line with William F. Buckley Jr.*, episode S0428, "Have We Learned Anything About Gun Control?," July 21, 1980.

106 *"revolt at Cincinnati":* Joseph P. Tartaro, *Revolt at Cincinnati* (Buffalo, NY: Hawkeye Press, 1981).

107 *murder a few months earlier of Allard Lowenstein:* "Ex-Rep. Lowenstein Killed by a Gunman," *New York Times*, March 15, 1980.

108 *"counterfeit zeal":* James Madison, *Federalist Papers*, no. 46, January 29, 1788.

109 *"mice and men":* Minutes of the NRA Board of Directors meeting, May 1, 1981, John D. Dingell Jr. Papers, Bentley Historical Library, University of Michigan.

108 "We must prepare now": Tartaro, Revolt at Cincinnati.

110 *laid out the case:* John Crewdson, "Hard-Line Opponent of Gun Control Wins New Term at Helm of Rifle Association," *New York Times*, May 4, 1981.

110 *"The motivation behind":* "Leader of Rifle Group Affirms That He Shot Boy to Death in 1931," *New York Times*, May 6, 1981.

110 *until his retirement:* Bruce Lambert, "Harlon B. Carter, Longtime Head of Rifle Association, Dies at 78," *New York Times*, November 22, 1991.

110 *President Reagan, looking polished:* Video of President Reagan's remarks to the National Rifle Association on May 6, 1983, Reagan Library.

110 *Carter had spoken approvingly: Firing Line*, episode S0428.

111 *"Committee for the Year 2000" report:* "Committee for the Year 2000," April 25, 1983, Dingell Jr. Papers.

111 *"repeated traumas":* Ibid.

112 *sometimes wore a pistol:* Marni Rose McFall, "How Many Presidents Have Owned Guns?," *Newsweek*, October 12, 2024.

112 *fifteen-day waiting period:* Kiron Skinner, Annelise Anderson, and Martin Anderson, *Reagan: A Life in Letters* (New York: Simon & Schuster, 2003).

112 *signed into law a ban:* Ibid.

112 *"the illegal use":* Letter to Ernest Henriques from Reagan, October 19, 1966, Duke Center for Firearms Law.

112 *banning Saturday night specials:* "Gun Control: Richard Nixon Wished for Total Handgun Ban," Associated Press, March 3, 2013.

112 *carrying of handguns:* Memo to Phil Buchen from Ken Lazarus, April 5, 1974, Gerald R. Ford Presidential Library.

113 *"The day could easily come":* Ronald Reagan, *Guns & Ammo*, September 1975, https://web.archive.org/web/20031030123844/http://www.gunsandammomag.com/classics/reagan_1007/.

113 *"felt a special bond":* Video of Reagan's remarks to the National Rifle Association.

113 *Firearm Owners' Protection Act:* Public Law 99-308, 99th Congress (Washington, DC: US Government Printing Office, May 19, 1986).

113 *"It's a nasty truth":* Ibid.

114 *women and children were killed:* Mark S. Hamm, *Apocalypse in Oklahoma: Waco and Ruby Ridge Revenged* (Boston: Northeastern University Press, 1997).

114 *NRA circulated a fundraising letter:* "NRA Apologizes for Calling Some Agents 'Thugs,'" Associated Press, May 18, 1995.

114 *some left-leaning groups:* Frank Langfitt, "More Liberals, People of Color, and LGBTQ Americans Say They're Buying Guns out of Fear," NPR, November 15, 2025.

115 *access to a private meeting:* Rick Hartford, "Taking the Pledge in Bullitt County: The Militia Opens the Door," *Hartford Courant*, November 24, 1997.

115 *"Evil is trying to take":* Ibid.

115 *survivalist/prepper convention:* Mike McIntire, "For Alienated Citizenry, Government Is the Enemy," *Hartford Courant*, November 23, 1997.

115 *A woman was selling:* Author's reporting at Preparedness Expo '97.

116 *"trainloads of tanks":* Ibid.

116 *"Ronald Reagan was the man!":* Ibid.

A COUNTERFEIT ZEAL

117 *"A well regulated militia":* US Bill of Rights, National Archives, www.archives.gov/founding-docs/bill-of-rights-transcript.

118 Heller, *the landmark 2008 case: District of Columbia et al. v. Heller*, US Supreme Court Docket #07-290, decided June 26, 2008.

118 McDonald v. City of Chicago, *limiting: McDonald v. City of Chicago*, US Supreme Court Docket #08-1521, decided June 28, 2010.

118 *"The right self-defence":* St. George Tucker, *Blackstone's Commentaries: With Notes of Reference to the Constitution and Laws of the Federal Government of the United States and of the Commonwealth of Virginia* (Philadelphia: Birch & Small, 1803).

119 *Tucker was a contemporary: Encyclopedia Virginia*, Virginia Humanities Council, under "St. George Tucker."

119 *"we may reasonably hope":* Tucker, Blackstone's Commentaries.

120 *"under the specious pretext":* Ibid.

120 *"As Tucker demonstrates":* David Kopel, "Our 2nd Amendment: The Original Perspective," *American Guardian*, July 1998.

121 *"The class of cases":* Justice Townsend Dickinson, concurring opinion, *The State v. Buzzard*, Arkansas Supreme Court, 1842.

122 *"When a gun control case":* "Committee for the Year 2000," April 25, 1983, John D. Dingell Jr. Papers, Bentley Historical Library, University of Michigan.

122 *In another memo: Planning for the Future: Report of the Executive Director of the NRA Institute to the NRA Executive Committee,* February 7, 1981, Dingell Jr. Papers.

123 *extensive legal work:* Résumé of Stephen P. Halbrook, November 10, 2022.

123 *voted to honor Halbrook:* Minutes of the Meeting of the Board of Directors of the National Rifle Association, January 7, 2021, in re: National Rifle Association of America, case cv30085, US Bankruptcy Court for the Northern District of Texas.

123 *mentions the NRA:* Curriculum vitae for Joyce Lee Malcolm, October 2019.

123 *bio doesn't refer:* Of Arms & the Law, https://armsandthelaw.com/aboutus.php.

123 *a prolific author:* David T. Hardy and John Stompoly, "Of Arms and the Law," *Chicago-Kent Law Review* 51, no. 1 (1974).

124 *underwrite writing projects:* Minutes of the Meeting of the Board of Directors of the National Rifle Association, September 8, 2018, in re: National Rifle Association of America, case cv30085, US Bankruptcy Court for the Northern District of Texas.

124 *hundreds of thousands of dollars:* Will Van Zant, "As SCOTUS Mulled *Bruen*, the NRA Lobbied in the Shadows," *Trace*, August 5, 2022.

124 *"the right of the citizens":* Majority opinion, *Bliss v. Commonwealth*, Kentucky Court of Appeals, 1822.

124 *"so obvious as to induce":* Chief Justice Daniel Ringo, opinion, *The State v. Buzzard.*

125 *"the great Palladium":* A. Bradford, "Sentiments on the Liberty of the Press," *American Weekly Mercury*, April 25, 1734.

125 *"sacred palladium":* Edward Lee, "Freedom of the Press 2.0," *Georgia Law Review*, Winter 2008.

125 *"palladium of public liberty":* Benjamin Austin, *Constitutional Republicanism, in Opposition*

to Fallacious Federalism (Boston: Printed for Adams & Rhoades, editors of the Independent Chronicle, 1803).

126 *When Tucker spoke:* Tucker, Blackstone's Commentaries.

126 *originalism and textualism:* James Burling, "What Is the Difference Between Originalism vs. Textualism vs. Living Constitutionalism?," Pacific Legal Foundation, April 27, 2022.

126 *"stretches to derive":* Justice John Paul Stevens, dissenting opinion, *District of Columbia et al. v. Heller*, US Supreme Court Docket #07-290, decided June 26, 2008.

126 *"greatest pieces of fraud":* Former Chief Justice Warren Burger, *PBS NewsHour*, December 16, 1991.

126 *"If I were writing":* Ibid.

127 *Breyer, in his dissent:* Dissenting opinion of Justice Stephen Breyer, *New York Pistol & Rifle Association v. Bruen*, June 23, 2022, US Supreme Court.

127 *"adapted to the various crises":* Majority opinion, *New York Pistol & Rifle Association v. Bruen.*

127 *"immutable rules":* Majority opinion, *McCulloch v. Maryland*, March 6, 1819, US Supreme Court.

128 *"The choice is not between":* Dissenting opinion of Justice Robert Jackson, *Terminiello v. Chicago*, May 16, 1949, US Supreme Court.

OUT OF THE JUNGLE

131 *Eugene Stoner was a:* Cameron McWhirter and Zusha Elinson, *American Gun: The True Story of the AR-15* (New York: Farrar, Straus & Giroux, 2023).

131 *as he explained later:* Eugene Stoner interview by Edward Ezell, Twentieth Century Small Arms Development Videohistory Collection, 1988–1990, Smithsonian Institution Archives.

131 *met his opposite:* Daniel T. McElrath, "The ArmaLite Story," *American Rifleman*, July 29, 2021.

131 *"we kinda started out":* Stoner interview by Ezell.

132 *drew up a concept car:* Benny Kirk, "Ford Nucleon: A Nuclear Concept Car That Accidentally Showed the Future of SMRs," *Autoevolution*, July 20, 2025.

132 *more than $1 billion: Review of Manned Aircraft Nuclear Propulsion Program, Report to the Congress*, Comptroller General of the US, February 1963.

132 *.22-caliber collapsible rifle:* Jeremiah Knupp, "The Unlikely Resilience of the AR-7 Survival Rifle," *American Rifleman*, December 27, 2016.

133 *M1 Garand, it was big:* David M. Fortier, "The M1 Garand Rifle, What Made It Great?," *Firearms News*, April 13, 2021.

133 *known as the M14:* Patrick Feng, "M14 Rifle," Army Historical Foundation, https://armyhistory.org/m14-rifle/.

133 *AR-10 was unlike:* McWhirter and Elision, *American Gun.*

134 *worse than the M1:* Steve Balestrieri, "M14: The 'Worst' Army Rifle Ever?," *National Security Journal*, May 28, 2025.

134 *"not a military weapon":* "AR-15 Used in Oklahoma Home Defense; Same Rifle 4th Circuit Court Says Americans Should Not Have," National Shooting Sports Foundation, www.nssf.org/articles/ar-15-used-in-oklahoma-home-defense-same-rifle-4th-circuit-court-says-americans-should-not-have/.

134 *letters to the editor:* "Should Massachusetts Adopt the Proposed Ban on the Manufacture of Assault Weapons in the State?," *Boston Globe*, July 18, 2021.

135 *sold its rifle patents:* McElrath, "ArmaLite Story."

135 *"a hush-hush thing":* Stoner interview by Ezell.

135 *marketing the AR-15:* www.ar15.com/forums/ar-15/Vintage_Colt_or_Armalite_Advertisements/123-714653/.

135 *An early Colt ad:* Ibid.

136 *Hollywood-ready SWAT:* "New! The AR-15 You Know Is Now Available in 9mm," Colt Firearms, 1985.

136 *"foreign military castoffs":* Carl Bakal, *The Right to Bear Arms* (New York: McGraw-Hill, 1966).

136 *By the 1960s and 1970s:* David Yamane, Paul Yamane, and Sebastian L. Ivory, "Targeted Advertising: Documenting the Emergence of Gun Culture 2.0 in *Guns* Magazine, 1955–2019," *Palgrave Communications*, April 15, 2020.

137 *"Our female-dominated":* Wayne R. Austerman, "Those Deadly, Depressing, Syncopated Semiautomatic Assault Rifle Blues," *Chronicles*, November 1, 1989.

137 *it took Charles Whitman:* Gary Lavergne, *A Sniper in the Tower* (Denton: University of North Texas Press, 1997).

137 *it took five minutes: Report of the State's Attorney for the Judicial District of Danbury on the Shootings at Sandy Hook Elementary School and 36 Yogananda Street, Newtown, Connecticut, on December 14, 2012*, Office of the State's Attorney, November 25, 2013.

137 *"U.S. Army semi-automatic":* www.ar15.com/forums/ar-15/Vintage_Colt_or_Armalite_Advertisements/123-714653/.

138 *as an assault rifle:* "The Colt AR-15, Performance Is Proof" (advertisement), *International Combat Arts Magazine*, 1983.

138 *"Out of the jungles":* "Now You Can Buy a Hot Combat Rifle for Sport," *Popular Science*, February 1965.

138 *"I suppose if the Vietnam War":* Stoner interview by Ezell.

138 *bar called Uncle Albert's:* Steve Graham, "Suspect in Six Killings Charged," Associated Press, July 26, 1977.

138 *earliest-known spree shooting:* "Mass Shooters," Violence Prevention Project, www.theviolenceproject.org/mass-shooter-database/.

138 *"This is war!":* Laura Richardson, "Man Opens Fire in Church, Killing 2," Associated Press, June 22, 1980.

138 *a former prison guard:* "New Competency Hearing Ordered in Killer's Case," *Allegheny Times*, January 1, 2008.

139 *Among the items found: Report of the State's Attorney.*

139 *"filled with lead":* "Fired into a Group of Children," *New York Times*, April 10, 1891.

139 *student in Camden, New Jersey:* "Youth, 15, Shoots Up Schoolroom," *Los Angeles Herald*, December 1, 1914.

139 *In Cleveland in 1933:* "Maniac Death Toll Up to 5," *Youngstown (OH) Vindicator*, March 7, 1933.

139 *"mass shooting" as opposed:* Jaclyn Schildkraut, H. Jaymi Elsass, Emily Greene-Colozzi, and Brent R. Klein, "Mass Shootings: Why Does Definition Matter?," Rockefeller Institute of Government, July 22, 2025.

139 *"four or more people shot":* "Mass Shooters," Violence Prevention Project.

140 *The data show:* Ibid.

140 *when Clemmie Henderson:* "Chicago Man Kills 4 and Wounds 2 Before Dying in a Shootout," *New York Times*, September 23, 1988.

140 *He fired all 105 shots:* Chief Dep. Atty. Gen. Nelson Kempsky, *A Report to Attorney General John K. Van de Kamp on the Patrick Edward Purdy and the Cleveland School Shootings*, October 1989.

140 *"national bans should be enacted":* Ibid.

141 *"Leadership always comes":* John D. Dingell Jr. interview for Edward M. Kennedy Oral History Project, June 16, 2005, Miller Center at University of Virginia.

141 *massive bill working:* 1994 Violent Crime Control and Law Enforcement Act, Office of Justice Programs, US Department of Justice, www.ojp.gov/ojp50/1994-violent-crime-control-and-law-enforcement-act.

141 *650 models of guns:* "Federal Assault Weapons Ban: Legal Issues," Congressional Research Service, February 14, 2013.

142 *"a vendetta dressed up":* Katherine Q. Seelye, "Assault Weapons Ban Allowed to Stay in Anti-Crime Measure," *New York Times*, July 28, 1994.

142 *Dingell also opposed:* "Remarks of Dingell on House Floor," August 21, 1994, *Congressional Record* (Washington, DC: US Government Printing Office).

142 *The two men were pitching:* Letter to White House Chief of Staff Leon E. Panetta from Dingell, April 17, 1994, John D. Dingell Jr. Papers, Bentley Historical Library, University of Michigan.

142 *"pressure needs to be brought":* Letter to Dingell from Jack Brooks, July 20, 1994, Dingell Jr. Papers.

142 *notably President Clinton:* Mike McIntire, "The Secret History of Gun Rights: How Lawmakers Armed the NRA," *New York Times*, July 30, 2023.

142 *late-in-life warming:* Steven A. Holmes, "Gun Control Bill Backed by Reagan in Appeal to Bush," *New York Times*, March 29, 1991.

143 *"After a great deal of thought":* Letter to Tom Washington from Dingell, August 21, 1994, Dingell Jr. Papers.

143 *"I violently disagree":* "Remarks of Dingell."

143 *"had to have police protection":* Deborah Dingell, interview with author.

144 *Voter anger:* Steven Greenhouse, "'Zombie-Like': The US Trade Agreement That Still Haunts Democrats," *Guardian*, October 28, 2024.

144 *ill-fated health-care reform:* Christopher M. Johnson, "Who Broke Health Care?," WNYC, December 14, 2017.

144 *there was little doubt:* Ron Elving, "The Nashville School Shooting Highlights the Partisan Divide over Gun Legislation," NPR, April 1, 2023.

144 *"We believe that a central theme":* Letter to Gingrich from Democratic congressmen, January 23, 1995, Dingell Jr. Papers.

144 *"People he made happy":* "The Gun Debate," undated memo, Dingell Jr. Papers.

144 *"cost us the election":* Dingell Jr. interview for Kennedy.

RAMBO ACQUISITION

145 *It took five hundred years:* Guy Martin, "The House of Beretta," *Garden & Gun*, December/January 2014.

145 *The 9mm Beretta M9:* Sam Lichtman, "Last Line of Defense: A History of the Beretta M9," Marine Corps Association, March 15, 2023, www.mca-marines.org/leatherneck/last-line-of-defense-a-history-of-the-beretta-m9.

145 *longer-term goal:* Tom Diaz, *The Last Gun* (New York: New Press, 2013).

145 *for about $225 apiece:* "Italian Gun Maker Beretta Hits U.S. Gun Market with a Bang," *Cleveland Plain Dealer*, April 18, 1993.

145 *lucrative civilian market:* Ibid.

146 *"My guess is":* Ibid.

146 *the homicide rate:* "Homicide Rate per 100,000 Population Where the Weapon Was a Firearm," Our World in Data, 2023, https://ourworldindata.org/grapher/homicide-rates-from-firearms.

146 *barrage of litigation:* Timothy Lytton, Suing the Gun Industry: A Battle at the Crossroads of Gun Control and Mass Torts (Ann Arbor: University of Michigan Press, 2005).

146 *combat-style features:* Michael Luo and Michael Cooper, "Lessons in Politics and Fine Print in Assault Weapons Ban of '90s," *New York Times*, December 19, 2012.

146 *Bushmaster was a small:* James Bandler and Doris Burke, "How a Maine Businessman Made the AR-15 into America's Best-Selling Rifle," *ProPublica*, November 21, 2023.

146 *"The rest of the rifle":* Ibid.

146 *defended its civilian sales:* Bushmaster statement regarding Brady Center–sponsored lawsuit, January 29, 2003, https://web.archive.org/web/20040827085609/http:/www.bushmaster.com/statement.asp.

147 *"would not agree":* Tom Jackman, "Gunmaker, Store Agree to Payout in Sniper Case," *Washington Post*, September 10, 2004.

147 *"I think we believe":* Mike McIntire and Michael Luo, "Gun Makers Saw No Role in Curbing Improper Sales," *New York Times*, May 27, 2013.

147 *affordable semiautomatic pistols:* Brad Fitzpatrick, "Taurus TX22 Compact: Full Review," *Guns & Ammo*, August 18, 2023.

147 *"nothing intrinsically evil":* Ibid.

148 *"not for us to enforce":* Ibid.

148 *"I don't even know":* Ibid.

148 *the fourteenth generation:* "Ugo Gussalli Beretta," Henokiens International Association of Bicentenary Family Companies, https://www.henokiens.com/content.php.

148 *"Common sense":* McIntire and Luo, "Gun Makers Saw No Role."

149 *reached a settlement:* "Clinton Administration Reaches Historic Agreement with Smith and Wesson," Office of the Press Secretary, White House, March 17, 2000.

149 *"Today's agreement":* Ibid.

149 *owned by Tomkins PLC:* Kenneth R. Bazinet, "British Firm Acquires Smith & Wesson," United Press International, June 10, 1987.

149 *"It was a business decision":* Jeffrey L. Seglin, "The Right Thing: When Good Ethics Aren't Good Business," *New York Times*, March 18, 2001.

149 *The NRA railed against:* "The Smith and Wesson Sell-Out," NRA Institute for Legislative Action, March 20, 2000.

150 *less than 1 percent:* "Firearm and Shotgun Certificates, April 2024–March 2025," UK Home Office, June 19, 2025.

150 *a third of Americans:* Cassandra McBride, "How Many Gun Owners Are in America? (2025 Statistics)," Ammo.com, November 18, 2025.

150 *"capitulation of Smith & Wesson":* "Report of the Executive Director, National Rifle Association—Institute for Legislative Action, to the Board of Directors," April 7, 2000, Bob Barr Papers, Ingram Library, Special Collections, University of West Georgia.

150 *"Run them out":* McIntire and Luo, "Gun Makers Saw No Role."

150 *Tomkins sold Smith & Wesson:* "Smith & Wesson Sold," *CNN Money*, May 14, 2001.

151 *"based on the tradition":* Seglin, "Right Thing."

151 *Mr. Second Amendment:* Bob Barr, interview with author.

151 *he drafted a bill:* Firearms Heritage Protection Act, H.R. 1032, 106th Congress.

151 *"absolutely zero interest":* Letter to Wayne LaPierre from Barr, October 21, 1999, Bob Barr Papers.

152 *"This is frightening":* Letter to Wayne LaPierre from Barr, November 9, 1999, Bob Barr Papers.

152 *"lawfully competing":* Firearms Heritage Protection Act.

152 *backed a similar bill:* Protection of Lawful Commerce in Arms Act, S. 659, 108th Congress.

152 *accused of lewd conduct:* "Senator, Arrested at Airport, Pleads Guilty," *New York Times*, April 28, 2007.

153 *"Mr. Dingell passionately":* Email to author from Michael Parker, February 3, 2006.

153 *"doing it as a member of Congress":* Barr, interview with author.

153 *"problem areas":* Letter to Heather Wingate from Stephen Halbrook, May 13, 1996, Clifford Stearns Congressional Papers, Special Collections Research Center, George Washington University.

153 *"open to any suggestions":* Memo to Tanya Metaska from Heather Wingate, May 31, 1996, Stearns Congressional Papers.

154 *"'close hold'":* Fax to Jessica from Heather, June 10, 1996, Stearns Congressional Papers.

154 *"does not require":* Mike McIntire, "The Secret History of Gun Rights: How Lawmakers Armed the NRA," *New York Times*, July 30, 2023.

154 *"your fight has become our fight":* Sharon Walsh, "Double-Barreled Fight Against Gun Litigation," *Washington Post*, February 1, 1999.

154 *favored extending the assault weapons ban:* Sheryl Gay Stolberg, "Effort to Renew Weapons Ban Falters on Hill," *New York Times*, September 9, 2004.

155 *After losing control:* Glenn Thrush, "Democrats Failed to Extend Assault Weapons Ban in 2004. They Regret It," *New York Times*, June 9, 2022.

155 *"There are so many issues":* Ibid.

155 *"It will expire Monday":* Ibid.

155 *A 2024 study:* Alex Lars Lunberg et al., "Public Mass Shootings: Counterfactual Trend Analysis of the Federal Assault Weapons Ban," *JMIR Public Health and Surveillance*, September 20, 2024.

155 *concluded in a 2019 study:* Charles DiMaggio et al., "Changes in US Mass Shooting Deaths

Associated with the 1994–2004 Federal Assault Weapons Ban: Analysis of Open-Source Data," *Journal of Trauma and Acute Care Surgery*, January 2019.

156 *"the number of deaths"*: Michael J. Klein, "Did the Assault Weapons Ban of 1994 Bring Down Mass Shootings? Here's What the Data Tells Us," *Ohio Capital Journal*, June 15, 2022.

156 *"The data shows"*: Ibid.

156 *one of its fact sheets:* "The Truth About So-Called 'Assault Weapons,'" NRA Institute of Legislative Action, https://www.nraila.org/the-truth-about-so-called-assault-weapons.

156 *what the Rand report said: The Science of Gun Policy*, Rand Corporation, 2018.

157 *Fourteen Democrats in the Senate:* S.397, 109th Congress, Recorded Vote no. 219, July 29, 2005.

157 *fifty-nine in the House:* S.397, 109th Congress, Roll Call no. 534, October 20, 2005.

157 *Rambo Acquisition LLC:* Affidavit of Roland Hlawaty, November 13, 2017, *Cade Liverman v. Remington Arms Co. et al.*, CV01192, US District Court, Western District of Texas.

157 *changing its name:* Ibid.

157 *three-headed beast:* Mark Reutter, "New York Hedge Fund Takes Investment Stake in Sparrows Point Owner," *Baltimore Brew*, January 18, 2012.

158 *estimated at $5 billion:* "*Forbes* Profile: Stephen Feinberg," www.forbes.com/profile/stephen-feinberg/.

158 *An experienced hunter:* Stephen Witt, "Big Gun's Big Fail," *New York*, November 14, 2016.

158 *used to purchase Bushmaster:* Natasha Singer, "How Freedom Group Became the Big Shot," *New York Times*, November 26, 2011.

158 *one of its annual reports:* Registration Statement of Freedom Group Inc., Securities and Exchange Commission, May 17, 2010.

158 *Cerberus bought Remington*: "Remington Arms Readies for 3rd Century of Business by Entering into Definitive Agreement for Sale" (Cerberus press release), April 5, 2007.

158 *"does not participate"*: "Firearms Three-Year Strategic Marketing Plan, 2004–2006, Remington Arms Co.," *Williams v. Remington*, CV1383, US District Court, Northern District of Texas.

159 *"legitimize the AR-15"*: Email to Eric Barnes from John Trull, September 4, 2007, *Soto v. Bushmaster*, CV15 6050025, Connecticut Superior Court at Waterbury.

159 *He lamented:* Ibid.

159 *"most photographed"*: Email to Alfred Russo et al. from Eddie Stevenson, June 12, 2008, *Soto v. Bushmaster*.

159 *"faster than the general firearms"*: Registration Statement of Freedom Group.

159 *more than doubled:* "Firearm Production in the United States, with Firearm Import and Export Data, 2020," National Shooting Sports Foundation.

159 *"significant long-term benefits"*: Registration Statement of Freedom Group.

160 *"relied on Bushmaster"*: Michael O. Humphries, "Remington R-15 VTR Series," *NRS Shooting Illustrated*, October 26, 2010.

160 *"Consider your man card"*: Mike McIntire, Glenn Thrush, and Eric Lipton, "Gun Sellers' Message to Americans: Man Up," *New York Times*, June 18, 2022.

160 *"same overall tone/attitude"*: Email to Roy Gifford et al. from Eric West, November 6, 2009, *Soto v. Bushmaster*, CV15 6050025, Connecticut Superior Court at Waterbury.

160 *"He went on to tell me":* Email to Jason Schauble et al. from John Trull, January 5, 2010, *Soto v. Bushmaster.*

161 *Donors at the $1 million level:* "Blood Money II: How Gun Industry Dollars Fund the NRA," Violence Policy Center, September 2013.

161 *charity whose ostensible purpose:* Mike McIntire, "Charity Takes Gun Lobby Closer to Its Quarry," *New York Times*, March 6, 2013.

161 *had evolved dramatically*: Nate Rawlings, "In the Shadow of Sandy Hook, a Powerful Pro-Gun Organization Keeps Silent," *Time*, December 15, 2012.

161 *days in the basement:* N. R. Kleinfeld, Ray Rivera, and Serge Kovaleski, "Newtown Killer's Obsessions, in Chilling Detail," *New York Times*, March 28, 2013.

162 *"courting him for years":* Elizabeth Williamson, "How They Did It: Sandy Hook Families Gain Long-Awaited Legal Wins," *New York Times*, February 20, 2022.

COMMON SENSE

164 *Newtown is relatively wealthy:* "Quick Facts," Newtown, CT, US Census Bureau, www.census.gov/quickfacts/fact/table/newtowntownwesternconnecticutplanningregionconnecticut/PST045224.

164 *average home costs more than $600,000:* "Newtown, CT Housing Market," Zillow, www.zillow.com/home-values/397566/newtown-ct/.

164 *Studies were starting to appear:* Dwight L. Evans et al., *Treating and Preventing Adolescent Mental Health Disorders: What We Know and What We Don't Know* (New York: Oxford University Press, 2017).

164 *Gun sales were skyrocketing:* Gregor Aisch and Josh Keller, "What Happens After Calls for New Gun Restrictions? Sales Go Up," *New York Times*, June 13, 2016.

164 *handwritten notes:* Handwritten notes of meeting, VP Task Force 01/14/13, John D. Dingell Jr. Papers, Bentley Historical Library, University of Michigan.

165 *"We don't want all the energy":* Ibid.

165 *Her group was ambushed:* Jonathan Marker, "'Undaunted' Congresswoman Jackie Speier Recounts Jonestown Massacre Survival," *National Archives News*, November 4, 2019.

165 *"I ask my colleagues":* "Jackie Speier: I Regret I Haven't Done More to Stop the Unspeakable," *San Francisco Chronicle*, December 21, 2012.

166 *"I do not think":* Handwritten notes, VP Task Force 01/14/13.

166 *shooting on the Long Island Rail Road:* Clyde Haberman, "Carolyn McCarthy, Who Turned a Gunman's Massacre into a Crusade, Dies at 81," *New York Times*, June 26, 2025.

166 *"I'm not going to be shy":* Mark Landler and Erica Goode, "Obama's Cautious Call for Action Sets Stage to Revive Gun Debate," *New York Times*, December 15, 2012.

166 *"We want something":* Handwritten notes, VP Task Force 01/14/13.

167 *Aurora, where the previous July:* "Aurora, Colorado, Theater Shooting Timeline, Facts," ABC7.com.

167 *"We need to be prepared":* Handwritten notes, VP Task Force 01/14/13.

168 *Matthew Beck. A thirty-five-year-old:* Mike McIntire, Al Lara, and Matthew Hay Brown, "Horrified Workers Witness Killings in Parking Lot," *Hartford Courant*, March 7, 1998.

169 *"I will regret that to my dying day":* Lynne Tuohy, "Killer's Parents Apologize," *Hartford Courant*, March 8, 1998.

169 *Nancy Lanza was another parent:* Matt Flegenheimer and Ravi Somaiya, "A Mother, a Gun Enthusiast and the First Victim," *New York Times*, December 15, 2012.

170 *President Obama's fifteen-page plan:* "Now Is the Time," January 16, 2013, obamawhitehouse.archives.gov.

170 *Polls showed:* Colleen Barry, "Majority of Americans Support Dozens of Policies to Strengthen U.S. Gun Laws," Bloomberg School of Public Health, Johns Hopkins University, January 28, 2013.

171 *We pored over medical examiner reports:* Michael Luo and Mike McIntire, "Children and Guns: The Hidden Toll," *New York Times*, September 28, 2013.

171 *We scraped data from a website:* Michael Luo, Mike McIntire, and Griff Palmer, "Seeking Gun or Selling One, Web Is a Land of Few Rules," *New York Times*, April 17, 2013.

171 *We collected court records:* Michael Luo and Mike McIntire, "When the Right to Bear Arms Includes the Mentally Ill," *New York Times*, December 21, 2013.

171 *We obtained confidential testimony:* Mike McIntire and Michael Luo, "Gun Makers Saw No Role in Curbing Improper Sales," *New York Times*, May 27, 2013.

171 *we shined a spotlight:* Mike McIntire, "Charity Takes Gun Lobby Closer to Its Quarry," *New York Times*, March 6, 2013.

172 *mostly kept silent:* Nate Rawlings, "In the Shadow of Sandy Hook, a Powerful Pro-Gun Organization Keeps Silent," *Time*, December 15, 2012.

172 *Dingell's notes of the meeting:* Dingell Jr. Papers.

173 *"good guy with a gun":* Aliyah Frumin, "NRA Breaks Silence: We Need Guns in Every School in America," NBC News, December 21, 2012.

173 *2 percent of all murders:* "Get the Facts: Assault Weapons, Large Magazines," National Rifle Association Institute of Legislative Action.

173 *a third of mass shootings:* Jennifer Mascia, "Are Handguns or Rifles Used More Often in Mass Shootings?," *Trace*, July 18, 2023.

173 *"criminalize all private firearms transfers":* Christopher W. Cox, "A Universally Bad Idea," *Hill*, March 18, 2013.

173 *designed to address the gun lobby's concerns:* Molly Moorhead, "NRA Says Manchin-Toomey Would Have Criminalized Some Gun Transfers Between Family, Friends," *Politifact*, April 18, 2013.

173 *"It's just common sense":* Gregory Korte and Jackie Kucinich, "Senators Reach Deal on Background Checks," *USA Today*, April 10, 2013.

173 *fear of losing their seats:* Will Simon, "Sandy Hook Parents Push for Changes in the Decade Since the School Shooting," CNN, December 14, 2022.

173 *the Senate failed to pass:* Jennifer Steinhauer, "Gun Control Measure Is Defeated in Senate," *New York Times*, April 17, 2013.

174 *failure by the Obama administration:* Bill Scher, "The Real Reason Obama Didn't Pass Gun Control," *Politico*, August 16, 2019.

174 *personally got on the phone:* Mike McIntire, "The Secret History of Gun Rights: How Lawmakers Armed the NRA," *New York Times*, July 30, 2023.

174 *"Our hearts are broken":* "President Obama Speaks on Common-Sense Measures to Reduce Gun Violence," Obama White House YouTube channel, April 17, 2013.

175 *bullet-resistant windows:* "Nearly Four Years After Massacre, Sandy Hook Builds New School," PBS, July 30, 2016.

175 *group eventually picked up:* Rob Ryser, "Gun Industry Trade Association Leaves Newtown; Gun Violence Prevention Group Says, 'Good Riddance,'" *Danbury (CT) News-Times*, January 6, 2023.

175 *was supposed to retire:* Davis Dunavin, "Newtown's Retiring 'Father Bob' Honored on Congress Floor," Connecticut Public Radio, March 4, 2024.

176 *"The first selectman's gone":* Interview with Msgr. Robert Weiss, *Still Newtown*, episode 10, WSHU Radio, December 5, 2022.

176 *"And I walked into church":* Ibid.

176 *"Sandy Hook showed":* Ibid.

177 *"Rarely in my lifetime":* John Paul Stevens, "John Paul Stevens: Repeal the Second Amendment," *New York Times*, March 27, 2018.

177 *led to a landmark settlement:* Erin Donaghue, "Sandy Hook Families Settle with Gunmaker Remington for $73 Million," CBS News, February 15, 2022.

177 *allowed a lawsuit to proceed:* Tommy Gallagher and Nate Benson, "Buffalo Shooting Survivors Can Pursue Claims Against Firearms Accessory Maker," WGRZ, July 26, 2025.

177 *more than eighty gun safety measures:* Lindsay Nichols, "Gun Law Trend Watch: 2025 Year-End Review," Giffords, December 18, 2025, www.giffords.org.

CHILDISH THINGS

180 *One found that 95 percent:* Heather Littleton, Mandy Kumpula, and Holly Orcutt, "Posttraumatic Symptoms Following a Campus Mass Shooting: The Role of Psychosocial Resource Loss," *Violence Victims* 26, no. 4 (2011).

180 *Other research suggests:* "The Mental Health Impact of Mass Shootings," Brady United Against Gun Violence, 2019.

180 *a posting by one of the teens:* "Harris Hinted at Violence to Come," CNN, April 21, 1999.

181 *perverse sense of community:* Ibid.

181 *men in their early forties:* "Mass Shooters," Violence Prevention Project, www.theviolenceproject.org/mass-shooter-database/.

181 *"There's a lot of research":* Ariana Eunjung Cha, Meghan Hoyer, and Tim Meko, "Young Men, Guns and the Prefrontal Cortex," *Washington Post*, June 3, 2022.

181 *Studies have shown:* Ibid.

182 *half of all homicides:* Rohit Acharya and Rhett Morris, "Why Did U.S. Homicides Spike in 2020 and Then Decline Rapidly in 2023 and 2024?," Brookings Institution, December 16, 2024.

182 *about 95 percent of whom:* "Mass Shooting Fact Sheet," Rockefeller Institute of Government, https://rockinst.org/gun-violence/mass-shooting-factsheet/.

182 *teenagers carried out:* "Mass Shooters," Violence Prevention Project.

182 *Jaylen Fryberg was fifteen:* Peter Foster and Josei Ensor, "US High School Gunman Shot Students 'over a Girl,'" *Telegraph*, October 24, 2014.

182 *Beau Wilson was eighteen:* Greg Norman, "New Mexico Police Reveal Beau Wilson's Arsenal During Deadly May Shooting Rampage," Fox News, June 2, 2023.

182 *"We see two clusters":* Glenn Thrush and Matt Richter, "A Disturbing New Pattern in Mass Shootings: Young Assailants," *New York Times*, June 2, 2022.

182 *They found 127 videos:* Moustafa Ayad, "Minors Exposed to Mass Shooter Glorification

Across Mainstream Social Media Platforms," Institute for Strategic Dialogue, January 24, 2024.

183 *Payton Gendron, eighteen:* "You Wait for a Signal While Your People Wait for You," manifesto of Payton Gendron.

183 *Adam Lanza had also spent: Report of the State's Attorney for the Judicial District of Danbury on the Shootings at Sandy Hook Elementary School and 36 Yogananda Street, Newtown, Connecticut, on December 14, 2012,* Office of the State's Attorney, November 25, 2013.

183 *"A child growing up in America":* "NRA: Full Statement by Wayne LaPierre in Response to Newtown Shootings," *Guardian*, December 21, 2012.

184 *meeting in January 1980:* Minutes of the Meeting of the Executive Committee of the National Rifle Association of America, January 12–13, 1980, Dingell Jr. Papers.

185 *fallen to sixty-five thousand:* Ibid.

185 *Director of Civilian Marksmanship:* "DCM, CMP and NRA Explained," NRA Shooting Sports USA, September 14, 2017, https://www.ssusa.org/content/dcm-cmp-and-nra-explained/.

185 *12 million rounds:* Ibid.

187 *total of $882,000:* Minutes of the Meeting of the Executive Committee.

187 *tens of millions:* Review of annual tax filings of NRA Foundation.

187 *"positive attitudes toward":* Nicholas Bogel-Burroughs and Mike Baker, "In Public Schools, the N.R.A. Gets a Boost from Junior R.O.T.C.," *New York Times*, December 20, 2022.

187 *"dangerous implications":* Rick Jahnkow, "The Gun Problem No One Talks About: Shooting Ranges in Schools," *Veteran* (Vietnam Veterans Against the War), Spring 2013.

188 *about thirty-five hundred JROTC units:* Bogel-Burroughs and Baker, "In Public Schools."

188 *$10,827 NRA grant:* Return of Organization Exempt from Income Tax, NRA Foundation Inc., 2016, Internal Revenue Service.

188 *$2 million the NRA distributed:* Ibid.

188 *February 2018 when the sound: Marjory Stoneman Douglas High School Public Safety Commission Initial Report*, January 2, 2019.

189 *"moody, impulsive, angry":* Rafael Olmeda, "Cruz Was on Radar Long Before Shooting," *South Florida Sun-Sentinel*, March 17, 2018.

189 *drunk gasoline:* Ibid.

189 *"My friends constantly":* Katie Zezima, "'People Need to Listen to Us': Demonstrators Gather Around the U.S. to Protest Gun Violence," *Washington Post*, March 28, 2018.

189 *Cruz was never committed:* Patricia Mazzei, "School Officials Wanted Florida Gunman Committed Long Before a Massacre," *New York Times*, March 18, 2018.

189 *received several awards:* "First Court Appearance for Fla. Teen Charged with 17 Counts of Premeditated Murder in School Shooting," *Fox 4 News*, WDAF, February 15, 2018.

189 *psychiatrist there had recommended:* Testimony in sentencing trial of Nikolas Cruz, August 16, 2022.

189 *"quiet and well-behaved":* Ibid.

189 *complaint being filed:* "FBI Statement on the Shooting in Parkland, Florida," Federal Bureau of Investigation, February 16, 2018.

189 *"a professional school shooter":* "Parkland Fallout: Should Gun Rights Advocates Be Concerned?," Fox News, February 19, 2018.

189 *firing 139 bullets:* "Parkland Shooting Reenacted Using 139 Live Bullets as Part of Lawsuit," CBS News, August 4, 2023.

190 *two other JROTC students:* "Florida Shooting: West Point Admits Murdered Hero Peter Wang," BBC, February 20, 2018.

190 *parents of Ethan Crumbley:* "Read the Prosecutor's Account of Events Before the Michigan School Shooting," *New York Times*, December 3, 2021.

190 *Colin Gray gave his son:* Sam Cabral, "Tough New Test of Parental Responsibility in Georgia Shooting Case," BBC, September 6, 2024.

190 *"interested in the outdoors":* Eric Levenson and Celina Tebor, "A Text, a Call, Then Gunfire: New Details Raise Questions About Efforts to Prevent Georgia School Shooting," CNN, September 9, 2024.

191 *"The point should be":* Mike McIntire, "Selling a New Generation on Guns," *New York Times*, January 26, 2013.

191 *"some frosty Christmas morning!":* Ibid.

191 *"opportunity to engage":* Bogel-Burroughs and Baker, "In Public Schools."

191 *"militarization of the kids":* Ibid.

192 *"You don't need a gun":* McIntire, "Selling a New Generation."

192 *In the summer of 2014:* Martin Gould, "'Devastated' Father of Girl, 9, Who Shot Dead Instructor in Uzi Gun Range Horror Is an Investment Banker," *Daily Mail*, September 5, 2014.

192 *loophole in the law:* Firearm Owners' Protection Act of 1986, Bureau of Alcohol, Tobacco, Firearms and Explosives, www.atf.gov/rules-and-regulations/laws-alcohol-tobacco-firearms-and-explosives/national-firearms-act.

192 *put the Uzi in her hands:* Kimberly McGee and Fernanda Santos, "A 9-Year-Old at a Shooting Range, a Spraying Uzi and Outrage," *New York Times*, August 27, 2014.

193 *"We might wonder":* Dr. Robert Young, "A Child and an Uzi," *National Review*, August 29, 2014.

193 *"I'm disgusted":* Matthew Hendley, "Arizona Lawmaker Proposes Ban on Giving Machine Guns to Children," *Phoenix New Times*, September 3, 2014.

193 *an "industrial accident":* Rebecca Cohen, "How Does a 9-Year-Old Come to Shoot a Fully Automatic Weapon?," *Mother Jones*, August 28, 2014.

193 *"What in the name of Jesus":* McGee and Santos, "A 9-Year-Old."

194 *In St. Louis in May 2022:* Joey Schneider, "Man Charged in Shootout After AR-15 Stolen Outside Wellston Food Market," *Fox 2 News*, June 1, 2022.

196 *offered by Staccato Vegas:* Staccato Vegas, https://staccatovegas.com.

196 *offers bachelorette parties:* The Range 702, www.therange702.com/shooting-experiences/vip-bachelorette-party/.

197 *"the phenomenon:* guntry club*":* Victoria L. Walker, "What Is a 'Guntry' Club?," *NRA Blog*, March 3, 2017, https://www.nrablog.com/articles/2017/3/what-is-a-guntry-club.

197 *ad for Bullets and Burgers:* Bullets and Burgers, https://bulletsandburgers.com/.

197 *"Machine gun and flame thrower":* Knob Creek Range, https://web.archive.org/web/19990202065824/https://www.knobcreekrange.com/.

197 *doctor's eight-year-old boy was:* "Father Twice Told Uzi Too Powerful for 8-Year-old Christopher Bizilj," ABC News, January 7, 2011.

198 *pushing import bans:* Joseph Michael Newhard, "'Bootleggers' and Gun Control," *Regulation* (Cato Institute), Fall 2015.

198 *earning more than $90,000:* "General Social Survey Report: Trends in Gun Ownership in the United States, 1972–2014," NORC at the University of Chicago, March 2015.

198 *"slightly less than half":* John Berrigan et al., "The Number and Type of Private Firearms in the United States," *Annals of the American Academy of Political and Social Science*, June 20, 2023.

198 *29 percent of gun owners:* Philip J. Cook and Jens Ludwig, "Guns in America: National Survey on Private Ownership and Use of Firearms," National Institute of Justice Research in Brief, May 1997.

198 *risen to 34 percent:* Kim Parker et al., "The Demographics of Gun Ownership," Pew Research Center, June 22, 2017.

198 *it was 40 percent:* "Percentage of Population in the United States with at Least One Gun in the Household in 2023, by Education Level," Statista, July 14, 2025.

199 *obtained a development agreement:* Mark Waite, "Front Sight Expansion Plans Include New Shooting Ranges," *Pahrump Valley Times*, June 14, 2014.

199 *exceed $200,000:* Robert M. Hausman, "Free Submachine Gun Class Offered at Front Sight!," *Small Arms Review*, June 2000.

199 *I found a list:* Front Sight bankruptcy case, No. 22-11824, US Bankruptcy Court, District of Nevada.

199 *"We've got people":* Waite, "Front Sight Expansion."

199 *What motivates them?:* Front Sight Firearms Training Institute, www.youtube.com/@gunsfirearmstraining/videos.

200 *Suppressors Adventure:* Desert Wolf Tours, https://desertwolftours.com/arizona-tours/machine-guns-suppressors-adventure/.

201 *"shoot a fully automatic":* Andrea Kelly and Rhonda Bodfield, "Her Plot Will Unfold at City Council Meetings," *Arizona Daily Star*, June 9, 2010.

201 *"to ensure that our limited government":* "4th District Candidate Plans AK-47 Social," WYFF News, June 3, 2010.

201 *"fight Obama's Democrat machine":* "Big Guns," Eric Greitens, July 31, 2016, https://www.youtube.com/watch?v=0-VfFi6Z14Q.

201 *"protected our monuments":* "Tough as Nails," Team Ivey, May 9, 2018, https://www.youtube.com/@teamivey1466.

202 *As Debbie had said:* John D. Dingell, *The Dean: The Best Seat in the House* (New York: Harper, 2018).

202 *"fight tyranny and evil":* "AR-15 Giveaway from U.S. Senate Candidate Josh Clark," Josh Clark, March 19, 2022, https://www.youtube.com/watch?v=rR6r99H6xlg.

202 *"We have a responsibility":* Statement of Robert F. Kennedy, July 11, 1967, www.rfkhumanrights.org.

WAR OF ATTRITION

205 *"shook and trembled":* Hiram Percy Maxim, *Horseless Carriage Days* (New York: Dover, 1962).

205 *patent for the device:* "Maxim's Gun Proves That It's Noiseless," *New York Times*, February 9, 1909.

205 *states started banning silencers:* Kel Whelan, "Noiseless Nightmares: How Fear Stamped Out Silencers," *Recoil*, June 17, 2022.

205 *Maxim finally stopped:* Ibid.

206 *"The government does not":* Opinion of the court, *Desimone v. United States,* May 1, 1970, US Court of Appeals for the Second Circuit.

206 *"suppressors are hard to get":* "You Wait for a Signal While Your People Wait for You," manifesto of Payton Gendron.

206 *"shooting industry by storm":* Transcript of Sturm, Ruger & Co. earnings call, February 25, 2016.

206 *President Trump's budget bill:* Stephen Gutkowski, "Congress Eliminates Taxes on Silencers, Sawed-Off Shotguns," *Reload,* July 3, 2025.

207 *5 million were registered:* Salam Fatohi, "Firearm Suppressor Registrations Outpace Historic Figures," National Shooting Sports Foundation, October 4, 2024.

207 *"We think the law-abiding citizen":* Knox Williams, interview with author.

207 *what is considered safe:* "Recreational Firearm Noise Exposure," American Speech-Language-Hearing Association, www.asha.org/public/hearing/Recreational-Firearm-Noise-Exposure/.

208 *operating a nail gun:* Natalie Musumeci, "Silencer Used in Virginia Beach Shooting Made It Deadlier: Survivor," *New York Post,* June 4, 2019.

208 *"thirty or sixty seconds more":* Ibid.

208 *does not guarantee:* ShotSpotter services agreements reviewed by author.

208 *ten years in prison:* Phil Ray, "10-Year Sentence Given in Gun Case," *Altoona (PA) Mirror,* May 16, 2024.

208 *a street in Istanbul:* "1 Dead in Assassination Attempt on Palestinian Businessman in Istanbul," *Türkiye Today,* August 19, 2024.

208 *kill protected rhinos:* Adrienne Carlisle, "Makhanda Judge Jails Three Rhino Poachers for 12 Years Each," *Cape Town (SA) Daily Dispatch,* October 10, 2024.

209 *"Silenced is a misnomer":* Thomas Chittum, interview with author.

209 *"all driven by commercialism":* Robert Spitzer, interview with author.

209 *produced a fact sheet:* "NSSF Fast Facts, Hearing Protection Act," National Shooting Sports Foundation, March 2023.

209 *"require the use":* "NSSF Welcomes State Department Removing Obstacles to Suppressor Exports" (press release), National Shooting Sports Foundation, July 10, 2020.

209 *"At this time":* Email to author from Mark Oliva, National Shooting Sports Foundation, October 28, 2024.

210 *extolling the benefits:* Dr. John Wipfler, "'Sound Arguments for the Purchase and Use of Firearm Suppressors': A Physician's Perspective and Recommendations," American College of Emergency Physicians, May 2016.

210 *French gun laws:* Republic of France Internal Security Code: Title I: Weapons and Ammunitions (Articles L311-2 to L317-12), www.legifrance.gouv.fr/codes/section_lc/LEGITEXT000025503132/LEGISCTA000025505560/#LEGISCTA000025508077.

210 *he could not recall:* Email to author from John Wipfler, October 21, 2024.

210 *"may be required":* Stephen P. Halbrook, "Firearm Sound Moderators: Issues of Criminalization and the Second Amendment," *Cumberland Law Review* 46, no.1 (2015/16).

210 *German laws governing:* Federal Republic of Germany General Administrative Regulation on the Weapons Act, www.verwaltungsvorschriften-im-internet.de/bsvwvbund_05032012_BMJKM5.htm.

210 *"authorities likely require":* Email to author from Stephen Halbrook, October 22, 2024.

210 *The Illinois lawsuit: Anderson v. Raoul,* Case no. 23-cv-00728, US District Court for the Southern District of Illinois.

210 *loud military weapons:* Scott E. Brueck et al., "Measurement of Exposure to Impulsive Noise at Indoor and Outdoor Firing Ranges During Tactical Training Exercises," National Institute for Occupational Safety and Health, June 2014.

210 *"has no policy statement":* Email to author from Melissa Dibble, October 23, 2024.

211 *"At the end of the day":* Email to author from Knox Williams, October 26, 2024.

212 *"defend and advance":* Return of Organization Exempt from Income Tax 2021, Center for Human Liberty, Internal Revenue Service.

212 *"We're pleased to tell you":* Letter to Center for Human Liberty from Internal Revenue Service, May 23, 2024.

212 *first significant contribution:* Return of Organization Exempt from Income Tax 2021, FPC Action Foundation, Internal Revenue Service.

212 *"to create a world":* Ibid.

212 *an amicus brief:* Brief of Amici Curiae William English, PhD, and Center for Human Liberty, July 19, 2021, *New York Pistol and Rifle Association v. Bruen*, US Supreme Court.

212 *largest of its kind:* Mike McIntire and Jodi Kantor, "The Gun Lobby's Hidden Hand in the 2nd Amendment Battle," *New York Times*, June 18, 2024.

212 *"shares English's interest":* Brief of Amici Curiae William English.

213 *ended up carrying weight:* McIntire and Kantor, "Gun Lobby's Hidden Hand."

213 *amicus in a Hawaii court:* Brief of Amici Curiae Angus Kirk McClellan, Firearms Policy Coalition, FPC Action Foundation, California Gun Rights Foundation, the Center for Human Liberty, and Citizens Committee for the Right to Keep and Bear Arms, *Wolford v. Lopez*, November 9, 2023, US Court of Appeals for the Ninth Circuit.

213 *in another Supreme Court case:* Brief of Amicus Curiae Center for Human Liberty, *United States v. Rahimi*, October 4, 2023, US Supreme Court.

213 *broke with tradition:* Gabrielle Berbey, *99% Invisible*, episode 584, "Fact Checking the Supreme Court," June 4, 2024, https://99percentinvisible.org/episode/fact-checking-the-supreme-court/.

214 *known as the Brandeis Brief:* "The Brandeis Brief—in Its Entirety," Louis D. Brandeis School of Law Library.

214 *formed in 2012:* Firearms Policy Coalition, https://web.archive.org/web/20121231010059/http://www.firearmspolicy.org/.

214 *"Superior firepower":* Firearms Policy Coalition X account, https://x.com/gunpolicy.

214 *in-your-face messaging:* Firearms Policy Coalition online store, https://fpcgear.com/.

214 *once told a newspaper:* Brandon Woolfolk, "New Zealand Banned Military Style Guns After Massacre. What About U.S.?," *San Jose (CA) Mercury News*, March 22, 2019.

214 *cases by Erik Jaffe:* "*CGF McDonald v. Chicago* Amicus: Fairman & Berger Are Wrong on the 14th," California Gun Rights Foundation, November 24, 2009, www.cagunrights.org/cgf-mcdonald-v-chicago-amicus-fairman-berger-are-wrong-on-the-14th/.

215 *as low as seventy thousand:* McIntire and Kantor, "Gun Lobby's Hidden Hand."

215 *dismissed English's findings:* Dr. Matthew Miller, interview with author.

216 *"sort of came out of nowhere":* Joseph Blocher, interview with author.

216 *"lie with data science":* William English, https://williamenglish1.wixsite.com/william english.

216 *"It kind of dawned on me":* Paul Bedard, "Georgetown Professor: AR-15 'Commonly Owned' and 'Incredibly Popular,'" *Washington Examiner*, September 19, 2022.

216 *did have prior connections:* McIntire and Kantor, "Gun Lobby's Hidden Hand."

217 *They emailed him, called:* Motion to compel, *Hartford v. Ferguson*, case CV05364, January 11, 2024, US District Court, Western District of Washington.

217 *published an op-ed:* William English, "Antigun Activists Ambushed Me," *Wall Street Journal*, June 26, 2024.

218 *"The Court agrees with the Government":* Order of the court, *Barnett v. Raoul*, case CV00209, US District Court, Southern District of Illinois.

218 *It was yet another amicus brief:* Benjamin Owen, "DOJ Says AR-15s, Ammo Magazines Protected by Second Amendment in Seventh Circuit Brief," *Reload*, June 19, 2025.

218 *full-blown lawsuits by:* Danica Coto, "Trump Administration Sues U.S. Virgin Islands, Accusing Officials of Violating 2nd Amendment," *Los Angeles Times*, December 17, 2025.

218 *"a second-class right":* Memorandum from Atty. Gen. Pamela Bondi to all DOJ employees regarding Second Amendment Enforcement Task Force, April 8, 2025.

219 *"in a country which has":* Testimony of Attorney General Nicholas Katzenbach before Senate Judiciary Committee, May 19, 1965 (Washington, DC: US Government Printing Office, 1965).

CONCLUSION: WHAT IS TO BE DONE?

222 *Only through litigation:* "Inside the Tobacco Deal, Full Chronology," PBS, www.pbs.org/wgbh/pages/frontline/shows/settlement/timelines/fullindex.html.

222 *"The law has been held":* Jonathan Lowy, "The Road to the Sandy Hook Settlement," *Second Thoughts Blog*, April 8, 2022, Duke Center for Firearms Law.

222 *"merely by selling":* Majority opinion, *Soto v. Bushmaster*, March 2019, Connecticut Supreme Court.

223 *"one narrow legal theory":* Ibid.

223 *law contains an exception:* "Gun Industry Accountability," Giffords Law Center, https://giffords.org/lawcenter/gun-laws/policy-areas/other-laws-policies/gun-industry-immunity/.

223 *"a wake-up call":* Patrick O. Dunphy, "Badger Guns Verdict, Lessons Learned," *Verdict, a Wisconsin Association for Justice Journal*, Fall 2016.

224 *Accidents at roadside work zones:* Mike McIntire, "Efforts Lag to Improve Safety at Work Zones," *New York Times*, December 21, 2009.

224 *"sensitivities to die down":* Mike McIntire, "The Secret History of Gun Rights: How Lawmakers Armed the NRA," *New York Times*, July 30, 2023.

225 *roughly forty thousand:* John Gramlich, "What the Data Says About Gun Deaths in the U.S.," Pew Research Center, March 5, 2025.

226 *A majority of Americans:* "Gun Violence Widely Viewed as a Major and Growing National Problem," Pew Research Center, June 28, 2023.

227 *"A full scan of American history":* Michael Walden, *The Second Amendment: A Biography* (New York: Simon & Schuster, 2014).

228 *dropped by half:* Daniel A. Cox, "American Men Suffer a Friendship Recession," Survey Center for American Life, American Enterprise Institute, July 6, 2021.

228 *"One could speculate":* Mary Kekatos, "As US Reels from Multiple Mass Shootings in California, Can Loneliness Be a Trigger for Violence?," ABC News, January 26, 2023.

229 *days after turning eighteen:* Eric Levenson et al., "Uvalde School Shooting Suspect Was a Loner Who Bought Two Assault Rifles for His 18th Birthday," CNN, May 27, 2022.

229 *receipt from Daniel Defense:* Dalia Faheid, "Maker of AR-15–Style Rifle Used in Texas Shooting Pulls out of NRA Convention," *Fort Worth Star-Telegram*, May 27, 2022.

INDEX

ABOUT THE AUTHOR

MIKE McINTIRE is an investigative reporter at *The New York Times* and the winner of three Pulitzer Prizes for his reporting. He shared Pulitzers in 2022 for reporting on the hidden financial incentives behind police traffic stops, and in 2017 for reporting on covert Russian interference in the US presidential election. During the 2020 presidential campaign, Mike was part of a team that obtained and published Donald Trump's long-concealed tax returns. In 2015, his investigation of corruption in college sports was a finalist for the Pulitzer Prize and was the basis for his book *Champions Way: Football, Florida, and the Lost Soul of College Sports* (Norton, 2017). He has taught journalism at New York University since 2004 and was a 2019 Ferris Visiting Professor of Journalism at Princeton University.